**New Businesses and Urban
Employment Opportunities**

New Businesses and Urban Employment Opportunities

Kenneth McLennan
Paul Seidenstat
Temple University

Lexington Books
D.C. Heath and Company
Lexington, Massachusetts
Toronto   London

HD
5724
.M22

Library of Congress Cataloging in Publication Data

McLennan, Kenneth
New businesses and urban employment opportunities.

    1. Job vacancies- United States. 2. Labor supply-
United States. 3. Manpower policy- United States.
4. Metropolitan areas- United States.
I. Seidenstat, Paul, joint author.
II. Title
HD5724.M22   331.1'0973   72-5198
ISBN 0-669-84525-6

This report was prepared for the Manpower Administration, U.S. Department of Labor, under research contract NO. 81-40-69-20 authorized by Title I of the Manpower Development and Training Act. Since contractors performing research under Government sponsorship are encouraged to express their own judgment freely, the report does not necessarily represent the Department's official opinion or policy. Moreover, the contractor is solely responsible for the factual accuracy of all material developed in the report.

To Barbara and Linda

Contents

List of Figures

List of Tables

Preface

Rapid demographic changes in urban areas and related geographic changes in racial and income distribution are among the most significant socioeconomic phenomena of the 1960s. The relationships among these new features of urbanization and the high rate of unemployment, poverty, deteriorated housing, and inadequate education are today only dimly understood.

Statistics which present only urban and nonurban comparisons in unemployment, growth of new job opportunities, crime, etc. are extremely misleading. The magnitude and relative importance of each major socioeconomic problem appears to vary with the size of the city or community within the city. In segments of every major urban area, thousands of people are crowded together in slums where the severity of socioeconomic problems is many times greater than the more affluent parts of the urban area. The differential in the socioeconomic conditions within urban areas is certainly a major contributor to the changing demography. It is less clear whether the slow growth of job opportunities within some sections of the urban area increase the severity of many of the serious socioeconomic problems which plague many parts of our inner cities.

During the latter part of the past decade, policy-makers have recognized the need for massive financial aid to our cities. This has led to heavy investments to rehabilitate the city. Investment has taken many forms. Renewal of dilapidated housing and to some extent commercial property, aid to educationally disadvantaged children, aid to ghetto businesses, and manpower retraining efforts have concentrated on the residents living in the most blighted sectors of the central cities. Despite the massive financial efforts the social indicators of human and physical well-being in the city have not improved. Crime rates have risen, the stock of deteriorating housing does not seem to be shrinking, and the educational, income, and employment opportunity differentials among residents of different geographic sectors within the urban areas do not seem to be narrowing. In fact, there is a widespread feeling of pessimism about the future role of the city in the nation's social and economic systems. Some have questioned whether the large city is a viable unit for providing the services and economic opportunities demanded by the population and have suggested that public policy should attempt to accelerate the current decentralization trends. In contrast, it is frequently pointed out that there are serious institutional and economic barriers (such as discrimination) which, given further decentralization, will simply worsen the plight of millions of slum residents. For the latter, rehabilitation of the inner city may be their only chance of economic improvement.

The choice of an effective urban policy requires a more complete understanding of the economic structure of the various segments which make up the metropolitan area. If it is assumed that economic opportunity is the appropriate linkage between the social decay of the poverty areas and the more affluent sections of the city and its suburban ring, it seems appropriate to make a comparative analysis of selected geographic parts of the metropolitan area. The emphasis should be on the potential economic solution to the problem rather than the crime rate, the level of poverty, inadequate housing, education and lack of skills among the residents, etc., since these are to a large extent symptoms of the basic problem of lack of access to employment opportunities. Some aspects of the symptoms do, of course, have to be considered but only insofar as they restrict access to available jobs.

Given this basic premise the microeconomic study of metropolitan areas should compare land-use patterns in the suburban ring and the city. Specific attention should be given to land values so that the cost of redevelopment may be assessed. The relationship between industrial land use and residential patterns must also be studied. It is important to know whether the economic forces shaping the location of industry and the movement of the population are increasing the isolation of segments of the population from the growing job centers. In this respect the public and private transit facilities linking residential and business locations is a relevant feature of the job opportunity system.

The development of a new urban policy should take account of which industries are likely to provide the greatest job opportunities for unemployed ghetto residents and whether it is feasible to make these industries part of an inner city renewal plan. The alternative policy of encouraging decentralization and providing programs to ensure that inner city residents are able to participate in the growing number of jobs outside the inner core must also be examined.

This book does not provide all of this information which is a prerequisite for a new urban policy. It is however, a preliminary examination of the employment structure of a city which is unfortunate enough to have many of the socioeconomic problems found in most urban areas. It is significant in that it is one of the few studies which has examined the geographic distribution of employment within the central city. It is unique in that it indicates some of the dynamic changes in demand caused by the entry and exit of firms among labor market segments of a large metropolitan area. It is in essence a detailed analysis of the industrial and geographic distribution of employment opportunities by socioeconomic areas of the city. In this sense it is an important contribution to the development of solutions to the problems associated with high unemployment within the inner city. As outlined in Chapter 1, some of the current public policy is supported by the results of the study while other policies are considered relatively ineffective. Some readers may find the conclusions drawn from analysis difficult to accept since they challenge certain aspects of conventional wisdom in the field of urban labor markets. The study was conducted, however, with the intention of providing an approach which would assist policy-makers in increasing employment opportunities in the nation's cities and reduce the extent of unemployment in ghettos to the lowest possible level. The nation currently has no higher obligation than to achieve this goal.

Acknowledgments

This study was made possible by the generous financial support of the Manpower Administration, U.S. Department of Labor. The authors are grateful for assistance throughout the project provided by many of the staff of the Manpower Administration. The confidence in the nature of the project shown by Dr. Howard Rosen, Director, Office of Research and Development, Manpower Administration, was most helpful during the execution of the research as was the constant assistance and advice provided by Joseph Epstein, Lester Rindler, and Harry Burton. Robert Manifold and John Ryan of the Manpower Administration were of great assistance in arranging and adjusting the budget to suit the needs of the research. Their patience and understanding were certainly appreciated.

The personnel of the city of Philadelphia also gave considerable support by providing much of the data used in the analysis. In this respect Bertram Todd, Milton Silverstein of the Management Information Systems Division, Department of Finance, and James Crummett, formerly of the Office of Economic Development, Department of Finance deserve special recognition for their time and effort in explaining and processing some of the data. Background information for the study was willingly provided by the staff of the Bureau of Employment Security, Pennsylvania Department of Labor and Industry.

The collection of original data from some two-hundred firms would not have been possible without the participation of senior company officials and a team of devoted and sometimes tenacious interviewers including David Binkley, Nancy Cliff, James Keddie, Rebekah Rosenberg, and Shelley Staller. The participation from Philadelphia businesses was very gratifying and to a large extent the assistance of the Greater Philadelphia Chamber of Commerce and its Executive Director, Thatcher Longstreth, ensured the business community's support.

The computer programmer for the project, Wayne Kaplan, displayed considerable skill and patience during the extensive processing of the data. His assistance was of great value to the project. Statistical advice in the design and execution of the project was willingly supplied by our colleagues John Flueck, Stanley Henemeir, and Bernard Siskin. Special thanks are due to the two research assistants attached to the project, Brian Dittenhafer and Stephen McDonough. They helped supervise the collection of data and the analysis of data. They also read sections of the manuscript and made valuable suggestions which were incorporated into the final version. Their role in the project went far beyond the requirements of their position and for this the authors are very grateful.

The help of the secretarial staff of the Department of Economics, Temple University, particularly that of Grace Tappert and Peggy Rawling, was essential in processing the manuscript. To Thomas Walsh and George Knecht of the Graphic Arts Department, Audiovisual Center, Temple University, we owe thanks for the quality and service provided in the preparation of the figures. The details of administering the research contract were ably carried out by Richard Harrington and Richard Smith of Research and Program Development, Temple University and Marshall Esterson of the School of Business Administration, Temple University. To Dean Seymour Wolfbein and Associate Dean Louis T. Harms of Temple, the authors owe a considerable debt for the encouragement and support they provided while the research was being executed.

Many persons in various federal government agencies and the academic community provided valuable comments on an earlier draft of the manuscript. In this respect the authors especially wish to thank Ellen M. Bussey, Gerald L. Duskin, Stanely Miller, Ellen Sehgal, and Thomas M. Stanback, Jr. None of these commentators or anyone named above is responsible for any shortcomings of this book.

New Businesses and Urban
Employment Opportunities

Introduction:
Urban Unemployment

Persistently high urban unemployment has been one of the most difficult unsolved socioeconomic problems of the 1960s, and it is one which is likely to be of urgent concern again in the 1970s. The problem is especially serious because it is geographically concentrated in a few subsections of the labor market. The sector where most of this unemployment is concentrated is in the nonwhite ghettos where the reinforcing links between joblessness and poverty, crime and social decay are painfully evident. The civil disturbances of the late 1960s are the most striking manifestations of these conditions.

The fact that the urban unemployment problem has sectoral characteristics is plainly seen by comparing the unemployment rates for the Philadelphia Standard Metropolitan Statistical Area (SMSA) in 1969 with that of the central city. The SMSA as a whole, which is usually considered to be the labor market for job information purposes, had an unemployment rate of 4.3%. The unemployment rate for the central city alone, however, was 5.3%. Surveys of other cities have shown that the unemployment rates in the racial ghettos are significantly higher than those in the central city. Table 2-4 shows this clearly. In Detroit, during 1968-69, the unemployment rate for whites in the entire SMSA was 3%, while the rate for nonwhites in the predominantly nonwhite ghetto areas was 13.5%.

The goal of low unemployment throughout all sectors of the urban labor market can be achieved by adjusting the supply and demand for labor in each of the sectors. Manpower legislation and programs which comprise the "Manpower Revolution" of the 1960s are designed to deal with unemployment problems primarily by changing the supply of labor skills in local areas. Consequently, in dealing with high unemployment in certain sectors within the nation's cities, programs have provided basic education, work experience, and some specific skill training. This approach assumes that if the unemployed can develop job skills and get some work experience, the private sector of the economy will be capable of supplying jobs for them.[1] Experience has shown, however, that the private sector, though actually generating a substantial increase in the aggregate number of new jobs and actively seeking to assist hard-core unemployed from ghettos, has had only a modest impact on the inner-city unemployment rate. The success of the private sector in absorbing graduates of manpower programs is, of course, likely to vary with the business cycle. Even in periods of strong aggregate demand, however, the inner city unemployment rate has remained substantially higher than the rate for the entire urban labor market area.

Rapid changes in both the demographic distribution of the population and the industrial structure of metropolitan areas offset the impact of changes in labor supply. The rapid growth in the size of the labor force and the migration of unskilled blacks from depressed rural areas to the urban slums appear to be factors which have negated any reduction that manpower programs might have made in the unemployment rates for these areas. Segregated housing patterns usually dictate that these migrants, because of their poverty and their race, must reside in the dilapidated housing stock of the central city ghettos. The geographic segmentation of the labor sup͏ is frequently strengthened by zoning laws and regulations which restr all but middle-to-upper-income residents from the suburban ring. Conseq ntly, workers with the skills necessary for many professional and highly skilled white-collar jobs most frequently reside in the suburbs. Segregation and income further segment the distribution of labor supply within the city, with employees having ability to perform the lowest skilled jobs living in ghetto areas, and the more skilled groups in the labor force residing in the nonghetto areas of the city.

Changes in the spacial arrangement of labor demand throughout the metropolitan area have not coincided with the geographic trend in the distribution of labor supply. The highly paid white-collar and professional jobs have grown fastest in the central business district at the heart of the central city, often quite near ghetto areas. In addition, most other types of jobs have grown fastest in the suburban ring, out of reach of the ghetto resident because of inadequate public transportation networks and/or the cost of commuting from the inner city to the suburban ring. The result is a shortage of service and blue-collar workers in suburban areas where unemployment is relatively low for all types of labor. This contrasts with the central city and ghetto where there is a surplus of low-skilled workers and, consequently, high unemployment rates.

If there are few job opportunities within the reach and capabilities of inner-city residents, it is difficult to place even those trained under government programs. Consequently, a manpower policy which concentrates solely on changing the nature of labor supply within the inner city is likely to result in only partial success. When faced with the lack of any prospect of finding desirable employment opportunities, one would expect an individual to adapt a "short-time horizon" in the sense that the individual's investment in himself as a potential wage earner would not be high.

Available evidence suggests that although there are economic benefits to the worker who does incur the costs necessary to acquire training and experience, the benefit to the ghetto resident may be substantially less than it is for other groups of workers. For example, the *Manpower Report of the President, 1971*, noted the smaller rewards from education for the central city nonwhite. According to 1965-66 data, the weekly wage of white high school graduates was nearly $25 higher than that of whites who had not attended high school; for nonwhites the difference was only $8.[2] Another study found that within sixteen slum areas the rate of unemployment did not have a significant relation with the level of education attainment.[3] Thus there is a weaker economic incentive for the ghetto youth to stay in school. Similarly, the prospect of a lifetime of "dead end" jobs would not encourage the individual to establish a stable work record, but rather to move from job to job at his convenience.[4] Such limited employment opportunities also reduce the opportunity cost of a police record. Indeed, criminal activities may compete favorably with "straight" society for young ghetto residents. As a way of earning a living, illegal income in the ghetto is not uncommon, nor is it grounds for social ostracism.

Ghetto residents face several socioeconomic disincentives when considering whether or not to continue their education or training, and these can result in such retraining and employment barriers as lack of education, motivation and regular work habits and, in many instances, the handicap of a criminal record. These barriers increase the difficulty and the cost of rehabilitating the worker in one of the nation's manpower programs. If future job opportunities were a more certain prospect for ghetto residents, some of these costs might be borne by the individual and therefore reduce some of the difficulties in changing the nature of labor supply in the central city.

A solution to the chronic nature of high sectoral unemployment within segments of metropolitan labor markets may therefore require changes in the demand for labor within the central city in addition to the emphasis of federal manpower policy which has almost exclusively concentrated on the supply of labor. The government's traditional role in stimulating labor demand has been through it's macroeconomic policy, with only a few very modest programs focused explicitly on creating jobs in specific localities. Examples of such programs are the Appalachian Regional Development Act and the Public Works and Economic Development Act,[5] both of 1965, which embody the concept of injecting public capital to stimulate economic development and create jobs in depressed areas. None of these programs, however, deal specifically with the sectoral unemployment of the urban area. The most prominent new approach is the one supported by the Nixon administration in which the ghetto businesses are given financial and training assistance. Minority businessmen are encouraged to start their own small businesses by receiving loans and counseling from the Small Business Administration. Another approach sometimes followed by state and local governments has been to offer locational subsidies to large, established corporations to induce them to establish plants within easy access of the ghetto worker. Still other proposals suggest community control of the ghetto's resources through cooperatives and community development corporations.

If an effective campaign of "job development" is to be mounted it is necessary to have some idea of the potential effectiveness of each of these proposals. In addition, an overall strategy must be developed. Should the ghetto areas be treated as underdeveloped nations which need to develop their own economies? A program with its major emphasis on starting new businesses, cooperatives, and community development corporations would constitute such an approach. The ghetto would strengthen its community identity, develop a stronger political organization, and pool its resources for investment and self-help. It is often contended that such a course of action, while it may improve the quality of life in the ghetto in many ways, may not be able to create sufficient numbers of jobs to solve unemployment problems. On the other hand, if there is a strong secular decline in the economic viability of urban ghettos, perhaps public policy should attempt to assist ghetto residents in moving out of the inner city and relocating in the sections of the metropolitan area where job opportunities are expanding most rapidly.

Bearing the above questions in mind, this project is designed to examine the geographic distribution of the urban demand for labor and its relationship with unemployment in the city.

Objectives

The first major objective of this study is to evaluate the feasibility of the approach to urban unemployment problems which would rehabilitate the ghetto areas of major cities through the development of new enterprises in the ghettos. Many believe that "such businesses will provide for many individuals another way out of the ghetto. They will create jobs [and] . . . in time, this process will replace the ghetto as an entity with flourishing inner cities."[6] The direct employment impact of all firms entering, exiting, or relocating within the city of Philadelphia during a one year period is assessed. Additional information is provided by a survey of the occupational structure of a sample of 200 new businesses. A large part of the analysis is performed by comparing the share of the dynamic change occurring in the ghetto and nonghetto areas of the city and within the central business district.

The justification for the geographic subdivision of the city is based on the existence of significant occupational and industrial immobilities which segment the urban labor market into "noncompeting" groups of workers. In a large city "the internal geographic arrangements of the labor market compliment and reinforce the occupational and industrial boundaries that have been found to exist in local labor markets."[7] The solution to high unemployment within some sections of cities therefore requires a micro approach which treats the urban labor market as a system of geographic "sublabor" markets.

The study also attempts to examine the relative attractiveness to industry of several geographic sections of the city. To facilitate this submetropolitan analysis, the city of Philadelphia was broken into eight geographic subdivisions which were grouped into three sections of analytic importance: the central business district, "ghetto" or low income residential areas, and "nonghetto" or high income residential areas. This method enabled the study to accomplish other objectives such as examination of the relative attractiveness of these geographic sublabor markets to different types of industry. In this manner it is possible to determine if the ghetto is an attractive site for new firms while questions on the survey instruments were designed to reveal whether these locational decisions necessarily mean employment opportunities to the potential labor supply residing near the new businesses' location.

A final purpose of this book is to present a cross-sectional analysis of the industrial employment structure by geographic subdivision of the city. The data for this analysis include the employment for all firms in Philadelphia in 1968. By providing this information on the geographic location of labor demand in relation to the potential supply, the study attempts to explain some of the reasons for the high sectoral unemployment found in Philadelphia and other cities.

Data Sources and Method of Analysis

The basic data for the study were derived from the mercantile license file and the wage tax records of the city of Philadelphia. Each new firm is required by law to obtain a license to operate within the city and changes of address and exits from business must be reported. In this way the location of the firm (by zip code), its Standard Industrial Classification, and its number of employees (from wage tax data) were obtained. Each firm was assigned to one of the eight geographic areas of the city, and since these areas were classified as ghetto, nonghetto or central business district, it was possible to compare the employment, industrial characteristics of firms, and so forth by type of geographic location.

Information was collected on the total population of firms in the city in 1968. In addition, the population of entrant, exit, and firms which moved within the city was studied for 1967. Although these were cross-sectional data, it did provide some indication of the dynamic changes which affect the demand for labor in the city.

To supplement these data, a mail survey and interviews were conducted on samples of firms entering the city and a suburban county. These instruments provided additional information on the characteristics of entrepreneurs, their locational decisions, and the race and residence of their employees. It also provided information on the occupational structure of new businesses.

The analysis of data is presented in three major sections. The discussion of some of the dynamic influences in the urban labor market includes chapter 2 which gives an overview of the employment situation in today's large metropolitan areas and of Philadelphia's in particular. The socioeconomic characteristics of the eight geographic sectors of Philadelphia to be used in subsequent chapters are discussed, as are the city's changing structure of the industry and labor force.

This information shows that the urban areas selected for the study is fairly diverse in its structure and not atypical of many of the nation's urban areas. Chapter 3 contains the data on the net effect on employment of firms entering, exiting, and changing location within the city. The relative importance of the net employment changes is assessed by geographic sector of the city. The occupational implications of the net employment changes are discussed in chapter 4.

The geographic distribution of employment in relation to the residential location of the potential labor supply is contained in Part II of the book. Chapter 5 presents an industrial breakdown of the dispersion of employment within the city. It also relates these dispersion patterns to the commuting time to the center of the city. Chapter 6 compares the industrial structure of each of eight sections of the city designated as the system of sublabor markets.

The reasons and implications of locational choices are discussed in Part III. The relationship between size of firm and commuting time to center city is discussed in chapter 7. The important factors in plant location decisions and the implications for the employment of local residents are presented in chapters 8 and 9. The personal characteristics of "new" entrepreneurs and the variation among industries and geographic locations are analyzed in chapter 10. The final chapter integrates the findings and points out some of the public policy implications.

Summary of Findings and Recommendations

The industrial and employment trends in the Philadelphia metropolitan area are quite typical of many of the nation's large urban areas. During the past two decades employment in the city expanded, but its rate of growth was about half as rapid as the rate for the entire SMSA. In addition, some industries located in the city have actually shown an absolute decline in employment. This has occurred for some manufacturing industries, transportation, and public utilities.

The study shows that at least for Philadelphia, the relatively slow employment growth in the city is not attributable to a large proportion of slow growing or declining industries being located in the city. In fact the highly diversified structure of the industry mix in the city has strengthened its economic base. The major reason for the city's sluggish growth in employment has been that in the recent past it has been unable to compete with the suburban counties in the metropolitan area for the location of new industry. This is probably a weakness common to many central cities. The employment trend would, of course, have been even more sluggish if Philadelphia had a higher proportion of "declining" manufacturing industries such as textiles and apparel. However, the diversified nature of its manufacturing has permitted it to sustain a slow rate of growth in employment during the past decade.

The Influence of New Business

The feasibility of a policy to rehabilitate the ghetto by providing incentives to new businesses which locate in the inner core of the city depends to a large extent on the current geographic distribution of firms which enter, exit, and relocate within the city. The findings of this study show that any policy designed to attract new businesses is operating against powerful economic forces and is unlikely to have a major impact on the employment problems of ghetto residents.

There is a considerable amount of change in the population of firms in all major geographic sectors (ghetto, nonghetto, and central business district) of Philadelphia. The extent of these changes is quite similar among geographic areas when compared to the population of firms in each area. The impact of these changes on the economic future of inner city business and its residents is more accurately assessed by the marginal change, that is the net increase (or decrease) in number of firms and employment opportunities. The entry and exit behavior of firms in the city during 1967 resulted in a net increase of 283 firms in nonghetto areas, 67 firms in the central business district, and only 76 firms in the ghettos.

The direct employment impact for the city as a whole was an increase of over 4,000 jobs which is about 0.5% of citywide total employment. There was a tendency, however, for nonghetto entrants to be larger and exits smaller than was the case for ghetto entrants and exits. As a result the increase in direct employment attributable to the marginal changes in the number of firms was concentrated in the nonghetto areas of the city. As a group the ghetto areas actually lost 450 jobs, although the net loss was entirely attributable to the largest ghetto area of the city which lost over 1,000 jobs. In contrast, the net employment impact in the nonghetto areas of the city resulted in an increase of some 3,800 jobs. In the central business district employment opportunities increased by about 750 jobs which, given the total employment in this area, was a rather modest increase and probably reflects the density of land use in the downtown area.

The industrial distribution of the increase in employment generated by the net increase in new businesses emphasizes the relative weakness of the ghetto areas. The long-run economic future of any section of the city is probably improved if the marginal increase in businesses and job opportunities is fairly diversified. Since the occupational structure in a geographic area is influenced by the industrial distribution of new firms, it is preferable for a sublabor market to be able to attract manufacturing industry as well as firms in the service sector. This will ensure job opportunities over a fairly wide range of wage rates.

The entry-exit behavior of firms throughout the city is heavily concentrated in the service sector. Almost 50% of the net increase in new businesses were service firms. There was only a net increase of 28 manufacturing businesses during 1967, and since the average size of exit firms was greater than the average size of entrants, the employment impact of this change resulted in a loss of almost i,000 manufacturing jobs. This loss is, however, attributable to the ghetto areas and the central business district which together lost over 1,700 jobs. There was actually a net gain of some 800 manufacturing jobs distributed throughout the nonghetto sectors of the city.

An analysis of the employment changes attributable to the entry-exit behavior of the various types of manufacturing firms does suggest that the central city, at least outside the ghetto, is still quite an attractive location for some types of manufacturing. The central city is still an acceptable location if production techniques do not require large-scale operations. Consequently, chemicals and petroleum refining are likely to decide against locating in the central city while small firms in the paper products, fabricated metals, electrical machinery industries are still attracted to the city as well as the suburban ring. Firms which use labor-intensive methods of production (e.g., textile and apparel industries) also find the central city an advantageous section for their operations. Although the ghetto appears unable to develop or even retain its manufacturing firms, the nonghetto areas within the central city are still able to attract small manufacturing firms using labor-intensive methods of production.

The ghettos and the central business district also showed considerable weakness in their ability to attract and retain jobs in wholesale and retail trade. It was only in jobs in the service industries, usually personal services, that the ghettos showed any strength. Employment growth in these types of jobs is of much less value than jobs in other industries since an expected low employment multiplier for the personal service industries is unlikely to result in a significant indirect employment growth in the future.

Considerable expansion and contraction of family businesses also occur within urban areas. Since these businesses do not employ a work force, their impact on the labor market is quite indirect. The entry or exit of an entrepreneur does, however, affect the employment status of some individuals, though in many cases it may be of a rather temporary nature. For example, in the construction industry the new entrepreneur may exit from the industry when building starts or job contracts are low and become a member of the labor force. Frequently, the exiting entrepreneur will find employment with another contractor in the urban area.

During 1967 several thousand new entrepreneurs without a work force registered in the city. About 40% of these family businesses were established in the ghetto sections of the city. This compares to only some 17% of the new firms with a work force locating in the ghettos.

The location of a high proportion of family business in any area is a dubious advantage since about 50% of such firms are in wholesale and retail trade and an additional 30% in service industries. Since many of these firms are rather transitory in nature and have a very uncertain future, the ghetto's success in attracting family business probably reflects a basic weakness in the existing industrial structure of the ghetto rather than an advantage which will bring long-run benefit to the residents of this section of the city.

The movement of existing firms from one section of the city to another changes the geographic distribution of jobs. In 1967 the ghetto areas did show some modest net increases in employment due to the movement of firms within the city, but the impact on employment was not sufficient to alter the conclusion that the locational patterns of firms reflect major economic pressures which make the ghetto a relatively unattractive environment for new businesses.

The lack of economic justification for a policy which attempts to attract and assist new businesses in the ghetto is further emphasized by the apparent relatively slow employment growth of ghetto firms during the first few years of operations. The new ghetto business does not only employ a much smaller number of workers than do the nonghetto city entrants and suburban entrant firms, but the rate of increase in the ghetto firms' work force is substantially less than the employment increase experienced by new nonghetto and suburban firms during the early stage of the firms' development. This difference applies to almost all types of occupations and industries.

There are apparently strong economic trends within the central city which will make it extremely difficult for the ghetto to become economically a "self sufficient" sector of the urban economy. New business is certainly not the appropriate vehicle to achieve a self-sufficient goal even if such a goal were desirable. New businesses locating outside the ghetto appear to do "better" than those locating within the ghetto, and if public policy is attempting to develop a new black business class (as distinguished from a policy to establish a self-sufficient ghetto economy), then any assistance to minority businessmen should encourage them to locate in nonghetto areas of the city or the central business district as well as the ghetto. The study produced little evidence that the ghetto provided relative locational advantages for any type of new business. It is possible that some manufacturing industries which provide a service to the firms in the central business district (e.g., printing) may successfully develop in the ghetto where space is available at low cost. However, the results show that it is most unlikely that new businesses established by individual blacks will generate a strong enough economic base to revitalize the ghetto economy. These entrepreneurs should therefore be advised to consider locations outside the ghetto. Not only will such a policy provide the minority entrepreneur with a greater chance of success, but it will generate more job opportunities for ghetto residents, provided the new business is located in nonghetto areas close to the core of the city.

The economic viability of the ghetto will only be achieved if the existing businesses retain their current level of output and employment. In some instances it may be feasible to provide new economic activity by locating government facilities in the ghetto. The solution to high sectoral unemployment does not necessarily depend on the economic expansion of the ghetto provided the ghetto resident can find employment opportunities close to the core of the city.

Occupational and Wage Differentials Among New Businesses

Occupational data was collected from a sample of new businesses in the city and the suburbs. A comparison of the occupational structure of the entrants shows some variation according to the location of the firm. The information was only collected from some 4,300 positions and the findings therefore cannot be considered definitive.

Ghetto entrants which are generally substantially smaller than either non-ghetto or suburban entrants tend to offer proportionally, and absolutely, fewer job opportunities which would be considered high in the skill hierarchy of occupations. Ghetto entrants have a lower proportion of professional and technical occupations, and among the service type occupations most opportunities are in personal services rather than business services. Consequently, ghetto entrants are more likely to offer proportionately more of the lower-paying jobs. However, for many of the higher skill level occupations (e.g., managerial and professional technical) the new ghetto firm is likely to pay a higher salary. A similar tendency exists for office clerical occupations. For some of the lower skilled occupations (e.g., plant clericals), the ghetto firms paid less than did the nonghetto firms.

As expected, the work force of the new ghetto firm is made up of a lower proportion of whites than the nonghetto entrants. For the high skill (and high pay) jobs, however, a high proportion of employees in ghetto firms were white. The salary differences between ghetto and nonghetto jobs in the same occupations is therefore a reflection of the lack of skilled labor and a surplus of semiskilled and unskilled labor residing close to the new ghetto businesses. It seems clear that ghetto residents should be trained for some of the skilled occupations in inner-city businesses. For example, some ghetto residents should be trained to compete for the office clerical opportunities in the inner city.

Employment Opportunities and the Geographic Distribution of Jobs

The geographic distribution of total citywide jobs was estimated for 1968. This analysis of over 850,000 jobs revealed that about 80% of these jobs were located within about 20 minutes highway-travel-time by automobile from the center of the city. The geographic area encompassed by this travel time was designated as the "core" or "inner" section of the city. It comprised the southern half of the city, including all three ghetto areas along with the central business district and one nonghetto section of the city.

The proportion of employment within the core of the city does vary from industry to industry. The high degree of employment concentration does suggest that ghetto residents are in close proximity of a substantial number of job opportunities requiring a wide variety of skills. It is for this reason that the approach of the Concentrated Employment Program, which is based on the target area concept in supplying manpower services, receives strong support from these findings. While this approach may be completely appropriate its success will depend on the administrative efficiency with which it is implemented and its relevance to the local demand for labor.

The policy which attempts to raise the labor productivity of residents of the inner city who experience the high unemployment rates will, of course, have a greater chance of success if additional steps can be taken to ensure that the ghetto resident will apply for jobs in the inner city and be hired for the vacant positions. In this respect, the findings suggest that improvements in the public transit system within the core of the city will make the large number of jobs in the inner city more accessible to ghetto residents. This policy is necessary because of the very low automobile ownership among ghetto families and because the degree of concentration of city jobs declines substantially when public transit time rather than highway travel time by private transportation is used in calculating the geographic dispersion of employment. Some parts of the ghetto areas are apparently somewhat isolated from the public transit routes, and as a result it may take some 40 minutes to travel to the center of the city by public transit compared to 20 minutes by automobile.

The geographic concentration of city jobs within the core implies that improvement in the inner city transportation network will make the vast majority of job opportunities accessible to ghetto residents. The feasibility of such improvements, of course, depends on the cost of the proposed changes. For example, the cost of developing new subway routes would be prohibitive given the expected benefits. However, substantial changes are possible in surface public transit without increasing substantial investments by the transit authority. Finally, it does seem desirable to experiment with changing the rate structure of the transit system including a low fare (or even zero fare) on reverse commuting during the high peak traffic hours.

The unemployed ghetto residents should be trained in the types of occupations which are expanding, or at least not declining, within the core of the city. In addition, industries which have a fairly high proportion of semiskilled and relatively unskilled occupations are most likely to provide employment opportunities for trainees.

If the inner city of Philadelphia is typical of many urban areas, then a strategy which permits the upgraded ghetto labor force to penetrate the work force of existing businesses is the approach which should be given highest priority.[8] The success of the penetration strategy requires more than simply supplying manpower services to areas with high sectoral unemployment. The choice of industries to penetrate is crucial since it influences the type of job training provided. In Philadelphia in choosing manufacturing industry, preference should be given to electrical machinery, paper, lumber and wood, printing and publishing. The situation will probably be different in other urban areas, but it is expected that when the criteria of geographic accessibility of jobs, occupational structure of industry, and industrial employment trend are applied, some industries will have greater potential job opportunities than others for unemployed ghetto residents who are entering manpower training programs.

The most attractive industrial sectors for the penetration strategy in most urban areas are the growth sectors of construction, transportation, finance, insurance, real estate services and, of course, government employment. With the exception of construction, a very high proportion of citywide jobs in these industries are likely to be located in the inner core of the city. The location and growth of local government employment is encouraging for ghetto residents and any national manpower policy which seeks to establish job opportunities in the public sector is, depending on the nature of the job opportunities created, likely to be of some assistance to unemployed inner-city residents. Such a policy may of course only be a temporary advantage since the number of job slots may vary with the unemployment level. The net impact of the public employment program under the Emergency Employment Act passed in July 1971 may not in fact result in a lower unemployment rate or in fact more job opportunities. It is possible, for example, that local authorities will use the public employment program jobs to offset an increase in new jobs which would have occurred irrespective of the federal program. In addition, the concept of public sector employment opportunities, as currently enacted, results in training or experience job slots rather than permanent employment positions. While the present public sector program is designed to place some of the enrollees in permanent positions the major benefit of such a program is likely to be in training ghetto residents rather than providing long-term employment.

The extent to which trained ghetto residents are able to gain entry into existing businesses depends partially on the reduction of discrimination in hiring. The policy which seeks to place unemployed ghetto residents in existing businesses will be more successful if the existing laws on discrimination on employment are effectively enforced. The government has "home town" plans in construction and "goals and timetables" in other industries. While these programs have improved employment for minorities it is now time to evaluate this policy so that all racial and ethnic groups are not subject to discrimination. Specific proposals to ensure nondiscrimination are, of course, clearly beyond the scope of this study and are only mentioned to illustrate their interdependence with the policy of retraining the unemployed for existing central city jobs rather than relying solely on the job opportunities created by new businesses.

The alternative policy of improving employment opportunities in existing businesses or developing jobs by encouraging new business are not mutually exclusive. Both approaches are likely to reduce high sectoral unemployment. The relative strength of the core of the city in the base industries (those which export a high proportion of their output) and the nonbase industries (those which supply services to the residents of the local area) is encouraging for those who are unemployed. If the base industries (usually manufacturing) show some signs of weakening in the central city and strengthening in the suburbs, the policy should be directed towards encouraging existing, or new, city businesses which will provide ancillary services to the expanding-base industries in the suburban ring.

The Entrepreneur and Ghetto Development

Minority entrepreneurs are most likely to enter business in the wholesale and retail trade and service sectors compared to manufacturing. They are also likely to locate in a ghetto section of the city. From the point of view of the economic success of the new venture, this is a rather disturbing finding and public policy should encourage minority businessmen to locate in nonghetto sections of the city which also provide considerable small business opportunities.

There is no evidence that the minority entrepreneur is at a disadvantage with the white businessman in financing the new enterprise. However, the black businessman tends to have less experience before entering business and a lower level of formal educational training. For this reason it is recommended that perhaps the highest priority in the strategy of assisting minority businessmen should be to provide entrepreneurial training services as part of the nation's manpower services.

Plant Location Decisions and Ghetto Unemployment

The trend in the pattern of location of existing business also has a potential impact on the high unemployment rates in the inner city. There are several reasons why firms with a large work force are likely to provide more potential job opportunities for the unemployed than do firms with a small number of workers. Large firms are likely to have a more formal approach towards recruiting and are expected to put less stress on recruiting through current employees. Since the unemployed ghetto resident may have few acquaintances who are employed regularly, the more formal hiring methods at least provide an opportunity to apply for a vacant position. In addition, larger organizations have to report the racial composition of their work force to the Equal Employment Opportunities Commission and this is likely to restrict extent of discrimination in hiring. Consequently, any trend for the larger firms to locate farther from the center of the city will create labor market difficulties for the unemployed ghetto residents seeking job opportunities.

The relationship of size of firm and distance from the core of the city was analyzed for manufacturing firms in Philadelphia in 1968. The findings suggest that in several industries there is a tendency for the larger firms to locate close to the center of the city. This was the finding for the apparel, lumber, printing and publishing, leather, and transportation manufacturing industries. On the basis of accessibility it therefore appears that these industries provide potential job opportunities for disadvantaged workers.

The geographic distribution by size of firm did not provide an indication of future trends. For this reason information on the factors influencing the choice of location was collected from a sample of city and suburban entrant firms. The disadvantages of current locations was also studied for both entrant and existing firms in ghetto and nonghetto locations.

The findings support the theory that nonmanufacturing firms are more market-oriented and stress economics of localization, while the availability of space and facilities, its price, and ability to expand are the major forces pulling manufacturing away from the center of the city. Ironically, however, these same forces attract small manufacturing and nonmanufacturing firms to the city's ghettos where cheap facilities are available close to the central business district. Despite these particular advantages of the ghetto, the inner city clearly has difficulty in supplying the locational characteristics preferred by new firms. The overriding issue, especially among smaller nonmanufacturing ghetto firms, is the fear of theft and vandalism. In addition, lack of room for expansion, lack of space for customer parking, and problems of transportation access are generally viewed as disadvantages which, unless dealt with by local authorities, may result in a substantial net outflow of businesses from the inner city or at least substantially inhibit the location of new firms in the city. It also appears that while improving the quality of the ghetto labor force will contribute to a reduction in high sectoral unemployment by making ghetto labor more competitive with the labor force in other sections of the city, this policy will not in itself be sufficient to attract or perhaps even retain jobs in the ghetto. Other environmental conditions which new businesses prefer may have to be supplied in the inner city.

The success of the "self-sufficiency" approach to reducing ghetto unemployment not only depends upon attracting new businesses but on the extent to which these firms employ residents from the surrounding area. From the interviews it was found that new businesses recruit a higher proportion of their employees from the immediate environment of the firm than do businesses which have been established for some time. For new ghetto firms, a higher proportion of employees live close to the firm than was the case for new nonghetto businesses. The relationship is reversed for *established* ghetto and nonghetto firms. Few existing ghetto firms had many employees residing close to the business; most employees resided outside the ghetto. On the other hand, established nonghetto firms had a fairly high proportion of employees living near the place of operations. Once the firm is established in the ghetto and its work force expands, it appears that the proportion of employees hired from the immediate environment declines. The established firm appears to enlarge the geographic dimensions of its search for workers. This may simply be the result of the increase in size of the work force, but it may also be due to the inadequate supply of labor of the quality preferred by businesses in the inner city.

The residential location of the firm's employees also varied among industries. There was some evidence to support the view that for manufacturing and service firms a fairly high proportion of the work force lives a substantial distance from the place of operations. Among wholesale and retail trade firms, especially for the new firms, there was a tendency for the work force to be recruited from the residential area close to the business.

The means of travel to work used by the employees of the firms surveyed reveal some interesting results. The automobile was the predominant method of getting to work and walking was relatively unimportant, though nonghetto firm employees did walk more than employees of firms in other geographic areas. As expected, employees working in central business district firms tended to use public transportation. This is because it is feasible to have such a transportation system in high density work-place areas. It was somewhat surprising that employees of nonghetto firms used public transit more frequently than employees in ghetto firms. The extremely heavy reliance of employees in ghetto firms on the automobile suggests that large sections of ghetto areas are isolated from public transit routes. The average daily travel time data utilized in studying the distribution of total employment in the city tends to support this finding. It appears that not only is the ghetto resident working in nonghetto sections of the city without adequate public transit, but those working in the ghetto (no matter where they reside) also experience the same problem and rely heavily on the automobile to travel to work.

Several general public policy implications seem to emerge from the results of this study. First, the problem of high unemployment in sectors of urban labor markets is only likely to be solved if several strategies are followed concurrently. For example, improvements in the public transit system in inner cities will reduce worker immobilities among various "sublabor" markets within the city and at the same time improve the locational advantages for firms considering locating in the city. A policy which attempts to raise the productivity of the ghetto labor supply is also likely to be more effective if the geographic boundary of the worker's preference for place of employment are enlarged through better transit facilities within the city.

A second major policy implication of the findings is that, despite the interdependence of policy strategies, there is clearly an order of priority among possible solutions to urban employment problems. Since the vast majority of job opportunities are located in the core of the city, raising the productivity of ghetto residents is clearly the policy which should be given top priority. The importance of this particular recommendation will, of course, vary with the industrial and residential structure of each urban area, but no other policy (e.g., enforcement of nondiscrimination in hiring, improved transit, etc.)—even in a city where job opportunities are not concentrated geographically—is likely to be of any consequence to hard core ghetto residents unless their labor skills are improved by job experience (e.g., wage subsidy to firms) or pure training.

A policy which attempts to create some urban environmental structural changes should also be given high priority. These changes include selective changes in urban transit systems within the inner city and a restructuring of the fare system in public transit. Programs to reduce the level of crime, especially crimes of violence and crimes against property should also make the central city a more desirable location for business. This particular policy should be given a high priority mainly because there is evidence to suggest that businessmen believe that environmental problems in the inner city are very serious and unless corrected may lead to a substantial migration of business. A reduction in the level of urban crime will not necessarily generate more job opportunities, but it will help retain existing jobs.

The findings strongly suggest that a policy which encourages new ghetto businesses should be given a low priority since they have a low payoff in terms of job opportunities for ghetto residents. If the policy goal is to increase the number of minority businessmen, then it is essential that minority businessmen be encouraged to locate in nonghetto areas. There may, of course, be exceptions to this general recommendation. There have been examples of successful community sponsored business projects in the ghetto and these may be worth supporting. Experience has shown, however, that the cost of subsidizing such projects is high and the increase in job opportunities very small. The policy of aid to minority businessmen, when given, should emphasize management training for the new entrepreneurs rather than a subsidy for starting business in a section of the city which has serious locational disadvantages. The rehabilitation of the ghetto, including the reduction of high unemployment, can clearly not be achieved through acts of heroism performed by individual minority entrepreneurs.

**Part I:
Dynamics of an Urban
Labor Market**

Trends in the Urban Supply and Demand for Labor

Statistics indicate that during the 1960s the unemployment rate for the population living in urban areas of the United States has fallen. This improvement has been experienced by both whites and nonwhites, as shown in table 2-1. Despite these advances in the aggregate, the demographic features of the urban population, residential segregation, and changing patterns of industrial location have combined to create high rates of unemployment in the racial ghettos of most large metropolitan areas. This situation is clearly one of sectoral unemployment, which, as explained earlier, exists when the unemployment rate in a particular sector is high relative to the rates experienced in the rest of the labor market.

Table 2-1
Unemployment Rates for Selected Groups

Group	1968 Metropolitan Areas (SMSA's)	1960 Metropolitan Areas (SMSA's)
White		
Male, 20 years and over	2.2	4.2
Female, 20 years and over	3.3	4.5
Youths, 16-19 years	11.1	10.4
Negro & Other Races		
Male, 20 years and over	5.5	9.4
Female, 20 years and over	6.4	9.3
Youths, 16-19 years	28.5	21.8

Source: Conrad Taeuber, U.S. Bureau of the Census, in testimony before the House Committee on Banking and Currency, October 14, 1969, Appendix.

Sectoral Unemployment Rates

The unemployment situation in metropolitan areas (which usually coincide with the boundaries of the statistical collection unit described as an urban labor market area) can perhaps best be appreciated by considering it as composed of three geographic sectors: the suburban ring, the nonghetto sections of the central city, and the ghetto sections. The most severe unemployment and associated poverty problems are in the ghettos. Here the population is largely nonwhite, poor, and living in dilapidated housing. Crime rates are much higher

19

than in other parts of the metropolitan area, and for many ghettos business and employment are declining. Public policy has established various manpower, education, housing, and economic development programs in many of these local communities. The second level of concern is the geographic area encompassing the ghettos. This sector, comprised of the nonghetto sections of the central city, frequently has the same external boundaries as the city itself. This sector is characterized by higher incomes and lower unemployment than among ghetto residents. Its population is largely white although it includes some nonwhites, especially those whose incomes are above the poverty level. Business and employment in the nonghetto sections of the central city have, in general, not shown the declines that mark many ghetto areas. This sector also generally contains a growing central business district. Finally the third primary sector, the suburban ring of the metropolitan area, is usually composed of counties outside the city limits. Here incomes are highest and unemployment lowest among the three geographic sectors in the metropolitan area. Business and employment have been expanding rapidly in this sector, in some instances creating a labor shortage.

The differences in the unemployment rate among these three sectors shown in five major metropolitan areas is shown in table 2-2. It should be noted that the figures for the central city include those unemployed in the ghettos. Similarly, the unemployment rates for the SMSAs include the unemployed in the central city and ghetto. This suggests very low unemployment rates in the suburban ring. It is, of course, likely that the suburban ring will contain geographic sections which have high unemployment rates and the characteristics of these "ghetto" areas may be similar in some respects to their counterparts within the central cities. However, the data suggest that for the most part the suburbs are either areas of sufficient or excess demand for labor. In contrast to both the metropolitan area and the central city, unemployment rates in the ghettos are two or three times higher.

Demographic Changes

The demographic changes in the population of central cities which have made it difficult to show that manpower programs have made significant inroads into urban unemployment have also tended to accentuate the sectoral nature of the problem. The most important demographic change, of course, is the increasing proportion of the central city population that is nonwhite. Table 2-3 shows that between 1960 and 1968 the central cities in the United States gained nearly two-thirds of a million people. As part of this net change the black population has increased by over two million, while the white population has declined by a little less than two million. About one-third of the increase in black central city population (800,000 persons) is due to net in-migration, while almost all of the

Table 2-2
Unemployment Rates for Selected Urban Areas: 1968-69

Labor Force Category	Chicago			Detroit			Houston			Los Angeles			New York City		
	SMSA	Central City[a]	Ghetto	SMSA	Central City[b]	Ghetto	SMSA	Central City	Ghetto	SMSA	Central City	Ghetto	SMSA	Central City	Ghetto
Male (20 yrs. and over)															
White	–	–	–	–	–	7.8	–	–	2.7	–	–	4.4	–	–	5.1
Black & Other	–	–	4.3	–	–	5.9	–	–	4.1	–	–	10.1	–	–	5.0
All Races	1.7	–	–	2.1	–	–	3.1	–	–	–	–	–	2.4	–	–
Female (20 yrs. and over)															
White	–	–	–	–	–	7.8	–	–	7.5	–	–	5.7	–	–	5.6
Black & Other	–	–	7.3	–	–	14.2	–	–	9.7	–	–	12.9	–	–	5.4
All Races	3.0	–	–	3.9	–	–	5.4	–	–	–	–	–	2.8	–	–
Youth (16 to 19 yrs.)															
All Races	12.7	–	31.1	13.6	–	36.4	–	–	30.2	14.3	–	31.8	11.1	–	25.3
Race															
White	2.3	2.7	4.0	3.0	–	9.1	–	2.5	5.9	4.2	4.6	6.3	2.9	2.9	6.9
Black & Other	7.6	7.4	8.8	7.5	–	13.5	–	5.8	9.5	8.5	8.6	15.2	3.9	4.0	6.7

Sources: Data were selected from U.S. Department of Labor, "Unemployment in 20 Largest Metropolitan Areas," news release, March 6, 1969 and from U.S. Department of Labor, *Urban Employment Survey* (BLS Report no. 376) October 1969.

[a] The Urban Employment Survey was conducted in Concentrated Employment Program (CEP) areas which are sometimes called poverty areas or slum areas. In New York City there are three CEP areas.

[b] The central city includes the CEP area and frequently includes other slum areas not included in the designated CEP area.

Table 2-3
Population of the United States by Residence and Race (in Millions)

Residence & Race	1968	1960	Percentage of Change
Total	198.2	178.5	11.1
Metropolitan Areas	127.5	112.9	12.9
Central Cities	58.4	57.8	1.0
Outside Central Cities	69.1	55.1	25.4
Nonmetropolitan	70.8	65.6	7.9
White			
Metropolitan	110.9	99.7	11.2
Central Cities	45.6	47.5	− 3.9
Outside Central Cities	65.3	52.3	24.9
Negro & Other Races			
Metropolitan	15.1	12.2	24.3
Central Cities	11.9	9.7	22.9
Outside Central Cities	3.2	2.5	29.8

Source: Data from Conrad Taeuber, U.S. Bureau of the Census, in testimony before the House Committee on Banking and Currency, October 14, 1969.

white decline is due to net out-migration. The unemployment rate for nonwhite Americans, despite improvements over the decade, is significantly higher than that for whites. This is due to numerous factors including racial discrimination and lack of skills and education. These latter disadvantages appear particularly serious among nonwhites who have recently migrated to the central cities from rural areas. The increasing proportion of nonwhites, therefore, would tend to raise the unemployment rate in the central cities. Another aspect of these demographic changes is the larger proportion of youth among the nonwhite urban population. The problem of youth unemployment is even more serious than for other labor force groups. While the overall unemployment rate has been falling since 1960, the rate for persons aged 16 to 19, although ordinarily high, has in fact risen and in some ghetto areas has at times reached the incredible rate of 35 percent.

Furthermore, recent studies in several cities have shown that there has been an increase in residential segregation since 1960, thus increasing the concentration of the unemployment problem in a few sections of the central cities. Conversely, in the suburbs residence is often restricted to middle and upper income white by zoning laws and other devices, resulting in that sector's low unemployment rate. In these ways, differences in unemployment rates by race and age group, when coupled with segregated residential patterns, have contributed to the development of variations in the unemployment among different sectors of the metropolitan area.

There are also considerable differences in occupational status among workers residing in different parts of the metropolitan area. Table 2-4 indicates that while 46% of all males in the labor force living in metropolitan areas are in white-collar jobs, only 11% of nonwhites living in selected poverty areas have these types of jobs. The proportion of nonwhite males holding these types of jobs ranged from a high of 25.5% in New York City to 11.1% in Detroit.

These data probably understate the occupational status differential between ghetto and nonghetto residents. This is because there is a significant occupational hierarchy within each of the broad occupational categories shown in table 2-4, and ghetto residents are likely to be concentrated at the bottom of the internal hierarchy. For example, managers in manufacturing plants are grouped with managers of small retail stores, barber shops, and so on. Ghetto residents who hold managerial jobs are likely to work in the latter type of firm.

The differential between female residents in ghetto and nonghetto sectors is even more pronounced; 65% of such workers in the metropolitan areas are in white collar jobs while less than 35% of the female workers living in the ghetto sector have white collar jobs. This finding has considerable socioeconomic implications for urban problems since close to one-third of ghetto families are headed by women.

The data clearly show that ghetto employees are concentrated in the service, laboring, and operative occupations. The explanation of this occupational distribution is mainly attributable to racial discrimination, low educational attainment, and lack of skill and experience among ghetto residents. However, inadequate labor demand in areas accessible to ghetto residents also contributes to the present occupational structure of ghetto workers.

Concurrently with the demographic and labor supply changes described above, there has been a geographic redistribution of jobs within urban areas. Advances in highway transportation and communications have made it feasible—and for many industries, more economical—for firms whose market is the metropolitan area to locate beyond the core of the city.[1] At the same time taxes, land costs, and crime rates have made the central city a more costly place of operation. As a result, there is a strong trend in metropolitan industrial location towards the suburbs.

The shifting pattern of industrial location within thirty large metropolitan areas is shown in table 2-5. Employment growth in the suburbs was found to be greater than in the central city in all industrial categories. In some industries, for example the service sector, there was an increase in central city jobs, but in other industries, especially manufacturing, there was a substantial decline in job opportunities. In the suburbs, employment in all industrial categories increased, with the rate of growth being most pronounced in nonmanufacturing. These findings are confirmed by Dorothy K. Newman's study of the distribution of new nonresidential building permits.[2] Her study shows that since 1954 there has been a steady trend in the movement of new factory and commercial buildings to the suburban ring of metropolitan areas. The trend toward decentralization of

Table 2-4
Distribution of Persons Employed by Occupational and Geographic Area: 1968-69 (Percentage Distribution)

Occupation	Metropolitan Areas (All Races)	Ghetto Areas (Negro & Other Races)				
		Chicago	Detroit	Houston	Los Angeles	New York City
Male						
White-Collar Workers	46	13.6	11.1	13.8	21.3	25.5
Professional, Technical & Managerial	31	4.3	5.7	6.9	10.4	9.5
Clerical & Sales	15	9.3	5.1	6.9	7.9	13.8
Blue-Collar Workers	46	75.0	77.1	71.4	61.1	52.3
Craftsmen & Foremen	20	16.9	12.4	12.9	15.8	13.9
Operatives	20	43.0	47.6	34.0	34.7	29.8
Laborers	6	15.2	17.2	24.5	10.5	8.6
Service Workers	8	11.4	11.8	13.9	16.5	22.1
Total	100	100.	100.	100.	100.	100.
Female						
White-Collar Workers	65	29.1	29.4	19.0	34.4	33.5
Professional, Technical & Managerial	20	6.0	6.6	7.6	10.9	8.3
Clerical & Sales	45	23.1	22.8	11.5	23.5	25.1
Blue-Collar Workers	15	46.4	18.2	12.9	27.9	25.4
Craftsmen & Foremen	—	2.3	.8	.8	1.4	1.5
Operatives	—	41.9	16.1	11.4	25.6	23.4
Laborers	—	2.2	1.3	.8	.9	.6
Service Workers	20	24.4	52.4	68.0	37.7	41.1
Total	100	100.	100.	100.	100.	100.

Sources: Data on ghetto areas from U.S. Department of Labor, *Urban Employment Survey*, BLS Report No. 370. 1969. Data for metropolitan areas from Conrad Taeuber, U.S. Bureau of the Census, in testimony before the House Committee on Banking and Currency, October 14, 1969, Appendix.

Notes: Distribution may not add to 100 because of rounding or omission of farm workers.

The data for the metropolitan areas include all races. The data on the ghetto exclude the occupational distribution of white ghetto residents. With the exception of Los Angeles, the proportion of whites in the ghetto is less than half the nonwhite proportion. White ghetto residents tend to have a slightly higher occupational status than do the nonwhites.

The occupational structure of ghetto residents does not include youths. The inclusion of youths would lower the occupational status of ghetto residents even more than shown in the table.

Table 2-5
Employment Distribution in Thirty Large Metropolitan Areas

| | 1958 | | 1963 | | Change | | Change Percentage | |
	Central City (000) (1)	Suburbs (000) (2)	Central City (000) (3)	Suburbs (000) (4)	Central City (000) (5)	Suburbs (000) (6)	Central City[a] (7)	Suburbs[b] (8)
Populous SMSA's								
Manufacturing firms	4,258	2,935	3,994	3,328	− 263	393	− 6.2	13.4
Wholesale firms	1,289	302	1,241	445	− 48	143	− 3.8	47.5
Retail firms	2,133	1,216	2,241	1,772	108	556	5.1	45.7
Service firms	1,252	460	1,415	665	173	205	13.9	44.7
Total	8,924	4,913	8,891	6,210	− 33	1,297	− 9.0	26.4

aColumn 7 is derived by dividing column 5 by column 1.
bColumn 8 is derived by dividing column 6 by column 2.
Sources: Bureau of the Census, 1958 and 1963 Census of Business (Area Statistics); 1963 Census of Manufacturers (Area Statistics). As quoted in Roger Noll, *Metropolitan Employment and Population Distribution and the Conditions of the Urban Poor*, The Brookings Institution, Washington, D.C., 1970.

metropolitan employment along with the increased segregation of the population by race and income has had serious implications for the urban labor market. It appears that the low skill jobs in manufacturing and trade for which ghetto residents would most easily qualify are expanding most rapidly in the suburbs while such jobs are growing slowly or even declining in the central city.[3] In this way the changes in the distribution of industry among sectors of the metropolitan area has run counter to shifts in the pattern of labor supply and has contributed to a highly sectoral pattern of unemployment.

Sectoral Unemployment and Demographic Changes in Philadelphia

The demographic changes and unemployment characteristics of the Philadelphia metropolitan area are quite similar to the experience in other urban areas. The proportion of the population of its central city that is nonwhite has increased from 18% in 1950 to 26% in 1960 and to an estimated 31% in 1965.[4] Over this period, racial ghettos in three sections of the city expanded significantly. The Philadelphia SMSA also had differential rates of employment growth between its central city and suburban ring which will be examined in detail below. Coinciding with these trends were differences in the unemployment rates among different sectors of the metropolitan area. In 1968 the unemployment rate in the suburban ring was 2.7%, while the rate for the central city was 3.9%. The figure for the suburban ring might have been lower had it not included the city of Chester, Pennsylvania, which had a ghetto of its own. A study of urban poverty areas conducted in November of 1966 showed that in the North Philadelphia ghetto the unemployment rate was 11% and the subemployment rate was 34%.[a] In contrast, the Philadelphia SMSA unemployment rate for 1966 (11 month average) was 3.4%.

Variations in Socioeconomic Conditions Among Sections of Philadelphia

In order to analyze the characteristics and employment impact of new and existing firms in this sectoral context, a major feature of this study is comparison of these firms according to their geographic location within the city. For such comparisons, the city was divided into eight geographic sections or

---

[a]The "subemployment" index includes: (1) the unemployed, (2) those working part time who are seeking full-time work, (3) heads of households working full time and earning less than $60 a week and those not heads of households working full time and earning less than $56 a week, (4) half the number of males aged 20 to 64 listed as not in the labor force, and (5) half the estimated number of "unfound" males.

sublabor markets. Neither this geographic division nor the term "sublabor market" is meant to imply that these are self-contained in terms of places of work and residences. This term refers only to geographic subsections of the larger labor market area. The relevance of these comparisons is due to the relation of firms' behavior to the differing socioeconomic characteristics of the sublabor market in which they choose to locate.

The geographic subdivision of the city of Philadelphia used for this study, as shown in figure 2-1, is based on the boundaries used by several federal and local agencies. Three of these sublabor markets, North Philadelphia, Spring Garden, and West Philadelphia, can be described as low-income areas and each contains a substantial ghetto. The boundaries used to demarcate these three sectors are quite similar to boundaries used by the Model Cities Program and the Concentrated Employment Program. Throughout the analysis, these three areas will be referred to collectively as ghetto areas, although, since their boundaries are based in part on administrative criteria, they contain sections which do not conform to the usual sociological meaning of the term "ghetto."

The remaining sections of the city—Center City, South Philadelphia, Northwest Philadelphia, Northeast Philadelphia, and Frankfort-Richmond—were selected according to the practice followed by the City Planning Commission and other local agencies. These sublabor markets are described as "high income" areas in the sense that none of them contain a substantial ghetto of low-income residents. One of these "nonghetto" areas, Center City, is the downtown section of the city and is designated as the central business district (CBD).

A statistical comparison of selected socioeconomic characteristics of these sublabor markets which highlights the differences among sections of the city is presented in Table 2-6. The data are adapted from a study by the Philadelphia City Planning Commission and based on the 1960 census. As mentioned above, Center City corresponds to the central business district which helps explain why it only had a population of 38,000, making it by far the smallest residential section of the city. Of the nonghetto areas it was the only one which had a substantial proportion of nonwhite residents. Center City is the only area where most of the residences are not owner-occupied. The median family income of its population is below the city median, although there is probably a considerable deviation from this average level.

The other four nonghetto areas of the city, South Philadelphia, Frankford-Richmond, Northwest and Northeast Philadelphia all tend to have a relatively high median family income, a very low percentage of nonwhite population, a high proportion of owner-occupied housing and, except for South Philadelphia and Frankford-Richmond, a population with a high median level of education. In contrast, the ghetto areas have a fairly large nonwhite population with a lower level of educational attainment, lower family income, and a smaller proportion of residents who own their homes.

The 1960 census data clearly show substantial differences in socioeconomic

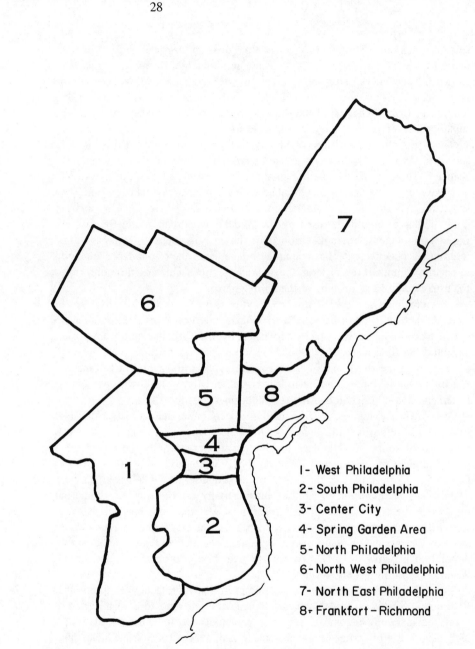

1- West Philadelphia
2- South Philadelphia
3- Center City
4- Spring Garden Area
5- North Philadelphia
6- North West Philadelphia
7- North East Philadelphia
8- Frankfort – Richmond

Figure 2-1. Geographic Division of Philadelphia into Sublabor Markets.

Table 2-6
Socioeconomic Characteristics of Residents in Local Area in 1960

	Total Population	Percentage Black & Other Races	Housing— Percentage, Owner Occupied	Median Income for all Families[a]	Median School Years
West Philadelphia	402,161	42.4	57.9	(a) 6,101 (b) 5,373	(a) 9.4 (b) 10.3
North & Spring Garden	463,773	52.6	46.6	(a) 4,029 (b) 5,535	(a) 8.6 (b) 9.0
Center City	38,323	21.6	14.6	5,574	12.0
South Philadelphia	260,767	25.8	61.5	5,204	8.6
Frankford-Richmond	136,693	0.6	76.6	5,869	8.8
Northwest	347,464	10.7	71.2	(a) 6,658 (b) 6,738 (c) 6,716	(a) 10.1 (b) 11.9 (c) 10.8
Northeast	353,432	2.0	81.6	(a) 6,796 (b) 7,077	(a) 10.3 (b) 11.0
Total	2,002,512	26.7	61.9	5,783	9.6

[a]In some instances, the income data was only available for sections of the local area, and it was not possible to aggregate these data for the total area.

Note: (a), (b) and (c) represent geographic divisions within the areas used in this study.

Source: Data adapted from City of Philadelphia, *Trends in Population, Housing and Socio-Economic Characteristics* (Philadelphia, Planning Analysis Sections, 1963).

characteristics of the ghetto and nonghetto areas. It is believed that during the past decade these differences have become even more pronounced as the proportion of whites in the ghetto areas has declined significantly.

The Current Employment and Industrial Structure of Philadelphia

The geographic and occupational dimensions of labor demand in the central city are related to the industrial structure of the Standard Metropolitan Statistical Area in which the central city is located. It is therefore necessary to identify the overall industrial and employment structure of the geographic area from which the empirical data are collected. Table 2-7 summarizes the employment structure for Philadelphia and the eight county[b] (two states) Philadelphia labor market and provides the relevant background information for the study.

The city of Philadelphia has one of the most highly diversified industrial structures of any city, having over 90% of the U.S. Census Bureau's categories of industries. Moreover, no one industry group is dominant among them. Non-manufacturing employment represents 70% of all nonfarm wage and salary employment as compared to only 30% for manufacturing.

Diversity is characteristic also of the manufacturing sector itself. Machinery, apparel, metals, foods, and printing collectively account for two-thirds of manufacturing employment. Machinery—the largest of these—has only about 19% of the total manufacturing employment.

More significant in terms of total jobs are nonmanufacturing activities. Trade is the predominant employer, but it is followed closely by service industries and government. Approximately 10% of total employment is accounted for by the self-employed, domestic workers, and farm employees.

The importance of the city of Philadelphia in its metropolitan area is evidenced by the fact that the city's establishments (including government) provided in excess of a million jobs in 1968, over one-half the employment in the entire labor market. There are some significant differences, however, between the industrial structure of the labor market as a whole and that of the city alone. In the metropolitan area, manufacturing is relatively important, representing almost one-third of all jobs. Of these manufacturing jobs, one-third are in the machinery or metals industries, while the remainder are widely scattered among other manufacturing activities. In contrast, city manufacturing jobs are concentrated in food, textiles, apparel and printing industries. In the nonmanufacturing industries, the city of Philadelphia has a higher concentration of jobs in finance, insurance and real estate, services and contract construction. These city-SMSA differences indicate that the geographic distribution of em-

---

[b]Besides Philadelphia County, included are Chester, Delaware, Montgomery, and Bucks Counties in Pennsylvania and Burlington, Camden, and Gloucester Counties in New Jersey.

Table 2-7
Employment Structure by Residence of Establishment—1968: City of Philadelphia and Philadelphia Labor Market (SMSA) (In Hundreds)

Industry	City of Philadelphia Employment	Percentage	Philadelphia Labor Market Employment	Percentage	City of Philadelphia Percentage of Philadelphia Labor Market
Contract construction	373	3.6	741	3.8	50.3
Manufacturing	2,705	26.4	5,799	29.5	46.6
Furniture and lumber	65	0.6	130	0.7	50.0
Metals	293	2.9	807	4.1	36.3
Machinery	514	5.0	1,354	6.9	38.0
Transportation equipment	68	0.7	299	1.5	22.7
Food	274	2.7	486	2.5	56.4
Textiles	170	1.7	273	1.4	62.3
Apparel	438	4.3	575	2.9	76.2
Printing	249	2.4	408	2.1	61.0
Chemicals	180	1.8	416	2.1	43.3
All Other	454	4.4	1,052	5.4	43.2
Transportation and public utilities	646	6.3	1,091	5.6	59.2
Trade	1,905	18.6	3,469	18.2	54.9
Finance, insurance, and real estate	693	6.8	938	4.8	73.9
Services and miscellaneous	1,585	15.5	2,837	14.4	55.9
Government	1,315	12.8	2,497	12.8	52.7
Total nonfarm wage & salary	9,221	90.0	17,372	88.5	53.1
Self-employed, domestics and farm	1,025	10.0	2,270	11.5	45.1
Total	10,247[a]	100.0	19,655	100.0	52.1

[a]Estimated.
Source: Pennsylvania Bureau of Employment Security.

ployment by industry follows the pattern typical of metropolitan areas throughout the nation.[5] The central cities tend to specialize in those types of industries,
such as finance, insurance and real estate, and many services which depend on
economies of agglomeration and which operate most efficiently at the hub of
regional communication and transportation networks. In addition the central
cities tend to specialize in those industries requiring a low-wage, low-skilled labor
force. This is exemplified by Philadelphia's dominance within the SMSA in
nondurable manufactures.

The Dynamic Shifts in Employment and
Industry in the City of Philadelphia

The 1968 pattern of employment in the city of Philadelphia as the central city
of the metropolitan area is the result of a dynamic process of change. Table 2-8
describes the industrial distribution of employment in the city for selected years
between 1951 and 1968. This shift in the employment pattern has takne place
against a background of a slightly downward trend in employment with cyclical
fluctuations around this trend line especially marked by the recessions of the
late 1950s and early 1960s.

Over the 1951-68 period the most significant change was the decline of
manufacturing relative to nonmanufacturing in the city. From a high of 35% of
total employment in 1951, manufacturing fell to slightly more than 26% by
1968. Although this decline has been felt widely in most manufacturing
categories, textiles and metals have been especially hard hit. Interestingly, the
most rapid increases in manufacturing employment have occurred in the durable
goods industries of metals products, machinery, and transportation, of which the
central city has a relatively smaller share.

Among the nonmanufacturing industries, major increases occurred in services,
finance, insurance, and real estate. There has also been a substantial increase in
the importance of government employment. This increase reflects the national
trend in the growing importance of public sector employment, especially at the
state and local levels. A major component of this government sector has
probably been in response to the demand for labor in education, especially in
the public school system. At the same time, smaller relative declines occurred in
contract construction, transportation, and public utilities.

While the unemployment rate in the central city has been higher than in the
metropolitan areas as a whole, the rise in city employment has occurred at only
half the rate for the entire metropolitan area. The comparative data by industry
for the period 1963-68, presented in table 2-9, reveals that the city increased
employment by about 7% or 65,8000 jobs compared to a 13% increase or
232,700 jobs for the SMSA. In absolute numbers of jobs, the city of
Philadelphia lost over 150,000 positions in manufacturing, transportation, and

Table 2-8
Distribution of Employment in City of Philadelphia for Selected Years

| Industry | Percentage of Employment | | | |
	1951[a]	1960[a]	1963[a]	1968[b]
Mining	–	–	–	–
Contract construction	4.2	2.8	2.9	3.6
Manufacturing	35.1	30.8	29.2	26.4
Furniture and lumber	0.8	0.7	0.7	0.6
Metals	4.4	3.4	3.0	2.9
Machinery	6.1	5.5	6.1	5.0
Transportation	0.5	0.4	0.2	0.7
Food	3.6	3.4	3.1	2.7
Textiles	3.9	2.3	2.0	1.7
Apparel	4.8	4.7	4.6	4.3
Printing	2.8	3.1	2.9	2.4
Chemicals	2.3	2.2	1.9	1.8
All other	6.0	5.3	4.7	4.4
Transportation and public utilities	7.9	7.4	7.3	6.3
Trade	18.9	18.8	18.3	18.6
Finance, insurance and real estate	5.0	6.0	6.5	6.8
Services and miscellaneous	10.7	14.3	15.4	15.5
Government	8.7	9.6	10.3	12.8
Total nonfarm wage & salary	90.5	89.9	90.0	90.0[c]
Self-employed, domestics and farm workers	9.5	10.1	10.0	10.0[c]
Total	100.0	100.0	100.0	100.0
Total number (hundreds of workers)	10,756	9,905	9,590	10,248[c]

Sources:
[a]Harms, L. and James, R. *Manpower in Pennsylvania*, vol. 2 Harrisburg: Commonwealth of Pennsylvania, Department of Community Affairs, 1967.
[b]Pennsylvania Bureau of Employment Security.
[c]Estimated.

public utilities. This decline was particularly acute in machinery, food, textiles, and printing, with over 140,000 jobs lost in these fields alone. Of the 23 major standard industrial classifications in manufacturing, it was only in one that the city exceeded the entire labor market in growth of employment. This occurred in transportation equipment with the success of the Budd Company of Philadelphia accounting for this exception to the general comparative disadvantage of the city. At the same time, over 460,000 jobs were created in these industries in the entire labor market. Both the city and the labor market area as a whole experienced important job gains in contract construction, trades, services, government, and to a lesser extent, finance, insurance, and real estate.

Table 2-9

Total Gain or Loss in Employment in City of Philadelphia and Philadelphia SMSA by Location of Establishment: 1963—68 (In Hundreds of Jobs)

Industry	City of Philadelphia		Philadelphia SMSA	
	% Change	Total Gain (+) or Loss (−)	% Change	Total Gain (+) or Loss (−)
Contract construction	33.7	+ 94	30.9	+ 175
Manufacturing	− 3.3	− 92	8.2	+ 441
Furniture and lumber	3.2	+ 2	20.4	+ 22
Metals	3.5	+ 10	8.6	+ 64
Machinery	−12.1	− 71	14.7	+ 174
Transportation equipment	195.7	+ 45	14.1	+ 37
Food	− 8.1	− 24	− 0.6	− 3
Textiles	−10.5	− 20	− 5.9	− 17
Apparel	− 0.7	− 3	1.4	+ 8
Printing	−11.7	− 33	12.1	+ 44
Chemicals	− 1.6	− 3	6.9	+ 27
All Other	0.9	+ 3	8.9	+ 86
Transportation and public utilities	− 8.0	− 56	2.2	+ 23
Trade	8.6	+151	17.2	+ 510
Finance, insurance, and real estate	10.4	+ 65	11.7	+ 98
Services and miscellaneous	7.4	+109	24.2	+ 552
Government	32.7	+324	27.9	+ 544
Total nonfarm wage and salary	6.9	+595	13.8	+2344
Self-employed, domestics, farm	−	+ 63	−	− 17
Total	6.9	+658	13.4	+2327

Sources: Harms, *Manpower in Pennsylvania*, and based on data from the Pennsylvania Bureau of Employment Security.

Only in the case of government and contract construction did the city move faster than the metropolitan area in creating jobs.

The growth rate of the metropolitan regions as a whole can be used as a standard for comparison or perhaps as a goal or measure of potential growth for the central city. If Philadelphia's overall job growth rate was the same as the entire regions', some 128,500 new jobs would have been created between 1963 and 1968. There were actually only 65,000 jobs created. This poor employment performance of the central city relative to the metropolitan area can be analyzed to determine its causes. The city's slow relative growth rate might be due to competitive disadvantages as an industrial location compared with the suburban counties. Such a competitive disadvantage may be due to higher crime rates, higher taxes, traffic congestion or lack of room for the expansion of facilities.

These factors would cause city firms to grow more slowly than their suburban counterparts and would also encourage new firms to locate outside the central city. A second possibility is that the industry mix of the city may contain a large portion of slow growing or declining industries. The relative importance of the competitive effect and the industry mix effect can be determined by comparing the actual performance of the central city with an employment growth "potential." This potential is the increase in employment that would have occurred in the central city if it had experienced the same growth rate as the entire labor market.

The total potential growth for Philadelphia between 1963 and 1968 for example is calculated by applying the Philadelphia labor market area growth rate to the city's employment base in 1963. The difference between the actual increase in jobs and this "potential" represents "lost jobs." To determine what part of this difference was due to the industry mix of the central city, the national growth rate for each industry is compared to the overall growth rate of the metropolitan area to obtain a differential growth rate which is then applied to the 1963 city employment in that industry. The result is a "gain or loss" of jobs due to the industry mix of the central city compared to the mix of the region as a whole.

The competitive effect, on the other hand, is determined by comparing the growth rate of the particular industry in the entire metropolitan region with its growth rate in the city alone. This procedure yields a differential growth rate which when applied against the 1963 employment base of the industry, designates the gain or loss of jobs owing to the relative sluggishness (or dynamism) of the city segment of the industry compared to that of the entire region. The sum of the mix and competitive effect yields the total overall effect on employment growth for each industry. The sum of these effects for each industry then equals the total "loss" of jobs, that is, the additional number of jobs that would have been created had the employment growth rate matched that of the labor market area as a whole.[6]

The result of this method of assessing the sources of job "loss" is shown in Table 2-10. The data show that it was the slower growth rate of local industries which caused the outward shift. The data was available only for the nonfarm wage and salary sector. Over the period 1963-68, this sector showed a new loss of 56,100 jobs. This net loss was the result of a loss of 75,100 jobs due to the competitive disadvantage of the city compared to the total metropolitan area and an offsetting increase in 190,000 city jobs attributable to a favorable industry mix in the city. The total job loss for the city was 62,700 which was made up of 56,100 lost in the wage and salary sector and the balance was lost in self-employment, domestic, family worker and farm categories for which no data was available.

In manufacturing, transportation, public utilities, and finance-insurance-real estate, both the competitive and mix effects were negative. Within the manufac-

Table 2-10

Sources of "Job Gain or Loss" for the City of Philadelphia Relative to Employment Gains for the Philadelphia Metropolitan Area, 1963-68 (In Hundreds)

Industry	Industry Mix	Effect of Geographic Competitition for Industry	Total
Mining	0	0	0
Contract construction	49	+ 8	57
Manufacturing	−145	−321	−466
Furniture and lumber	4	− 11	− 7
Metals	− 14	− 14	− 28
Machinery	8	−157	−149
Transportation equipment	−	42	42
Food	− 42	− 22	− 64
Textiles	− 37	− 9	− 46
Apparel	− 53	− 9	− 62
Printing	− 4	− 67	− 71
Chemicals	− 12	− 16	− 28
All Other	+ 5	− 58	− 53
Transportation and public utilities	− 79	− 71	−150
Trade	67	−151	− 84
Finance, insurance, and real estate	− 11	− 8	− 19
Services and miscellaneous	159	−248	− 89
Government	144	48	192
Total nonfarm wage and salary	+190	−751	−561

turing category, moreover, there were industries in which the mix effect was negative and sizeable—especially in food, textiles, and apparel. The changing nature of labor supply in the central city may be related to this result.

Relevance of Findings to All Large Cities

This review of the employment and industrial structure of the Philadelphia labor market area provides not only the background for this study, but also a basis for relating its results to the unemployment situations in other metropolitan areas. A primary contention of this study is that the performance of new businesses and their impact on sectoral unemployment in a given labor market is closely related to the industrial structure and pattern of growth, both in the aggregate and especially by subsection of the metropolitan area. Thus the degree to which the Philadelphia results will apply to other areas will be directly related to the degree to which the problem of sectoral unemployment and the factors determining the employment impact of new firms observed in Philadelphia are duplicated. As the above analysis has shown, the Philadelphia area is undergoing the pattern of changes in demography, and industrial and spatial structure which have been noted as characteristic of metropolitan labor markets.

As a rough approximation, it is possible to restrict the group of cities which the situation in Philadelphia fairly represents to a set considerably smaller than that of all SMSAs. A recent study by Stanback and Knight emphasized that manpower policy must recognize the differences in industrial structure and dynamics among cities.[7] Using 1960 census data, the authors found that these characteristics varied considerably with a metropolitan area's size and the function it performs within the national economy. In their analysis, Philadelphia's industrial structure was found to have a comparatively large concentration of employment in manufacturing, ranking in the top third of the 368 metropolitan units studied (SMSAs and counties with cities over 250,000 population). Of the thirteen SMSAs with populations over 1.6 million in 1966, four others were found to have similar concentrations in manufacturing. Of the remainder, six were in the top quartile for four of six business or consumer services sectors,[8] thus qualifying as "model" type cities. The other two large SMSAs were classified "mixed" type. Philadelphia was placed in this last category, rather than manufacturing because it had some model characteristics (high concentration in three of the six service sectors). The rate of employment growth for the Philadelphia SMSA was 14.4% between 1950 and 1960, considerably above the median rate 10.6% for large manufacturing SMSAs as well as the 12.3% median rate of growth for large model cities. Philadelphia's rate of growth was still well below the growth rates of most median size metropolitan areas in all categories.[9]

Information on industrial structure and size as presented by Stanback and Knight is certainly important in tailoring training and recruitment programs to a metropolitan area's manpower needs. In order to plan demand-oriented programs, however, this information must be complemented with data on the spatial structure of the area's industry and growth.

Employment in the Philadelphia central city (Philadelphia county) increased slightly during the 1960s. In the 1950s however, employment in the central city declined by some 4.7% while the Philadelphia SMSA experienced a moderate growth in employment. It is the central core of the metropolitan area which is of greatest concern in developing demand-oriented programs since most sectoral unemployment is located nearby and it is the area in which jobs will probably need to be created. Roger Noll, in a recent analysis of employment distribution in metropolitan areas,[10] found that two characteristics clearly associated with central core decline were large size and an early date at which prominence was attained. Noll's study found that during 1958-63 ten of the thirteen most populous SMSAs lost employment in a group of industries consisting of four major sectors—manufacturing, wholesale, retail, and services (exclusive of government, public utilities, domestic services and professions). Also, of the eleven cities with populations exceeding 300,000 in 1900, ten (including Philadelphia) showed declines in employment in this same group of industries.

Noll points out that the age at which the central core was developed has important implications for its attractiveness as a location for business. A large number of the commercial and industrial structures currently standing in the central area of the SMSA will date from this period. Philadelphia's central core contains many buildings erected before 1900. These structures are inefficient for many modern uses, thus contributing to the employment problems in this section of the city. These older structures, primarily due to the more intensive use of land before the automobile and truck, also make assembly and clearance of the size usually required for modern enterprises difficult, expensive, and sometimes impossible without government action.

The high density of work places and residences found in the older central cores is likely to indicate a higher reliance on public transit. This appears to have been the case in Philadelphia which has a subway system and several trolleys which still operate. Consequently the transportation system in many cities will influence the success of programs aimed at reducing high unemployment among central city residents.

The degree of racial segregation and the proportion of nonwhite population in the city also affect the central cities' employment problem. The effect of residential segregation of employment opportunities in Detroit and Chicago indicates that a greater degree of segregation reduces the employment opportunities available to the nonwhite.[11] Cities with a high proportion of blacks are therefore likely to have somewhat similar employment problems among its residents in the core of the city.

The findings and policy recommendations of this study apply to those SMSAs which most resemble Philadelphia in its industrial and demographic characteristics. It is suggested that Philadelphia best represents those large SMSAs whose central cities were developed near the turn of the century and which have relatively large, residentially segregated nonwhite populations. Among these, SMSAs which have a large concentration of employment in manufacturing would be most similar.

Such "new" cities as Houston or Los Angeles which were developed in the era of the automobile present different problems in the urban labor demand and supply since their central city building stocks are of more recent vintage and would present fewer obstacles to new firms. The existence of high sectoral unemployment in these cities suggests that perhaps the effects of racial discrimination and residential segregation by race and economic status along with the geographic extensiveness of the urban labor market are quite important causes of their high sectoral unemployment.

Despite the differences between Philadelphia and some of the newer cities, the study of urban employment and the role of new business provides valuable insights to the unemployment problem in all cities. This is because most cities, no matter their age or industrial composition, face many similar problems. A high level of crime and physical deterioration is characteristic of all of the ghettos in the nation. The geographic segmentation of the urban labor market with a severe mismatch between labor supply and demand in some segments of the labor market is also common in most cities. It is for this reason that although many features of the findings concern the Philadelphia labor market, they are also applicable to all large urban labor markets.

Employment Impact of Firm Entrants, Exits, and Relocatees

In any metropolitan area the population of business enterprises is constantly changing. New businesses enter and some existing ones leave the geographic area. The entry and exit behavior of firms is likely to vary from industry to industry, with the number of entrants and exits varying with the degree of competitiveness in the industry. The rate of entry is also affected by the average capital requirements of firms in the industry, and the number of entrants is likely to be inversely related to the amount of capital required. The capital structure of firms in the industry is also likely to affect the rate of exits. If an industry has a high rate of fixed to variable capital, the rate of exit of firms in this industry is likely to be relatively low.

The dynamic flow of entrants and exits includes firms which have changed their legal ownership status either by incorporation or by sale and purchase of businesses. This flow is presented diagrammatically in Figure 3-1, and the relationship of this continuing process to job opportunities is depicted. The graphical presentation shows that there are essentially two entry and exit flows. New businesses which consist of new economic entities clearly constitute an employment increase in the citywide employment. Similarly, firms which exit by moving to a location outside the city or simply stop operations without selling the business as a going concern reduce total city employment.

The second entry-exit flow is not likely to have any impact on employment since the unit of economic activity remains unchanged while the legal description of the firm changes. For example, a new business which becomes an entrant by the change in an established firm's legal status either through incorporation, change in partnership, or simply a change in name of firm will not change the size of its labor force. The business which exits by selling to new ownership is also not expected to change citywide employment. It is of course possible that in the long run the purchaser of the existing business, and perhaps also the changed partnership or business name, etc., will lead to increased output and consequently more employment. It is equally possible that the new legal entity will eventually change the method of production by using more capital-intensive techniques which may reduce the amount of labor required. In any event these are long-run changes, and it can be assumed that in the short run the employment impact of a change in the businesses legal status will be negligible.

The decision to enter or exit from the city involves a choice of geographic location as well as a choice of type of industry. Figure 3-1 categorizes the geographic possibilities into the three broad groups of central business district,

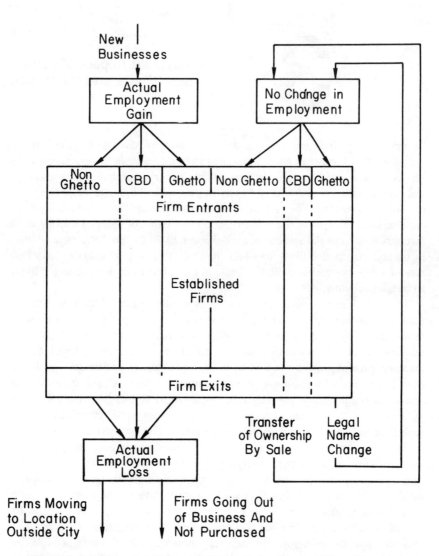

Figure 3-1. Urban Job Opportunities and the Flow of Firm Entrants and Exists.

nonghetto or high-income, and ghetto or low income which are appropriate for testing hypotheses concerning the geographic employment impact of entrants and exits.

An additional feature of the dynamic movement of firms in a metropolitan area is the constant relocation of firms among geographic areas within the city. The net effect of these relocatees may result in a differential employment impact in each of the three broad geographic groups, although there will be no change in total citywide employment. This sectoral impact should therefore be studied in any assessment of the change in employment in geographic areas of the city. Finally, it is again emphasized that although the expansion and contraction of established firms is largely beyond the scope of the present study, this substantial change in total employment also has industrial and geographic dimensions which will affect job opportunities in ghetto and nonghetto areas both absolutely and relatively. In terms of total job opportunities, it is indeed likely that the net impact of the expansion and contraction in the employment level of established firms is greater than the net change produced by firm entrants and exits.

Employment Impact Hypotheses

The major hypothesis which is tested in this chapter is that decisions made by firms in regard to location result in an increase in employment in the nonghetto areas of the city and a decrease in ghetto employment. Several factors are likely to contribute to the acceptance of this hypothesis. It is expected that more firm entrants, absolutely and proportionally, locate in the nonghetto areas and conversely more exits leave from the ghetto areas. A difference in the average size of firms will also affect the employment impact. It is possible that the number of exits in any geographic area is greater than the number of entrants. If, however, the average number of employees in the entrant firms exceeds average number in the exit firms, the net employment impact can be positive. The average size may of course vary by geographic area. For example, because of several factors such as financial resources of entrepreneur, potential for expansion, and so forth, the nonghetto entrant firm is likely to be larger than the ghetto entrant.

The industrial structure is expected to vary by geographic area, and it is hypothesized that proportionately more manufacturing entrants will be located in nonghetto areas compared to ghetto areas. A high proportion of ghetto entrant firms are likely to be in the nonmanufacturing sector with wholesale and retail trade likely to predominate. The data also permit this hypothesis to be explored.

Employment information on the firms which entered, exited, and relocated was collected for 1967. According to the city agency which issues building permits to industry, this was not a year in which there was an unusual increase or decline in this type of building. It was also close to the end of a period of general economic expansion but there was still no sign of weakness in economic activity which might affect the rate of entry and exit. The data on each type of firm are presented in a comparative framework so that the net difference between entry and exit is highlighted. For the purpose of estimating the employment potential of the dynamic behavior of firms, it is important to distinguish between enterprises which hire a work force (one or more employees) and those which have no employees and are essentially family operations. An additional distinction is made for firms which have relocated within the city, and their employment impact is discussed separately.

Firms Employing A Work Force

New firms entering and leaving the city during 1967 are shown in Table 3-1. The results show that there were some twenty-five hundred legal entrants and about two thousand legal exits which constitute a net citywide increase of a little over 400 firms. The entry and exit of firms in any year is not widely distributed among industries; most entry and exit behavior is concentrated in the wholesale, retail trade, and service sectors with about 70% of all entrants and exits in these industrial categories. Manufacturing firms and contract construction each account for about 10% of the firms, while finance, real estate, and insurance firms constitute some 6% with transportation, trucking, and natural resource firms of negligible importance.

As discussed earlier, the rate of entry and exit depends on several factors such as capital requirements, capital structure, degree of competition, and future profit expectations. The industrial distribution of entrants and exits in Philadelphia suggests that since both the wholesale and retail trade and service sectors are relatively competitive and do not require substantial amounts of capital, the importance of these factors in influencing the rate of entry and exit is supported. The geographic distribution of wholesale and retail trade firms shows that the Northeast, Northwest, and West Philadelphia areas received the largest number of this type of new firms. However, when each area's proportion of wholesale and retail trade entrants are compared to its share of all entrants, there is no significant difference between the ghetto and nonghetto areas. The hypothesis that ghetto areas are more likely to receive this type of entrant is therefore not supported.

The geographic distribution of firms shows that the central business district and nonghetto areas usually experience greater entry and exit activity than the ghetto areas. The geographic areas are of different sizes and consequently it is misleading to compare the areas by absolute number of firms entering and leaving. If, however, the number of firms entering are compared to the 1968 total employment in each area, the nonghetto areas receive a relatively higher proportion of entrants than the ghetto areas and the relative importance of the central business district declines significantly. This result supports the contention that, for firms hiring a work force, the ghetto areas appear somewhat less attractive to entrants than do the nonghetto sectors in the city. The geographic comparison also shows that there is a net inflow of firms for each area except

Table 3-1
Industrial and Geographic Distribution of Legal Entrant and Exit Businesses Employing a Work Force

Type of Industry

Geographic Sector	Natural Resources Entrant %	Natural Resources Exit %	Contract Construction Entrant %	Contract Construction Exit %	Manu- facturing Entrant %	Manu- facturing Exit %	Trans- portation Entrant %	Trans- portation Exit %	Trucking Entrant %	Trucking Exit %	Wholesale & Retail Trade Entrant %	Wholesale & Retail Trade Exit %	Finance, Ins. & Real Estate Entrant %	Finance, Ins. & Real Estate Exit %	Services Entrant %	Services Exit %	Total Entrant #	Total Entrant %	Total Exit #	Total Exit %
West Phila.	0	0	1.1	1.1	0.5	0.9	0.1	0.1	0.2	0.3	4.9	7.6	0.6	0.8	3.4	2.6	262	10.9	263	13.9
Spring Garden	0	0	0.3	0.2	0.8	1.1	0	0.1	0	0.1	2.1	2.5	0.2	0.2	1.0	0.9	108	4.5	97	5.0
North Phila.	0	0	1.0	0.5	2.7	2.2	0.2	0.3	0.2	0	5.8	6.3	0.5	0.4	1.7	1.5	288	12.0	222	11.1
Center City	0.1	0	0.3	1.9	2.8	2.6	0.4	0.1	0.2	0	6.0	7.0	2.6	2.4	10.2	10.3	544	22.6	477	24.3
South Phila.	0	0.1	1.4	0.8	0.8	0.9	0.2	0.3	0.1	0.3	5.2	5.5	0.4	0.4	2.1	1.7	246	10.2	198	9.9
Frankford Richmond	0.2	0	0.5	0.2	1.2	0.9	0.1	0.1	0	0	1.7	2.6	0.3	0.5	1.2	0.7	129	5.4	96	4.9
Northwest Phila.	0.2	0.3	2.5	1.4	1.0	1.2	0.2	0.1	0.2	0.1	6.4	8.2	1.0	0.7	5.0	4.9	395	16.4	336	16.9
Northeast Phila.	0.3	0	2.1	1.4	1.0	1.1	0.4	0.3	0	0	8.4	8.1	0.8	0.6	5.0	3.2	435	18.1	292	14.6
Sub total	0.8	0.4	9.1	7.4	10.9	10.7	1.6	1.3	0.9	0.8	40.5	47.8	6.4	5.8	29.7	25.8	2407	100	1931	100
No. of firms	19	6	219	124	263	235	39	22	24	17	976	947	153	117	712	513	2407		1981	

Note: The term "legal" entrant is used throughout this chapter since, as discussed earlier in the chapter, some entrants and exits do not have any employment impact in the labor market. The term, "legal" entrant therefore includes firms which affect employment ("economic" entrant) and those which reflect only a change in firm ownership.

West Philadelphia. In a period of high general economic activity, this exception suggests possible locational disadvantages for this particular ghetto district.

Size of Firms Entering and Leaving

Table 3-2 presents the average number of employees for both entrants and exits by industry and geographic location. A comparison of the size of entrants and exits is important since the net gain in number of entrants over exits which is characteristic of most geographic areas and industries may be offset if the average size of the exits exceeds the average of entrants in any particular area.

The average size of all entrants and exits is almost identical—each with about eleven employees. When the firms are classified by industry and geographic location, there are significant differences in the size of the two groups of firms. For example, the average size of exits was substantially larger than entrants in manufacturing and contract construction, while in transportation, trucking, natural resources, and to a lesser extent services, the entrants were larger. There were similar differences when firms were compared by geographic area. Exits were larger than entrants in North and Northeast Philadelphia and in the central business district, while the reverse was true in the remaining locations.

It appears that for many industries entrants are smaller and exits larger in ghetto areas compared to nonghetto locations. This is especially the case for manufacturing industry. In this industrial group the ghetto entrants are smaller than the entrants in most nonghetto locations. In addition, it appears that the average size of ghetto exits exceeds the size of nonghetto entrants by a fairly wide margin. This is particularly true for North Philadelphia which is the largest ghetto employment area. This suggests that the net employment impact of manufacturing entry and exit behavior will be negative within the ghetto sector of the city and positive in the nonghetto areas. This finding is particularly important since the average number of employees in manufacturing entrants is about twenty-five, while the average for wholesale and retail trade firms is some nine employees. The manufacturing exits also tend to employ substantially more workers than do the exits from other industries.

There is probably an upward bias in the average number of employees in all industrial and geographic categories in Table 3-2. This is because the firms which have changed their legal status either by change of name or sale of business, and so forth, are included in both the entrant and exit estimates of employment. It is possible that the firms which enter and exit by this legal status change employ more workers than entirely new economic enterprises and as a result will raise the average size of all entrants and exits. From the interviews conducted with the entrant firms, the available evidence suggests that the size of this overesti-mate in average number of employees is quite small and in any event it does not

Table 3-2

Average Number of Employees Among Legal Entrant and Exit Businesses Employing a Work Force

Geographic Sector	Type of Industry																	
	Natural Resources		Contract Construction		Manu-facturing		Trans-portation		Trucking		Wholesale & Retail Trade		Finance, Ins. & Real Estate		Services		All Industries	
	Entrant	Exit	Entrant	Exit	Entrant	Exit	Entrant	Exit	Entrant	Exit	Entrant	Exit	Entrant	Exit	Entrant	Exit	Entrant	Exit
West Phila.	–	–	8.6	21.2	2.7	6.0	5.7	1.5	15.0	9.6	8.9	6.1	10.7	4.2	10.5	7.6	9.5	7.6
Spring Garden	–	–	17.6	6.5	9.7	7.3	–	1.0	–	4.5	7.1	9.4	4.3	2.0	11.2	10.6	9.1	8.6
North Phila.	–	–	7.0	4.0	24.4	66.1	9.5	11.8	25.0	0	7.9	9.2	3.3	6.0	7.4	6.6	11.6	19.9
Center City	11.5	–	44.9	20.2	31.2	32.4	14.4	5.0	9.8	0	13.4	16.1	7.2	8.9	9.4	5.9	13.5	13.7
South Phila.	–	2	24.6	5.6	47.6	51.5	11.0	33.2	3.7	4.3	8.3	5.6	2.5	5.6	6.3	2.5	11.4	9.4
Frankford Richmond	15.6	–	5.8	15.7	34.9	24.6	3.0	1.0	26.0	0	13.7	5.9	9.4	3.1	5.4	6.1	15.5	8.9
Northwest Phila.	15.6	7	5.9	4.6	19.5	19.1	2.3	1.5	4.3	4.5	6.3	5.9	3.5	3.4	6.4	4.2	7.0	6.0
Northeast Phila.	11.1	–	10.2	27.2	10.5	10.5	40.0	6.0	4.0	0	8.2	7.3	2.8	3.3	5.1	6.1	8.2	9.0
Sub Total	13.5	5.6	10.1	14.2	25.3	32.4	17.3	10.8	12.5	6.0	8.9	8.2	5.8	6.0	7.9	5.7	10.5	10.7

affect the major findings since any overestimate appears to be randomly distributed.

Net Employment Impact of Entry and Exit

The data source did not distinguish between the two entry and exit flows previously discussed in connection with Figure 3-1. New economic entities and firms which move to another location outside the city have an employment impact, while firms changing their legal status without affecting the production of goods and services have no impact since the firm's employment appears as an exit under the old firm's name and again as an entrant under the firm's new name. The employment increase of the legal change of name entrants included in the entrant statistics is therefore exactly offset by the employment decrease of the same firm included in the exit statistics since the change is only in ownership status. Consequently, the net employment change is a reliable estimate of the impact of the gain and loss of entirely new economic entrants and exits from the city, even though the total entrant and exit employment obtained from the city wage tax records is an overestimate of the number of employees affected by entry and exit behavior.

The net employment impact for firms employing a labor force is shown in Table 3-3. The total job creation resulting from the entry of new economic units and the loss of others during 1967 is estimated to be about 4,000 jobs. This represents less than 0.5% of the city's 1968 total employment. This positive employment-generating force, though small, is encouraging, and if it represents a typical annual change is quite significant at a time when the decline in importance of the city as the major geographic location of job opportunities is currently being predicted. It is of course necessary to emphasize two qualifications. The relative importance of entry-exit activity in reducing urban unemployment also depends on the net changes in the labor supply available to the city which in turn is influenced by migration, internal population changes, and labor force participation rates. It is quite possible that the increase in job opportunities created by firms entering and leaving is not enough to offset the increase in labor supply. In addition, net changes in the level of employment in established firms, including the opening and closing of branches of multiestablishment firms, are of considerable significance to the trend in job opportunities within the city.

The results show that the job creation effect varies by type of industry with more than half of the net gain in jobs occurring in the service sector. In fact the service and wholesale and retail trade sectors account for over 80% of the net increase in employment. Modest job increases are traced to the remaining industries, with manufacturing being the only industry which experienced a decline (a little less than 1,000 jobs) as a result of the entry-exit activity.

The geographic distribution of employment gains indicates that the non-

Table 3-3
Net Employment Effect of Legal Entrant and Exit Businesses Employing a Work Force

Geographic Sector	Natural Resources	Contract Construction	Manufacturing	Transportation	Trucking	Wholesale & Retail Trade	Finance, Insurance & Real Estate	Services	Total Net Employment	% of Area Employment	Total Employment in Area
West Phila.	0	-256	-22	14	42	118	87	484	467	0.45	103,180
Spring Garden	0	97	54	-1	-9	-107	20	90	144	0.32	45,338
North Phila.	0	127	-1297	-21	100	-56	-12	98	-1061	0.80	132,972
Center City	23	193	-473	134	39	-282	36	1088	758	0.24	317,848
South Phila.	-4	368	81	-122	-19	442	-20	232	958	1.97	48,626
Frankford Richmond	78	22	620	7	26	273	38	77	1141	1.20	57,365
Northwest Phila.	43	205	48	6	8	19	34	375	738	0.98	75,718
Northeast Phila.	78	-282	32	362	4	506	16	224	940	0.92	102,921
Sub Total	218	474	-957	379	191	913	199	2668	4085		
% of Industry Employment	30.24	1.16	-0.35	0.49	2.77	0.43	0.29	1.42			
Total Industry Employment	721	40,806	277,591	76,903	6,904	213,249	68,363	188,435			866,068

ghetto locations gained considerably more jobs than the ghetto areas. This was the case for absolute number of jobs as well as the relative increase in employment as a proportion of the total employment in each geographic section of the city. A second feature of the geographic distribution of the net employment impact was the relatively poor performance of the central business district compared to the other nonghetto areas, despite the fact that the central business district accounted for about 17% of the total citywide increase in jobs. The results showed the relative weakness of the central business district was particularly pronounced in wholesale and retail trade. This finding suggests that although the center of the city is still an extremely important focal point for this industry, there appears to be a decentralization trend to other parts of the city. The nonghetto areas also displayed some weakness in their ability to attract and retain wholesale and retail trade firms and consequently to generate new job opportunities in this industrial sector. This supports the view that the trend in urban population distribution has attracted consumer-oriented industries such as retail trade to the suburban ring in preference to the central business district and nonghetto areas of the city as well as the ghettos within the central core.

North Philadelphia was the only area which experienced an actual decline in employment attributable to entry-exit activity in 1967. This location showed declines in several industrial categories, but the largest decline was in manufacturing which experienced a net loss of some 1,300 jobs. This is an important finding since North Philadelphia is an important manufacturing area of the city. The apparent inability of the inner city to maintain a self-generating manufacturing economy has important manpower implications for inner-city residents. The central business district also experienced a similar weakness. The lack of job creation in manufacturing is perhaps the single most important finding in the net employment effect of firms entering and exiting. The nature of the job loss by type of manufacturing firm is explored in a later section.

Family Businesses

Many firms which entered and left the city during 1967 did not employ any workers during the first year of operations. Some of these firms may of course hire employees at some future time, but for most it is likely that the family will supply the labor required and for this reason they are classified as family businesses or owner-operated firms. The number of new owner-operated firms is surprisingly large; there were well over 5,000 such firms which is about twice as many as the entrant firms which employed a labor force. During the same period, about two thousand owner-operated firms left the city, giving a net gain of about three thousand firms. As shown in Table 3-4, almost 80% of the entrants and exits are either in the wholesale and retail trade or service sectors with a very low proportion in natural resources, transportation, and manufacturing. Contract construction is a relatively important industry for new firms, with over 600 firms representing more than a tenth of all entrants being registered in 1967. Finance, insurance, and real estate was also a relatively popular field for new entrepreneurs.

The family business entrants are widely dispersed among the geographic areas of the city with the ghetto and nonghetto areas each receiving almost the same proportion of both entrants and exits. A comparison of the geographic distribution of family business and firms with a work force reveals an important difference. The central business district which was relatively important for both entrants and exits employing a work force is proportionately much less important in the geographic distribution of family businesses which entered and exited during 1967. In contrast, about 35% of all new family businesses located in the two large low-income areas of North and West Philadelphia. In addition, only about 22% of the entrants with a work force chose these geographic areas in which to start their business operations.

There are also important industrial differences between firms with a work force and family businesses. Family businesses are proportionately, and in terms of absolute number of firms, more important in wholesale and retail than are firms which enter the labor market. Almost one-half of the family business entrants and exits are in this industry compared to about 40% for firms with a work force. In contrast, manufacturing firms are relatively unimportant for family businesses.

The employment impact of family businesses is difficult to assess because of the problem of counting the contribution of members of the family working for the firm. It is quite conceivable, for example, that in some industries, especially retail trade, the employment impact of an entrant or exit is two or more jobs since the spouse or close relatives of the entrepreneur works for the firm without being considered an employee. Consequently, if each firm is allocated one job slot, this would probably understate the employment impact.

This underestimate is likely to be offset since many family businesses may represent a second job for individuals regularly employed in a firm with a labor force. In the process of developing a sample of entrants and exits to be interviewed, there was substantial evidence to suggest that this moonlighting activity was most pronounced in construction and some types of service firms. In construction it appeared that for many entrepreneurs it was not unusual for the skilled tradesman to work "for himself" at various times of the year and when business was slow he would work for another firm in the industry. It was also found among some new firms in the business service industries that the entrepreneur was a professional employee of a larger organization and for tax purposes his outside income from consulting and other work done in addition to his regular job was channeled through a business organization.

On the assumption that each family firm entrant and exit affects one employment position, the net impact is over 3,500 jobs. The magnitude of the

Table 3-4
Industrial and Geographic Percentage Distribution of Legal Entrant and Exit Family Businesses

Geographic Sector	Natural Resources		Contract Construction		Manu-facturing		Trans-portation		Trucking		Wholesale & Retail Trade		Finance, Ins. & Real Estate		Services		Total			
	Entrant	Exit	Entrant	Exit	Entrant	Exit	Entrant	Exit	Entrant	Exit	Entrant	Exit	Entrant	Exit	Entrant	Exit	Entrant %	#	Exit %	#
West Phila.	0.1	0.1	2.3	0.8	0.3	0.3	0.1	0.1	0.2	0.1	8.1	8.2	0.5	0.4	5.7	7.1	17.2	949	16.9	330
Spring Garden	0	0	0.1	0.4	0.2	0.2	0	0	0	0	1.9	1.3	0.2	0.2	1.1	1.3	3.5	191	3.5	65
North Phila.	0	0.1	1.6	1.0	0.4	0.6	0.1	0.1	0.1	0.1	10.0	8.2	0.5	0.1	4.4	3.8	17.1	940	14.0	272
Center City	0	0.1	0.1	0.3	0.7	0.9	0.1	0.3	0	0	3.5	4.1	1.7	1.8	5.1	6.8	11.2	614	14.1	275
South Phila.	0.3	0.1	1.7	0.8	0.5	0.3	0	0	0.1	0.2	7.3	6.4	0.4	0.4	3.4	2.5	13.7	756	10.6	207
Frankford Richmond	0	0	0.5	0.3	0.3	0.4	0	0.1	0	0.1	2.7	3.4	0.1	0.2	1.1	1.3	4.8	264	5.6	110
Northwest Phila.	0.1	0.2	2.2	1.2	0.3	0.5	0.1	0.2	0.2	0.1	7.2	8.9	0.7	0.9	5.4	5.2	16.2	892	17.1	333
Northeast Phila.	0.1	0.1	2.8	1.5	0.6	0.7	0.2	0.1	0.1	0.1	6.8	9.2	1.2	1.1	4.5	5.5	16.3	897	18.2	355
Sub total	0.7	0.5	11.4	6.3	3.3	3.7	0.5	0.8	0.7	0.6	47.5	49.6	5.3	4.9	30.5	33.6	100	5503	100	1946
No. of firms	41	11	627	122	182	72	29	14	41	13	2609	965	293	95	1681	654		5503		1946

employment generated by this activity is surprisingly large. The importance of this in the labor market is of course of much less significance since in several industries it is unlikely that many new firms will engage in continuous activity throughout the entire year. In this sense, the net employment impact is an overestimate. It is also possible that there is an upward bias in the excess of entrants over exits, since there is less pressure on the family business to report that they have exited from business than is the case for exits with employees. The reason for this is that family businesses result in negligible revenue from the wage tax and consequently their exit is of little consequence to the revenue department of the city. It is, however, clear from the findings that a substantial proportion of the entry activity occurs in wholesale and retail trade and a disproportionately large number of entrants locate in the ghetto areas of the city. From a policy point of view, this shows an ease of entry for new entrepreneurs, but it is of questionable long-run advantage to ghetto areas since the industrial nature of most of the new jobs generated makes it unlikely that there will be any future increase in the employment associated with these firms. In fact, a high rate of failure is usually associated with new family businesses and the net employment effect of these particular entrants will probably decline in the next few years.

Firms which Have Relocated within the City

During 1967 many firms changed their location within the city. The employment significance of these moves depends on the distance involved in the relocation of the firm. If the firm's operations are moved several blocks from their original location, the labor market implications are negligible. On the other hand, a change in the site of operations from a ghetto district to a nonghetto area perhaps five miles apart may have considerable impact on the employees of the firm. For this reason, in a study concerned primarily with manpower implications, it does not seem appropriate to be concerned with short-distance relocations. For this reason, the total employment involved in moves within a sublabor market—though of considerable interest to problems of land values, availability of building structures and so on,—was not included in assessing the impact of relocatees.

The length of time the relocatee has been in business may also affect the labor market impact of firms moving. The interviews conducted with a small sample of relocatees suggest that in some instances the original address of the firm was only a temporary location and that it was always intended that the permanent location would be selected shortly after the firm started operations. The labor market impact of this type of relocation is not likely to be significant, however, since the vast majority of moves occur within the same sublabor market.

The magnitude of the geographic flow in job opportunities among sublabor markets was obtained from a special change of address file prepared by the city of Philadelphia. The results categorized by industry are shown in Table 3-5. During 1967 some 5,000 firms relocated within the city; most of these firms did not employ a labor force and their labor-market impact is therefore limited. It is in fact likely that some of these firms are operated out of the enterpreneur's home and a change in residence also involves a change in the firm's location.

There were about 2,000 relocatees with a work force and the geographic movement of these firms affected many employees. The total citywide number of jobs affected by firms relocating was 73,000—about 8% of citywide employment. Relocation activity is concentrated primarily in manufacturing, transportation, services, and wholesale and retail trade. The location of some 65,000 jobs was affected by the relocation activity in these industries.

The important employment implications of firms changing their location are reflected in the geographic areas of the city. The results suggest that Center City is the area which in terms of number of employees employed by firms moving into and out of the area is the most important sublabor market. Despite the fact that over 80,000 workers were employed by firms either moving in or out of Center City, the net employment impact was only an increase of some 200 employees in the area. In terms of employment opportunities the net change rather than the absolute number of jobs involved in the relocation is probably a more significant statistic.

The ghetto areas all showed small net gains in employment due to relocation of firms within the city. Some nonghetto areas also showed modest increases in employment while others, the Northwest and Northeast sections of the city lost some employment because of the relocation of firms. Firms which relocate within the city do not of course affect citywide employment but may have a slight impact on the geographic distribution of jobs within the city.

Since the study is cross-sectional, it is not possible to imply definitive manpower conclusions from the findings. If it is assumed that the 1967 pattern of relocation of firms within the city did not display any unusual characteristics, it appears that the employment impact of relocatees will affect the total employment by sublabor market either by supplementing or offsetting the net employment impact of entrants and exits. For a particular sublabor market, a relocatee which moves to the area from another city sublabor market has the same positive employment impact as does an entrant firm. Similarly, the relocatee which moves out of the sublabor market is like a firm exit. The impact of the relocatees in 1967 therefore offset the net entrant-exit employment gain which occurred in the Northwest and Northeast sublabor markets.In most other areas the relocatees increased the employment generated by the excess of entrant jobs over exit jobs.

It is not possible to discern any definite industrial pattern to the employment changes in the geographic sublabor markets. For example, in manufacturing

Table 3-5

Employment Effect of Firms Relocating within the City (Number of employees for Firms with a Work Force)

Geographic Sector	Natural Resources			Contract Construction			Manufacturing			Transportation			Trucking			Wholesale & Retail Trade			Finance, Insurance & Real Estate			Services			All Industries		
	From	To	Net	From	To	Net	From	To	Net	From	To	Net	From	To	Net	From	To	Net	From	To	Net	From	To	Net	From	To	Net
West Phila.	16	15	1	345	210	−135	264	491	227	61	63	2	8	13	5	896	969	73	50	115	65	785	796	11	2425	2672	24
Spring Garden	0	0	0	56	82	26	238	274	36	1	0	−1	0	11	11	689	1058	369	65	62	−3	449	249	−200	1498	1736	23
North Phila.	13	13	0	155	166	11	1673	1671	−2	33	35	2	23	55	32	1362	1363	1	123	46	−77	476	655	179	3858	4004	14
Center City	30	30	0	101	85	−16	11525	11979	454	14433	13985	−448	15	17	2	1930	2123	193	5292	5264	−28	6697	6752	55	40023	40235	21
South Phila.	0	0	0	117	278	161	1699	1474	−225	85	390	305	4	3	−1	1077	1378	301	45	73	28	743	610	−133	3770	4206	43
Frankford Richmond	1	1	0	126	133	7	8823	8937	114	0	155	155	136	112	−24	760	574	−186	16	16	0	246	497	251	10108	10425	33
Northwest Phila.	3	3	0	754	809	55	606	427	−179	14	3	−11	21	4	−17	1447	1011	−436	128	145	17	1126	1032	−94	4099	3434	−66
Northeast Phila.	12	13	1	497	388	−109	3287	2862	−425	90	86	−4	43	35	−8	1503	1188	−315	214	212	−2	1271	1202	−69	6917	5986	−93
Sub total	75	75	0	2151	2151	0	28115	28115	0	14717	14717	0	250	250	0	9664	9664	0	5933	5933	0	11793	11793	0	72698	72698	0
No. of Firms with Labor Force	6			153			266			38			20			616			199			778			2076		
No. of Firms without Labor Force	7			235			182			13			33			1655			289			729			3143		

55

where relocatees caused the greatest shift in employment, the nonghetto areas of South, Northwest, and Northeast Philadelphia lost some employment, while Center City, Frankford-Richmond and West Philadelphia gained. In wholesale and retail trade, Frankford-Richmond, Northwest, and Northeast Philadelphia lost jobs with net increases being registered by Spring Garden and North Philadelphia. The only generalization which seems to emerge is the rather obvious conclusion that for the sublabor markets which lost jobs, their net loss by firms relocating was primarily due to a net outflow of jobs in manufacturing and wholesale and retail trade.

Entry-Exit Behavior among Manufacturing Firms

The failure of the inner city to show a net increase in manufacturing jobs due to the entry-exit behavior of firms is consistent with industrial employment trends occurring in metropolitan areas. Since manufacturing usually accounts for more jobs in metropolitan areas than any other industrial sector, it is important to recognize differences within manufacturing. It may be that some manufacturing industries are in fact expanding within the central core of the city despite the general decline in citywide manufacturing employment.

The analysis of manufacturing firms entering and leaving a geographic area is only a proxy for the changes which may be occurring in the level of employment among firms which do not change their locational status. It is recommended that the total population of firms in manufacturing and other industries be studied on a longitudinal basis over a period of several years to analyze employment trends in detail. In the meantime, the following analysis of the firms which enter and exit gives some insight into the changes taking place in manufacturing within the city.

The findings showed 445 manufacturing firms entering the city and 307 firms leaving, resulting in a net gain of 138 firms.[a] This represents about a 3% increase based on the total number of manufacturing firms in the city at the end of 1968. Standard industrial classifications with the highest net gains in number of firms were printing and publishing with a net gain of 45 firms, fabricated metal with 25, machinery with 21 and electrical machinery with 11 more firms. Both food and leather had net losses of 8 firms each, and in rubber and plastic the number of exits equalled the number of entrants, as was the case for the chemical industry.

The sum of the number of firms entering the city and the number of firms leaving the city in this period is 752 which, on the basis of the 1968 total in manufacturing, indicates that about 16% of this total were involved in movement in or out of the city. Even though many of these entrants and exits were

---

[a]This includes the entry of some 75 family businesses and the exits of a similar number of family manufacturing enterprises.

firms changing their legal status or involved in the purchase of an ongoing operation, it still represents a good deal of flexibility and adjustment to changing economic conditions occurring within the manufacturing sector in Philadelphia.

The effect on employment of the entry and exit of firms into and out of the city provides greater insights into the nature of those movements and an idea of future employment prospects in manufacturing. The net employment effect due to these factors was a loss of 941 jobs in manufacturing industries, even though more manufacturing firms entered the city than left it.

The industrial and geographic distribution of the net employment impact is shown in Table 3-6. The industries showing the greatest net loss in number of jobs are the machinery and chemical industries. More moderate losses were experienced by the leather, textile, and apparel industries. These losses were not widely distributed among the sublabor markets of the city. The net loss in the machinery industry was almost completely attributable to the ghetto area of North Philadelphia, and in fact the Northeast and Northwest sectors of the city showed small net gains in number of jobs in this industry. Similarly, the decline due to entrant-exit behavior in the chemical industry occurred primarily in Center City with no part of the city making any noticeable gain in employment. The loss of apparel jobs was mainly in Center City, while both North Philadelphia and Frankford-Richmond made significant gains in this type of employment. The performance in the textile industry indicates that, although North Philadelphia lost employment, the nonghetto area of South Philadelphia gained a substantial number of jobs.

Although there was an overall decline in manufacturing employment, it is important to notice that many industries within this sector actually experienced net gains in the number of jobs. The gains were moderately strong in electrical machinery, food products, primary metals, and fabricated metals. In addition, ghetto and nonghetto areas appear to have benefited equally from these increases.

The following conclusions can be drawn from the industrial and geographic distribution of net employment effect of entrants and exits. It is misleading to assume that all types of manufacturing are declining within the city. Even in the inner city occasional examples of expanding manufacturing employment exist. In Philadelphia the nonghetto areas, except the central business district, all showed small increases in employment with the sections outside but close to the central core of the city showing a greater increase than the areas close to the perimeter of the city.

In manufacturing there appears to be a trend towards a larger total number of firms within the city but with a smaller average size of firm and consequently lower total employment. The average size of exiting firms was about 25 employees while for manufacturing firms which entered the average size was 15 employees. In addition, the percentage of exiting firms which reported no employees was 21, while about 40% of the firms which entered reported no

58

Table 3-6
Net Employment Effect of Manufacturing Legal Entrants and Exits Employing a Work Force

	West Phila.	Spring Garden	North Phila.	Center City	South Phila.	Frankford Richmond	Northwest Phila.	Northeast Phila.	Total
Food	+39	+51	+631	−14	−42	−203	−36	+66	+492
Tobacco	0	0	0	0	0	0	0	0	0
Textile mills	0	−10	−326	−26	+227	−4	−40	+18	−161
Apparel, fabrics	−1	−8	+121	−466	−71	+309	−31	−22	−169
Lumber & wood	0	0	0	0	+7	−18	+10	0	−1
Furniture & fixture	0	+12	+12	−9	−1	0	−11	−34	−31
Paper & paper products	−2	−2	−355	+191	−15	+23	+51	+182	+73
Printing & publishing	+19	−24	+18	−43	+5	+3	+5	−20	−37
Chemicals	0	0	−51	−908	−18	0	+50	−2	−929
Petroleum refining	+1	+2	+12	+16	+7	+16	+13	†2	−68
Rubber, plastics	−1	−2	−18	−72	−5	−2	+13	−1	−88
Leather	−3	−5	−138	−100	−30	−14	−16	−8	−314
Stone, clay, glass, concrete	−2	0	−36	−4	0	0	−27	−22	−91
Primary metals	+3	+7	+50	+68	+29	+34	+16	+2	+209
Fabricated metals	−17	+12	−29	0	+31	+238	+36	+33	+304
Machinery	+6	−9	−1026	−90	−5	+3	+15	+63	−1043
Electrical machinery	−1	−1	+191	−10	−5	−2	+19	+66	+257
Transportation	0	0	+22	+26	−3	+25	−1	−16	+52
Professional, scientific instruments	+1	+1	+4	+27	+2	+3	+2	+1	+41
Miscellaneous	−43	+18	+121	+466	−138	+20	−7	0	+437
Total	−21	+55	−1298	−457	+79	+619	+51	+31	−941

employees. These trends lend some support to the hypothesis that manufacturing in large cities such as Philadelphia is shifting its orientation toward more specialized products to take maximum advantage of their location at the center of a region and in close proximity to firms performing special functions for the region with unique product needs. Conversely, the orientation is moving away from supplying products of large demand which require production on a large scale. Industrial classifications in which this effect was particularly large were chemicals, in which the average size of exiting firms were 47.8 employees while that of entrants was only 5.5 employees, and machinery, where exiting firms averaged 58.8 employees and entering firms averaged 3.2 employees.

Such trends—if they continue—are important for the development of manpower programs in the future. An industry characterized by large firms with organized employment procedures affects labor market practices differently from one in which the average firm is small and hiring is more likely to be on a personal, informal basis.

Conclusions

The extent and nature of movement of firms into and out of the major geographic sections of the city clearly shows that encouraging new businesses to locate in the ghetto is not the most appropriate policy to increase employment opportunities within the ghetto. The results showed that in one year there was a net increase (a positive gain of entrants over exits) of some 400 firms. Almost 70% of this net gain in firms was from firms locating in nonghetto sections of the city; the remainder were divided fairly equally among the ghetto sections and the central business district. Given the number of existing firms in the ghettos and the central business district both geographic sectors of the city did poorly in attracting new businesses. The high density of firms and the small geographic area in the central business district explain its relatively poor performance. On the other hand, no such explanation can be applied to the geographically larger ghetto areas.

The entry-exit behavior of businesses resulted in an increase of some 4,000 new jobs in the city. As a group, the ghettos made no gain in job opportunities and in fact lost some 450 jobs, while the increase in jobs in the nonghetto areas was about 3,800 jobs and some 750 jobs in the central business district. The employment impact did vary among ghetto sections of the city. The poor performance in the ghettos was entirely attributable to one ghetto which showed a net loss of some 1,000 jobs. The poor performance of the ghettos was partially attributed to the much smaller size of entrant firms and the larger size of the exit firms when compared to firm size in the nonghetto sections of the city.

The industrial distribution of the change in the population of firms was heavily concentrated in the service and wholesale and retail sectors. The comparative weakness of the ghetto areas was also evident in the entry-exit behavior of nonmanufacturing firms. The net increase in manufacturing firms was small, although the average size of an entrant firm in this industry was much greater than the size of firms entering other industries.

The small size of entrant firms, especially in the ghetto, was paradoxically not without some advantages. This finding seemed to support the hypothesis that the city and the ghetto areas in particular serve as "hot houses" for new firms and products. This argument contends that such firms are attracted by the availability in these areas of inexpensive plant space in small quantities. The central core of the city can normally provide older structures which have been vacated by expanding firms, and a wide variety of business services which the small firm cannot easily or economically provide for itself. This area also affords the small business with an efficient market for products where a large number of buyers can be reached on a face to face basis at minimal cost in travel and time. Consequently, although there were some notable job losses in the manufacturing industries of machinery, chemicals, leather, textiles, and apparel, there were also some job gains from small firms in specialized manufacturing industry.

A substantial number of firms changed their location within the city during the year of the study. This change in the geographic distribution of job opportunities did not appear to improve the poor performance of ghetto areas in attracting or retaining jobs. Similarly, although the ghettos received a very high proportion of the net gain in new family businesses (about 40% of net increase in the city), their role in improving the employment status of ghetto residents is not encouraging. This is because a particularly large proportion of the owner-operated firms which locate in the ghetto areas are in wholesale and retail trade, and the prognosis for their future expansion is not hopeful. The evidence presented in this chapter all tends to point to the view that new businesses, while in some instances increasing ghetto employment, are likely to have their greatest impact outside the ghetto areas of the city. In this respect a policy which subsidizes new businesses in urban areas is not likely to result in a productive payoff by increasing employment of ghetto residents. Such a policy must be highly selective by type of industry and should probably be justified on grounds other than reducing high sectoral unemployment.

4

Occupational Structure and Employment Characteristics of New Businesses

The information input necessary for urban manpower policy decisions will be much more complete if, in addition to the number of jobs created by new business, something is known about the nature of these jobs. The characteristics of the new firm's industrial classification has a major influence on the nature of the job. It is also likely that features of new jobs will vary depending on whether the firm locates in the suburbs, the city, or a ghetto area within the city, since the industrial distribution of new firms will vary by geographic area. This chapter deals with the occupational and wage structure of several groups of new firms and also discusses the growth in occupational employment during the early years of a new firm's development. The racial characteristics of employees who work for new enterprises are studied as well as the criteria and method of recruitment used by new entrepreneurs.

Occupational Hypotheses

There is no well-developed body of theory which discusses the relationship between the location of the firm and the occupational structure and other job features of the new firm. Labor market theory, however, does provide a framework which permits a series of hypotheses to be suggested:

1. It is expected that ghetto entrant firms for a given size will have a lower proportion of its employees in the managerial-professional and clerical occupational categories than the nonghetto entrant firms. The sizes of these two occupational categories are not likely to be greatly affected by the nature of the firm's product, except in industries such as banking and insurance which are primarily white-collar in nature. The major factor affecting the size of the managerial and clerical structure of new firms is likely to be the ability of the firm to attract employees with the necessary skills and the size of the firm. Since ghetto employment is apparently less desirable than nonghetto employment and ghetto firms are smaller in size, the occupational structure of ghetto firms is likely to have a relatively low proportion of their employees in these broad occupational categories. For similar reasons there is likely to be a tendency for suburban firms to have a slightly larger managerial-professional and clerical structure than found among firms locating in the city.

2. Salaries and wages in most occupational categories are likely to be higher in ghetto firms compared to nonghetto city firms and higher for all city firms compared to suburban firms. This tendency is expected to be particularly strong for higher level manpower occupations and white-collar jobs in which a high proportion of the job holders are women. Research studies have shown that women with clerical skills are willing to travel a considerable distance and accept a lower wage rate in order to secure employment in a nonghetto area.[1] Consequently, ghetto firms will have to offer additional remuneration to hire clerical labor. The residential pattern among managerial-professional employees is likely to involve a substantial commuting distance from ghetto area. Therefore, although these employees have a larger "normal preference area" for employment than other occupational groups, it is necessary for entrant firms in the ghetto, which are likely to be located at the boundary of the managerial employees' preference area, to pay a differential in salary over the salary paid by new firms which locate closer to the center of the employees' preference area.

The location of the supply of labor in a particular occupation in relation to its demand will also affect the relative wages paid to employees. If, for example, an adequate supply of labor which can perform the skills required in any occupation is available within the ghetto, then ghetto entrant firms may deviate from the overall tendency for higher wages and salaries in the ghetto. Even in these circumstances, it is possible for ghetto entrepreneurs to prefer nonghetto labor and be prepared to pay a premium for this labor.[2]

3. The ranking of occupations by wages paid (wage structure) for all groups of entrant firms is likely to be quite similar. Despite expected absolute wage differences among groups of firms for particular occupations, it is likely that differences in the ranking of occupations will not be great. Because of the availability of labor supply, it is possible that in the ghetto relatively low-skilled occupations will have a lower ranking than in the structure of wages among nonghetto entrant firms.

4. During the early development stage of new businesses (first three years), it is expected that for most occupations employment opportunities will increase more rapidly in nonghetto firms compared to ghetto firms. A similar relationship between suburban and city firms is also expected, though the employment growth differential in favor of suburban firms is expected to be relatively small.

Most new enterprises are small-scale operations, and during the first few years the degree of success in the new venture is likely to vary substantially from firm to firm. Consequently, the growth rate in employment will also vary considerably. However, some groups of firms are likely to fare better than others. For example, the growth rate is likely to vary from industry to industry. It is also expected that firms in some geographic areas will expand quicker than in others. In the short run, small businesses serve their immediate local market. As a result, firms in the suburbs and nonghetto areas of the city are likely to be in an advantageous geographic position since residential and economic development has tended to be greatest in these areas. Employment growth among new entrants is therefore likely to be higher for nonghetto and suburban firms during this initial development stage than for other groups of firms.

5. The racial characteristics of employees in new firms are likely to vary significantly among the various groups of entrant firms. A higher proportion of nonwhite employees will be found in ghetto firms compared to nonghetto firms. Similarly, there will be proportionately more nonwhites in city firms than found in suburban firms. The proportion of nonwhites will also vary among occupations irrespective of geographic locations of new entrant firms. The proportion found in managerial-professional and occupations in construction will be particularly low. Within manufacuring, nonwhites will also tend to be concentrated in particular occupations which require only a moderate amount of skill and where entry restrictions are not present.

6. The formal educational entry requirements for most occupations in new businesses are not likely to be high. This is because in relatively small firms there is rarely a professional personnel policy which formalizes training requirements for specific occupations. In addition, the number of applicants for jobs in new firms is not likely to be as large as in existing firms and there is therefore less opportunity to apply educational achievement as a selection criteria.

7. In the recruitment of employees for jobs in new businesses, personal contacts are likely to be the most important type of method of attractive potential employees. It is also expected that city firms will make more use of newspaper advertising than suburban firms.

These hypotheses which have been stated in very general terms cannot be subjected to rigorous analysis which will yield definitive conclusions. The small sample of employees in many occupational groups restricts the extent of comparative analysis possible. In instances where the number of respondents was small, it was necessary to merge occupational categories to permit analysis of the occupational information. The specific occupational categories used in the analysis are discussed below.

Framework for Occupational Analysis

The occupational information was collected through interviews conducted with the entrepreneurs of 44 suburban entrant firms and 113 firms which located within the city. Of the city entrants, 29 were located in the designated ghetto areas and the remaining 84 were from nonghetto parts of the city. Since the new businesses had only been in operation a little less than three years, the average number of employees in the firm was relatively small. The average number of employees for the suburban entrants was 29, for city entrants it was 26; for those located in the ghetto, the average size was smallest with some 22 employees, while for firms in the nonghetto city areas the size of firm was substantially higher with an average of 37 employees.

In the interviews, information was collected on the job description of each occupation within the firm. In addition, the range of weekly wage rate corresponding to each occupation was collected. The number of employees in each occupation at several dates was also obtained along with the age, race, and sex of these employees.

The interviews resulted in occupational information covering some 4,300 employees in a wide variety of occupations. An occupational code was developed to present enough categories of jobs so that significant differences in the type of work could be reflected and at the same time ensure that each item contained enough employees to allow comparative analysis by geographic location of the entrant firm.

As a first step each occupation identified by the interviewee was classified according to the three digit Dictionary of Occupational Titles (DOT) based on the job title, job description, wage rate, and industrial classification of the firm. From the range of DOT numbers of occupations in the survey, it was decided to reduce this range of 22 occupational categories. The specific DOT numbers contained in each of the 22 occupations used for analysis are presented in Appendix C. This list of 22 occupations formed the basic unit for the occupational analysis contained in the study. For some parts of the analysis, in order to achieve a general description of the data, the 22 occupations are reduced to the 7 major occupational categories as shown in Table 4-1.

Occupational Structure of New Businesses

Table 4-1 presents the occupational structure for the employees in city and suburban entrant firms. A comparison of the occupational structure in both types of firms reveals that suburban firms have a higher proportion of employees in managerial-professional occupations than do the city firms. The difference between the two types of firms is particularly pronounced for professional occupations; the proportion of employees in this category in suburban firms is three times as high as in city firms. There is also a higher proportion of suburban employees in clerical occupations, especially in accounting and business machine operation occupations.

These findings provide some support for the hypothesis that suburban

Table 4-1

Occupational Structure of New Businesses in the Metropolitan Area

	City Firms		Ghetto Firms		Nonghetto Firms		Suburban Firms	
	No. of Empl. (N=3,015)	% Dist. of Empl.	No. of Empl. (N=524)	% Dist. of Empl.	No. of Empl. (N=2,491)	% Dist. of Empl.	No. of Empl. (N=1,268)	% Dist. of Empl.
Managerial-Professional	251		18		233		198	
Professional	91	3.0	12	2.3	79	3.2	125	9.9
Mgr: Admin. specialist	44	1.5	2	0.4	42	1.7	21	1.7
Mgr: General	116	3.8	4	0.8	112	4.5	52	4.1
Clerical	256		46		210		138	
General office clerical	144	4.8	25	4.8	119	4.8	63	5.0
Acct. & bus. mach. oper.	50	1.7	7	1.3	43	1.7	61	4.8
Plant clerical	62	2.1	14	2.6	48	1.9	14	1.1
Sales	267		24		243		405	
Sales & sales related	138	4.8	22	4.2	116	4.7	26	2.1
Retail food & drink	129	4.3	2	0.4	127	5.1	379	30.0
Service	422		60		362		126	
Personal service	179	6.0	36	6.9	143	5.8	107	8.5
Building service	243	8.1	24	4.6	219	8.8	19	1.5
Operatives & Craftsmen	1597		331		1266		319	
Metal processing	169	5.6	23	4.4	146	5.8	47	3.7
Mach. op. & repair	68	2.3	19	3.6	49	2.0	148	11.7
Paper & printing	33	1.1	9	1.7	24	1.0	5	0.4
Wood & stone mach.	–	–	–	–	–	–	5	0.4
Textiles	401	13.3	2	0.4	399	15.9	–	–
General benchwork	60	2.0	41	8.0	19	0.8	92	7.3
Fabrication & repair	31	1.0	–	–	31	1.2	8	0.6
Fabrication textile	836	27.9	238	45.5	598	24.0	14	1.1
Construction related	102		13		89		32	
Structural work	45	1.5	6	1.2	39	1.5	8	0.6
Construction	57	1.9	7	1.3	50	2.0	24	1.9
Materials Handling	119		31		88		50	
Transportation	40	1.3	10	1.9	30	1.2	39	3.1
Packaging & material handling	79	2.6	21	4.1	58	2.3	11	0.9

entrants have a higher proportion of high level manpower in their employment structure than do city entrants. The larger average size of the suburban firms may be a partial explanation of this result, although the managerial occupational hierarchy is usually regarded as a fixed cost of operations and is therefore considered part of the firm's initial investment. The proportion of professional employees in a firm's occupational structure is, no doubt, partially a function of the type of industry. This may explain why the sample of suburban firms had such a high proportion of professional employees compared to firms in the city. In the chemical, petroleum, rubber, leather industry group there were some 13% of the suburban entrants compared to 2% for the city firms. In the category designated electrical, transportation, equipment, instruments, which is also likely to require a highly skilled labor force, there were 9% of suburban respondents in contrast to only 2% of the city entrants. However, even if the professional employees are considered separately from managerial employees, the suburban firms continue to have a higher proportion of managerial employees.

The remaining differences in the occupational structure of the two samples of entrant firms are probably closely related to the industrial structure of the two groups of firms presented in Appendix A. Suburban firms have a higher proportion of employees in sales, especially in sales jobs in retail food and drink. This is to be expected since a much higher proportion of suburban entrants were in wholesale and retail trade than were city firms. In the service category of occupations, the city entrants had a relatively high proportion of employees in the building service type of jobs.

In the broad occupational category of operatives and craftsmen, there is an important difference between the two samples of firms. In the city, a very large proportion of the employees are concentrated in the textile and textile fabrication occupations, while in the suburbs many employees are in the machine operator and repair, and benchwork occupations. This reflects the fact that about 15% of the city respondents were in the textile and apparel industries and some 20% of the suburban firms were in the machinery and electrical industries. It may be speculated from this finding that new firm skilled and semiskilled jobs in the city are likely to continue to be in industries which have traditionally located in the central city where it is possible to establish an operation on a site which does not provide a large amount of space. In contrast, the skilled and semiskilled jobs created by suburban entrants are more likely to be in industries which require considerably more space for their operations.

The ghetto-nonghetto comparison of occupational structure, shown in Table 4-1, suggests that nonghetto firms have a larger managerial-professional group of employees than the ghetto firms. The difference in average firm sizes, with the ghetto firms averaging 22 employees and the nonghetto averaging 37 employees, may account for the differences in the managerial-professional hierarchy in the new businesses. The remaining differences in occupational structure are probably related to the industrial composition of each group of firms. The nonghetto firms, and these include firms in the city center, have a higher proportion of their employees in sales jobs especially of the retail food and drink type. Among jobs in the service sector, a higher proportion of nonghetto firm employees were in building service occupations than in personal service jobs.

In the operatives and craftsmen category, there is a good deal of similarity in the relative importance of the specific types of occupations. For example, in ghetto areas over two-fifths of the employees in new businesses are in textile fabrication occupations, while for nonghetto about two-fifths of the employees are either in textile fabrication jobs or in textile jobs involving the production of the basic textile material.

The hypothesis that a higher proportion of nonghetto employees are in occupations in the managerial-professional hierarchy is supported. However, as in the case of the similar hypothesis discussed in the city-suburban comparison, this conclusion must be considered tentative since the size of the sample of ghetto firms is quite small and the theoretical basis of this hypothesis is not entirely clear.

Wages and Salaries in New Businesses

Table 4-2 presents data on the average weekly wage for each of the occupational categories for city, suburban, ghetto, and nonghetto city employees. In the city-suburban comparison, it appears that city wage and salaries are slightly higher than for suburban entrants. An exception to this trend is found in some clerical and construction occupations where suburban employees had a higher average weekly salary.

Based on the weighted average for the broad occupational category,[a] it was found that managerial-professional salaries in the city were about 10% higher than in the suburbs. In the suburbs, professional employees were paid slightly more than in the city, but for the managerial types of jobs the differential was substantially higher in the city. Differences in salaries for similar jobs are a function of the supply and demand for the particular skill, including some estimate of the employees' normal preference area for employment. In addition, certain institutional factors such as seniority or age of employee will influence the rate of pay. On the whole, suburban managers tended to be slightly younger than city managers; managers in administrative specialties were quite a bit younger with a differential of some eight years. This may account for part of the salary difference in the managerial-professional category but since the manager-administrative specialist occupation accounts for less than 2% of employees in both the city and the suburbs, it is not expected that the difference in the age of

---

[a]The weighted average wage for the broad occupational groups is the average wage for the component occupations weighted by the number of employees in each component occupation divided by the total number of employees in the broad occupational group.

Table 4-2
Wage Structure of New Businesses in the Metropolitan Area

Occupational Group	City Firms		Ghetto Firms		Nonghetto Firms		Suburban Firms	
	No. of Empl. (N=3,015)	Aver. Weekly Wage in $	No. of Empl. (N=524)	Aver. Weekly Wage in $	No. of Empl. (N=2,491)	Aver. Weekly Wage in $	No. of Empl. (N=1,268)	Aver. Weekly Wage in $
Managerial-Professional	251		18		233		198	
Professional	91	181	12	162	79	188	125	208
Mgr: Admin. specialist	44	263	2	a	42	205	21	146
Mgr: General	116	302	4	a	112	261	52	283
Clerical	256		46		210		138	
General office clerical	144	97	25	90	119	100	63	114
Acct. & bus. mach. op.	50	114	7	128	43	111	61	98
Plant clerical	62	104	14	77	48	107	14	150
Sales	267		24		243		405	
Sales & sales related	138	245	22	386	116	205	26	85
Retail food & drink	129	76	2	–	127	75	379	94
Service	422		60		362		126	
Personal service	179	99	36	134	143	94	107	60
Building service	243	75	24	77	219	73	19	100
Operatives & Craftsmen	1597		331		1266		319	
Metal processing	169	103	23	121	146	98	47	73
Mach. oper. & repair	68	160	19	176	49	153	148	133
Paper & printing	33	132	9	146	24	125	5	–
Wood & stone mach.	–	–	–	–	–	–	5	128
Textiles	401	104	2	125	399	102	–	–
General benchwork	60	115	41	67	19	143	92	118
Fabrication & repair	31	87	–	–	31	87	8	110
Fabrication textile	836	114	238	125	598	111	14	–
Construction related	102		13		89		32	
Structural work	45	153	6	119	39	187	8	112
Construction	57	159	7	121	50	197	24	208
Materials Handling	119		31		88		50	
Transportation	40	110	10	121	30	106	39	85
Packaging & material handling	79	94	21	96	58	91	11	80

aNumber of responses too small to provide meaningful data.

these employees is significant enough to affect the general conclusion that managers and professionals are paid more in city entrants than in new businesses in the suburbs.

Clerical salaries were about 7% higher in the suburbs than in the city. An exception to this was the salaries paid in accounting and business machine operator occupations which were paid more by the city entrants. However, the suburban firms paid more than city firms in the other two clerical occupations. An age differential between the groups of employees is unlikely to affect the finding since the average age of the employees in both the city and suburbs was quite similar for each occupation, and the differential in average age was never more than four years.

In the broad occupational group which includes the sales occupations, the city paid substantially more than the suburbs. The difference in one type of sales occupation, sales and sales-related, is so large that it seems most likely that the jobs in the city in this category are in a different industrial category than similar occupations in the suburbs, with the city jobs being much more technical in nature.

Despite the general finding that wage and salary rates are higher in the city than the suburbs, it is important to note that in sales occupations of the retail food and drink type the city actually paid a lower rate than the suburbs. The larger supply of unskilled labor available in the city probably explains this finding.

In the service category the weighted average salary in the city was higher than in the suburbs. For personal service occupations, the city rate was substantially higher than the suburban rate. The reverse relationship existed for building service occupations; the lower city rate for these jobs is likely to be a function of the relatively adequate supply of manpower for this type of occupation compared to the lack of supply in suburban areas. The weighted average salary for operatives and craftsmen occupation was also slightly higher for employees of city entrants than among suburban entrants. However, lack of wage data for some occupations within this broad occupational group restricted the extent to which it was possible to compare specific occupations.

In construction-related occupations, there was little overall difference in the weighted average salary paid by firms in each geographic area. In the structural occupations, the city employees were paid more than the suburban employees. The opposite result was found for construction occupations. Lack of information on the specific nature of construction jobs does not permit the higher rate in the suburbs to be explained in terms of relative supply of semiskilled labor available in the city and suburban areas. The city employees were paid substantially more than suburban employees in the materials handling occupations. This finding supports the general tendency for city entrant firms to pay higher salaries than entrant firms in the suburbs.

The ghetto-nonghetto comparison of salaries by occupation group, also shown in Table 4-2, indicates some similarities with the city-suburban results. In this case the ghetto entrants tended to pay higher wages and salaries in all broad occupational groups except clerical and construction related. Professional employees were paid slightly more in the nonghetto areas, however, the size of the sample of ghetto managers is too small to be confident of this conclusion.

The weighted average salary for all clerical occupations was about 10% lower in the ghetto than in the nonghetto. The difference was most pronounced in plant clerical occupations with nonghetto firms paying some 30% more than ghetto firms. In contrast, the ghetto firms paid more than nonghetto firms to employees in accounting and business machine operation. Age differentials in the employees in the two groups of firms did not explain these differentials in salaries.

Inadequate wage data within the sales occupational category restrict the comparison possible. In sales and sales related occupations, the ghetto employees were paid substantially more than nonghetto employees. An age differential between the two groups of employees may account for part of the difference, but the major explanation is probably in the technical nature of the sales jobs in ghetto entrant firms.

In both the service and materials handling occupational sectors, the ghetto employees were paid substantially more than nonghetto employees. By a similar magnitude, the ghetto firms also paid more to employees in the major group of operatives and craftsmen. This was true for all occupations within the general category except general benchwork occupations. In the occupations within the construction related category the relationship was reversed with the nonghetto firms paying wages about 40% higher than the firms in ghetto areas. This suggests that there is a substantial difference in the type of work performed by the construction firm which starts operations in the ghetto compared to construction firms in other geographic areas. Perhaps the ghetto-based firm concentrates on repair and renovation work which requires a lower level of labor skill, while the nonghetto based firms do more basic types of construction and require a more highly skilled labor force of tradesmen.

Employment Growth during Development Stage of New Businesses

The percentage increase in employment in each occupation for the first few years after the new business was established is shown in Table 4-3. This is, of course, only a very rough measure of each group of firm's performance since growth in employment is a function of the employment base which each firm has at the start of operations as well as the economic climate faced by firms in particular industries and geographic areas. Some entrepreneurs may refrain from entering a new business until they have considerable capital to invest. As a result,

Table 4-3
Employment Increase during Development Stage of New Businesses in Metropolitan Area

Occupational Group	City — No. of Empl. (N=3,015)	City — % Increase in Employment 1967-69	Ghetto — No. of Empl. (N=524)	Ghetto — % Increase in Employment 1967-69	Nonghetto — No. of Empl. (N=2,491)	Nonghetto — % Increase in Employment 1967-69	Suburbs — No. of Empl. (N=1,268)	Suburbs — % Increase in Employment 1967-69	Rank of Occupation by Employment Increase — Ghetto	Rank of Occupation by Employment Increase — Nonghetto	Rank of Occupation by Employment Increase — Ghetto	Rank of Occupation by Employment Increase — Nonghetto
Managerial-Professional	251		18		233		198					
Professional	91	105	12	47	79	122	125	115	4	4	3	2
Mgr: Admin. specialist	44	48	2	0	42	54	21	3	19.5	6	5	13.5
Mgr: General	116	21	4	33	112	21	52	3	7.5	11	9	13.5
Clerical	256		46		210		138					
General office clerical	144	38	25	11	119	57	63	14	13	5	6	9
Acct. & bus. mach. op.	50	20	7	7	43	35	61	34	16	8	10	5
Plant clerical	62	4	14	3	48	5	14	0	17	17.5	14	17
Sales	267		24		243		405					
Sales & sales related	138	18	22	7	116	21	26	0	15	10	11	17
Retail food & drink	129	-9	2	0	127	13	379	15	19.5	13	19	8
Service	422		60		362		126					
Personal service	179	49	36	59	143	49	107	16	3	7	4	7
Building service	243	237	24	9	219	630	19	12	14	2	2	10
Operatives & Craftsmen	1597		331		1266		319					
Metal processing	169	3	23	76	146	0	47	21	2	19.5	15.5	6
Mach. oper. & repair	68	30	19	46	49	32	148	76	5	9	7	3
Paper & printing	33	23	9	42	24	30	5	8	6	12	8	11
Wood & stone mach.	—	179	—		—	—	5	0	—	—	—	—
Textiles	401		2	33	399	181	—		7.5	3	—	—
General benchwork	60	1	41	1	19	9	92	1	18	15	18	15
Fabrication & repair	31	a	—	92	31	a	8	0	—	1	1	17
Fabrication textile	836	14	238		598	5	14	122	1	17.5	12	1
Construction Related	102		13		89		32					
Structural work	45	5	6	16	39	4	8	5	10	16	13	12
Construction	57	2	7	25	50	0	24	47	9	19.5	17	4
Materials Handling	119		31		88		50					
Transportation	40	3	10	14	30	10	39	-5	11	14	15.5	19
Packaging & material handling	79	4	21	10	58	2	11		12	21	—	—

aPercentage increase was very large but this is primarily attributable to the small number of employees hired in 1967.

the initial scale of production may be quite large and little expansion of activities anticipated during the first few years of operations. Consequently, wide variation in rate of employment expansion is to be expected. The existence of large differences in average employment increase between groups of entrant firms is not expected, and if such differences occur it probably indicated differences in the short-run employment potential of various groups of new firms.

The results show that overall rate of growth in employment is slightly higher for city entrants than for suburban entrants. The occupations which expanded most rapidly during this two-to-three-year development stage are not the same for each group of firms. For city firms, the largest increase occurred in the occupational groups of fabrication and repair, building services, textiles, and professional employees. In contrast, the suburban entrants appear to result in the greatest expansion among fabrication, textile, and professional jobs.

The lack of consistency in occupational growth between city and suburban firms is shown by the marked difference in the ranking of occupations by growth for both groups of firms. In fact, the rank correlation between the two rankings shows that there is virtually no relationship in occupational growth. The rank correlation value is 0.08, significant at the 63% level of confidence.

In the ghetto-nonghetto comparison, the occupational employment growth rate is much greater for the nonghetto firms in most types of occupations. However, it was also found that the nonghetto occupations experiencing the greatest growth were different than the ones which expanded most rapidly in ghetto firms. The greatest growth in nonghetto firms' occupations occurred in fabrication and repair, building services, textile, and professional jobs. In contrast, for ghetto firms, fabrication, textiles, metal processing, and personal services were the occupations with the greatest growth. There was virtually no similarity between the occupational rankings for ghetto and nonghetto firms. The rank correlation showed a very low negative relationship (value of −0.09 at the 66% level of confidence), which means that whenever a relationship did exist, those occupations which were ranked relatively high by one group of firms were generally ranked low by the other group.

The degree of similarity in the ranking of occupations by growth rate did increase somewhat when the major occupational categories were compared as shown in Table 4-4. The city and suburban rankings resulted in a small positive rank correlation (value of 0.21, significant at the 70% level), with the managerial-professional category showing greatest growth and materials handling the slowest short-run rate of increase in employment. A larger positive correlation existed for the ghetto-nonghetto rankings with a rank value of 0.4, significant at the 83% level. The managerial-professional employment again was one of the largest growing sectors with materials handling and sales occupations growing least rapidly. However, it must be concluded that even among broad occupational groups there was no great similarity in expansion rate of employment among new businesses in different geographic areas.

Table 4-4

Comparison of Employment Increase during Development Period of New Businesses in the City and the Suburbs for Major Occupational Categories

Major Occupational Category	Rank of Weighted Mean Rate of Employment Increase			
	Metropolitan Firms		City Firms	
	City Entrants	Suburban Entrants	Ghetto Entrants	Nonghetto Entrants
Managerial-Professional	2	1	2	2
Clerical	4	4	6	3
Sales	5	6	7	5
Service	1	5	3	1
Operatives and craftsmen	3	3	1	4
Construction related	7	2	4	6
Materials handling	6	7	5	7

Despite inconsistencies in the short-run occupational growth pattern of the various groups of firms, the results suggest some important implications. The relatively higher growth rate of the managerial-professional category is mainly attributable to the rapid expansion rate for professional employees. It appears that for most groups of firms the size of the managerial labor force is part of original investment decision of the new firm and does not expand rapidly in the early development stage. Early in the new businesses' development, however, highly skilled manpower which brings professional skill and knowledge to the new enterprise is required, and proportionately this resource becomes more important in the firm's occupational structure. This tendency appears much more pronounced among suburban and nonghetto city entrants than it does among new businesses in the ghetto. There are, of course, other occupational categories which showed more rapid rates of expansion than professional employees (for example, fabrication and repair, textiles, building services), but these increases tend to be concentrated in one group of firms and growth is to be expected if the firm is successful.

The generally higher rate of increase among city firms compared to suburban firms is partially explained by the smaller average size of firm in the city. Such an explanation does not apply, however, to the less rapid growth of ghetto firms compared to all other groups of firms. The ghetto firm has a substantially smaller average number of employees than the nonghetto firm (22 employees for ghetto entrants and 37 for nonghetto city entrants), and any increase in ghetto employment would appear proportionately quite large. It therefore appears that the ghetto entrant does not increase employment opportunities very rapidly during the first few years of operation. This finding has obvious implications for any public policy which deliberately directs financial assistance to ghetto enterprises.

Racial Characteristics of Employees in New Businesses

The proportion of white employees in each occupational category for the city and suburban firms is shown in Table 4-5. In addition, the significance of the difference between the city and suburban proportions for each occupation is indicated as either statistically significant or nonsignificant based on the Chi Square test at the 90% level of confidence.

The proportion of nonwhites in many occupational groups is quite high. Unfortunately, no data was available to compare the proportion of nonwhites in a sample of existing firms stratified by industry and location in the same manner as the entrant samples. The results intuitively suggest that nonwhites are employed in a slightly higher proportion of total employment in entrant firms than in existing firms.

The proportion of nonwhite employees varies considerably from occupation to occupation. Nonwhites find employment much more frequently in the service, craftsmen and operatives, construction and materials-handling occupations than they do in the managerial-professional, clerical and sales occupations. They also occupy a higher proportion of jobs in city firms than in suburban firms. There is a significantly higher proportion of whites in suburban firms in the broad occupational categories of managerial-professional, sales, service, operatives, and craftsmen and materials handlings. In some of the more specific occupations within these broad types of jobs, there is no significant difference in the proportion of white employees, and for a few occupations there is a significantly higher proportion of whites in the city firms. However, the general tendency is for the suburban firms to have proportionately more whites than the city firms. If the metropolitan area was a unified labor market in which the supply and demand for labor operated under perfect market conditions so that ability to perform the work was the only criterion for entry into the employment position, then although a higher proportion of whites may work in the more highly skilled occupations, the rank of the occupations by proportion of white employees for both groups of firms should show a high positive correlation. Table 4-5 shows that the rankings are quite dissimilar, and in fact there is statistically no relationship between the two rankings (rank correlation value of 0.09, significant at the 66% level).

The imperfections in the metropolitan labor market which the data indirectly suggest may occur on either the demand side through employer restrictions on hiring, or on the supply side because the suburbs are outside the black workers' normal preference area for employment. No matter the reason, it is clear that the geographic location of new entrant firms has a differential effect on the potential employment opportunities of blacks and whites.

The comparison of ghetto and nonghetto entrant firms, shown in Table 4-6, also suggests different racial characteristics in the occupational structure of both groups of firms. There is a higher proportion of whites employed in nonghetto

Table 4-5
Comparison of Racial Characteristics of Occupational Structure of New Businesses in the Metropolitan Area

Occupational Group	City Firms No. of Empl. (N=3,015)	City Firms % of Employees White	Suburban Firms No. of Empl. (N=1,268)	Suburban Firms % of Employees White	City-Suburban White-Nonwhite Differences (Chi Square)	Rank of Occupation by % of White — City	Rank of Occupation by % of White — Suburban
Managerial-Professional	251		198				
Professional	91	85	125	99	S	7	6
Mgr.: Admin. specialist	44	98	21	81	S	1.5	11
Mgr.: General	116	85	52	92	NS	7	8
Clerical	256		138		NS		
General office clerical	144	85	63	76	NS	7	13
Acct. & bus. mach. op.	50	88	61	70	S	4	15
Plant clerical	62	63	14	93	S	11	7
Sales	267		405		S		
Sales & sales related	138	98	26	100	NS	1.5	3
Retail food & drink	129	76	379	58	S	10	20
Service	422		126		S		
Personal service	179	27	107	66	S	20	17
Building service	243	46	19	63	S	17.5	18.8
Operatives & Craftsmen	1597		319		S		
Metal processing	169	52	47	85	S	14	9.5
Mach. oper. & repair	68	82	148	85	NS	9	9.5
Paper & printing	33	87	5	100		5	3
Wood & stone mach.	–	–	5	60	–	–	18.5
Textiles	401	55	–	–	–	–	–
General benchwork	60	53	92	63	NS	12.5	3
Fabrication & repair	31	48	8	100	S	16	14
Fabrication textile	836	53	14	71	NS	12.5	
Construction Related	102		32		NS		
Structural work	45	51	8	100	S	15	3
Construction	57	95	24	67	S	3	16
Materials Handling	119		50		S		
Transportation	40	46	39	79	S	17.5	12
Packaging & material handling	79	44	11	100	S	19	3

firms, especially in the broad occupational groups of clerical, sales, and service jobs. Within each broad occupational category, there are important variations among the more specific occupations. For example, in the ghetto firms the managerial hierarchy is almost exclusively white even though some of the ghetto firms were owned by black entrepreneurs. Similarly, of the clerical jobs in ghetto firms, only in the plant clerical occupations did black workers predominate. Employees in accounting and business machine operator occupations were all white even though the firm was located in a ghetto area. This suggests the possibility of a lack of indigenous skills within the ghetto for some types of jobs, and as indicated in the discussion of occupational wages the salary paid to accounting and business machine operators was substantially higher in the ghetto than in any other geographic area. On the basis of the small number of responses, the tentative conclusion is that a premium is frequently paid by ghetto firms to attract some types of labor which are not in adequate supply in the immediate geographic environment of the new entrant.

The correlation between the rank of occupations by wages paid and proportion of white employees in each occupation for the various groups of firms supports these findings. For example, the r_s value for the ghetto firms was a positive value of 0.69, indicating that high rank in proportion white employees was associated with high level in the occupational wage structure. In nonghetto firms there was little relationship between the ranks for these two variables, suggesting that blacks employed in nonghetto firms are distributed evenly among occupations and not concentrated in low-paying occupations. A similar result was found in suburban firms where the r_s value was actually a negative (-0.05). These results are interpreted to reflect the strength of occupational demand and supply in different geographic areas rather than conscious wage discrimination in ghetto firms, since many ghetto firms are headed by black entrepreneurs.

The results indirectly suggest that for many occupations there is an adequate labor supply within or close to the ghetto areas of the city. This seems to be the case for jobs in the service type occupations and in some jobs within the operatives and craftsmen category, such as metal processing and general benchwork occupations which for ghetto firms are mostly performed by blacks. Blacks also tend to be concentrated in the materials-handling types of jobs, and this is the case for entrant firms located in both ghetto and nonghetto areas.

Table 4-6 also shows the lack of similarity between ghetto and nonghetto in the racial structure of the respective work forces. Even when the broad occupational categories are considered as in Table 4-7, the degree of similarity in ranking of occupations by racial characteristics of employees is quite small (rank correlation value of 0.25, significant at the 73% level).

The comparison of the ghetto-nonghetto rankings for the twenty-two occupations actually shows a negative correlation value of -0.12, significant at the 69% level. If the ghetto and nonghetto areas together constituted a single labor market in which the skill of the labor supply was the criterion for employment,

Table 4-6
Comparison of Racial Characteristics of Occupational Structure of New Businesses in the City

Occupational Group	Ghetto Firms No. of Empl. (N=524)	Ghetto Firms % of Employees White	No. of Empl. (N=2,491)	% of Employees White	Ghetto-Nonghetto White-Nonwhite Differences (Chi Square)	Rank of Occupation by % of White Ghetto	Rank of Occupation by % of White Nonghetto
Managerial-Professional	18		233		NS		
Professional	12	80	79	86	NS	8.5	8.5
Mgr: Admin. specialist	2	100	42	82	NS	3.5	13
Mgr: General	4	100	112	85	NS	3.5	11
Clerical	46		210		S		
General office clerical	25	80	119	86	NS	8.5	8.5
Acct. & bus. mach. oper.	7	100	43	86	NS	3.5	8.5
Plant clerical	14	33	48	71	S	17.5	15
Sales	24		243		NS		
Sales & sales related	22	100	116	97	NS	3.5	4
Retail food & drink	2	0	127	78	S	–	14
Service	60		362		NS		
Personal service	36	44	143	99	S	14.5	2
Building	24	44	219	92	S	14.5	6
Operatives & Craftsmen	331		1266		NS		
Metal processing	23	15	146	55	S	19	16.5
Mach. op. & repair	19	73	49	86	NS	10	8.5
Paper & printing	9	100	24	83	–	3.5	12
Wood & stone mach.	–	–	–	–	NS	–	–
Textiles	2	100	399	55	NS	3.5	16.5
General benchwork	41	33	19	100	S	17.5	1
Fabrication & repair	–	–	31	–	–	–	5
Fabrication textile	238	58	598	51	S	13	18
Construction Related	13		89		NS		
Structural work	6	83	39	46	S	7	20
Construction	7	71	50	98	S	11	3
Materials Handling	31		88		NS		
Transportation	10	70	30	36	S	12	21
Packaging & material handling	21	38	58	47	NS	16	19

Table 4-7

Comparison of Racial Characteristics of Major Occupational Categories of New Businesses in the City and the Suburbs

| Major Occupational Category | Rank of Weighted Mean % White | | | |
| | Metropolitan Firms | | City Firms | |
	City Entrants	Suburban Entrants	Ghetto Entrants	Nonghetto Entrants
Managerial-Professional	2	1	2	3
Clerical	3	4	4	4
Sales	1	6	1	2
Service	7	5	7	1
Operatives and craftsmen	5	2	5	6
Construction related	4	3	3	5
Materials handling	6	7	6	7

then the rankings should show a strong positive correlation. It appears that there are labor market restrictions which tend to segment the citywide market. For some highly skilled occupations (such as some managerial and clerical occupations) and perhaps some highly unionized occupations (paper and printing), the market is apparently not segmented by the ghetto and nonghetto difference, but for many occupations the results provide indirect evidence of the existence of sublabor markets based on geographic boundaries.

Educational Entry Requirements for New Positions

In the interviews, most entrepreneurs said that the formal educational requirements for entry into almost all occupations in their firms were extremely low. Among the city entrant firms, the formal requirements for the occupations were generally high school graduation or less. It was only in the managerial-professional, clerical, and sales (excluding retail food and drink) that actual graduation from high school became important. College or technical school experience was only mentioned for about 10% of the professional and managerial jobs.

Suburban entrepreneurs viewed formal education as a more important entry requirement to new positions than did their counterpart in the city. On the average, high school graduation or above was required for about 50% of the new suburban jobs. For managerial-professional jobs in the suburbs, college or technical school graduation was seen as a prerequisite for over one-third of the positions.

The comparison of ghetto and nonghetto responses revealed that nonghetto firms required slightly higher overall educational entry requirements, but for some specific occupations the ghetto firms' requirements were slightly higher. In any case, for both groups of firms the formal educational requirements were surprisingly low and substantially lower than the suburban firms' requirements.

It is difficult to explain the difference between the suburban firms and all other groups of firms. A possible explanation is that the suburban firms have been exposed to a different segment of the potential labor supply for each occupation and that the applicants they interview and recruit have a higher level of formal education which becomes the standard required in the firm's job specifications. In addition, the suburban firms were on the average larger than the other groups of firms, and a more formal approach to personnel policy (which specifies standards of entry) may be more typical of suburban firms. The generally low educational requirements for jobs in all firms is probably a reflection of the small size of entrant firms and the relatively small number of applicants (compared to established firms) from which the work force has been selected during the first few years of operations.

Method of Recruitment for New Positions

The recruitment techniques used by new enterprises are expected to involve similar channels of contact with potential employees as those used by firms which have been in business for some time. Since the new firm is relatively small, it is expected that considerable reliance will be placed on informal employee contacts through relatives and present employees. In the study the interviewee was asked to indicate on a check list the most important source of new employees for each job title in the firm's occupational structure. It was found that government supported training programs and educational placement services (schools and colleges) were rarely mentioned as a source and were therefore dropped from the analysis.

For purposes of analysis, the occupational groups were merged into the major categories as shown in Table 4-8. Since several recruitment methods were clearly the most important for all occupations, there was a high degree of consistency of response among the occupations within each of the major occupational groups in Table 4-8. The comparison of the findings for city and suburban entrants indicated some different recruitment practices between the two groups of firms.

For city entrants, newspaper advertising, present employees, and advertising on the premises are generally the most important methods of recruitment, with members of the family and private employment agencies the least important. Suburban firms rely mainly on present employees as well as newspaper advertising and the State Employment Service. In the suburbs less reliance is placed on newspapers probably because of the limited readership in most suburban papers. Advertising on the premises and private employment agencies are of least importance in suburban recruitment. The degree of consistency in the overall relative importance of the methods was relatively high for both city

Table 4-8
Methods of Recruitment Used by New Businesses in the City and the Suburbs for Major Occupational Categories

Major Occupational Category	Rank Order of Importance of Methods of Recruitment												City-Suburbs Comparison	
	Members of Family		Employment Service		Private Agency		Present Employees		Advertising on Premises		Newspaper Advertising		r Value	Level of Confidence
	City	Suburbs	City	Suburbs	City	Suburbs	City	Suburbs	City	Suburbs	City	Suburbs		
Managerial-Professional	5	3	4	4	6	5	2	1	3	6	1	2	.54	89
Clerical	4	5.5	5.5	1.5	5.5	3.5	2	1.5	3	5.5	1	3.5	.00	50
Sales	5.5	3.5	5.5	2	3.5	5.5	3.5	1	2	5.5	1	3.5	-.29	74
Service	5.5	2	3.5	4.5	5.5	4.5	3.5	1	2	4.5	1	4.5	-.11	60
Operatives and craftsmen	5.5	3	2	4	5.5	5	3	2	4	6	1	1	.56	89
Construction related	4.5	4	4.5	4	4.5	1	2	4	4.5	6	1	2	.43	83
Materials handling	3.5	4.5	5.5	4.5	5.5	4.5	2	2	3.5	4.5	1	1	.89	97

and suburban firms. For the city firms, the consistency in ranking as measured by the coefficient of concordance was 0.67, where 0 is complete disagreement among the occupational groups as to the relative ranking and 1 signifies complete agreement. For the suburban firms, the consistency in the overall ranking of the methods was also fairly high with a value of 0.45 for the coefficient of concordance.

When the two groups of firms are compared for particular major occupational groups, the differences are even more apparent. For example, when the rank orders of importance of the methods for both types of firms are correlated, there is no relationship for clerical occupations. Suburban firms ranked the employment service and present employees as the two most important methods. The rank correlation values for sales and service occupations actually showed a negative relationship.

Strong positive correlations in the ranking of importance were found for materials-handling jobs, operatives, and craftsmen and professional-technical jobs. This indicates a similarity between new city and suburban firms in the techniques used to recruit employees. There are enough differences, however, in the approach used by the two groups of firms to conclude that the method of recruitment varies with the geographic location of the new firm.

The ghetto-nonghetto comparison in Table 4-9 also shows the similarities and differences in the methods of recruitment used. The overall ranking for all occupational groups in both ghetto and nonghetto firms resulted in newspaper advertising being the most important method of recruitment. The ghetto firms made considerable use of present employees and private agencies and less use of advertising on the premises. In contrast, the nonghetto firms relied much more on advertising on the premises as well as present employees and made little use of private employment agencies. The consistency of these overall rankings among the major occupational groups was relatively high.[b]

For the most part there was agreement between the ghetto and nonghetto rankings for each individual occupational group. The values of the rank correlation ranged from a low of 0.43 for clerical occupations to a high of about 0.87 for managerial-professional and construction related occupations. The major differences between the firms were in the clerical and service occupations. In recruiting clerical employees, ghetto firms used private agencies more than nonghetto firms, which relied more on advertising on the premises. Recruitment of service employees in ghetto-based firms was frequently through the employment service, while the nonghetto firms relied more on recommendations from present employees. It therefore appears that the ghetto-nonghetto differences in recruitment methods used are restricted to one or two occupational groups and are generally much less pronounced than the city-suburban differences.

---

[b]The value of the coefficient of concordance of the overall rankings among occupational groups was 0.63 for both groups of firms and this value was significant at the 99% level.

Table 4-9

Methods of Recruitment Used by New Businesses in the City for Major Occupational Categories

| Major Occupational Category | Rank Order of Importance of Methods of Recruitment | | | | | | | | | | | | Non-ghetto-Ghetto Comparison Level of | |
| | Member of Family | | Employment Service | | Private Agency | | Present Employees | | Advertising on Premises | | Newspaper Advertising | | | |
	Ghetto	Nonghetto	Ghetto	Nonghetto	Ghetto	Nonghetto	Ghetto	Nonghetto	Ghetto	Nonghetto	Ghetto	Nonghetto	r	Val. Conf.
Managerial-Professional	4.5	5.5	4.5	4	4.5	5.5	2	2	4.5	3	1	1	.87	97
Clerical	3.5	4	5.5	5	3.5	6	2	3	5.5	2	1	1	.43	83
Sales	4.5	5.5	4.5	5.5	4.5	3	2	4	4.5	2	1	1	.59	90
Service	4.5	5	2	5	4.5	5	4.5	2.5	4.5	2.5	1	1	.50	87
Operatives and craftsmen	6	5	4	2	4	6	2	3.5	4	3.5	1	1	.67	93
Construction related	4.5	4	4.5	4	4.5	4	2	4	4.5	4	1	1	.86	97
Materials handling	5	3.5	5	5	3	6	2	1.5	5	3.5	1	1.5	.60	91

Conclusions

The survey of firms produced findings which were fairly consistent with the regularities expected from a comparison of entrant firms by geographic area. Most variations in the occupational structure of different groups of firms appear to be related to the industrial structure of each group of entrants. Some occupational categories, such as managerial jobs, tended to be proportionately most important to suburban firms and nonghetto city firms. The size of ghetto entrants and perhaps difficulties in attracting high-level manpower seem to restrict the size of the managerial hierarchy.

It was found that wages perform their traditional labor market role in the allocation of labor among the various occupations and groups of entrant firms. The ghetto firms have to pay more to attract managerial-professional labor and some types of clerical employees who are likely to reside some distance from the ghetto and who for many reasons prefer nonghetto employment. Similarly, for some lower-skilled occupations for which the labor supply is likely to be more plentiful near the central core of the city, the ghetto firms offer a lower wage.

The data suggested an additional hypothesis which was not discussed at the outset. The industrial distribution of entrants resulted in an occupational bias in the new-skilled and semiskilled jobs so that in both the ghetto and the city as a whole, most of the new jobs in this skilled level were in industries which have traditionally been located in the central city and probably do not require much single level floor space for operations. In contrast, most of the skilled and semiskilled blue-collar jobs created by new businesses in the suburbs seemed to be biased towards machine work in industries which probably require a large amount of plant floor space.[c]

The findings on the occupational structure and employment characteristics of new businesses have some important implications for urban manpower policy. One of the major problems in employment policy has been the high rate of sectoral unemployment in many urban areas. Minority groups are particularly affected by this high rate, and as a result many programs are designed to improve the skills and find employment for unemployed ghetto residents. In addition, an attempt has been to assist minority group entrepreneurs establish new businesses in the ghetto area.

The data on the occupational structure and characteristics of new businesses suggest some difficulties which make the success of such a policy doubtful. The urban labor market consists of a series of sublabor markets, and the employment opportunities for minority group members appear to decline outside the central

---

[c]The testing of this hypothesis obviously requires a different type of data than collected for this study. The comparative samples of firms should also be chosen from the same population of firms. As was pointed out in the methodology section, the suburban sample was selected from the unemployment compensation list of firms, while the city firms were samples from wage-tax data. There are some differences in these sources of entrant data.

core of the city with the suburban labor market providing the least opportunities. Suburban and nonghetto city entrant firms tend to hire more employees than ghetto firms, and during the first few years of operations nonghetto and suburban employment expands more rapidly. Consequently, the establishment of new businesses may provide proportionately less new employment opportunities for nonwhites than it does for whites.

These findings suggest that the policy of "gilding the ghetto"[3] through encouraging new minority ghetto entrepreneurs should perhaps be redirected towards more assistance to minority entrepreneurs in nonghetto and suburban areas where there is some evidence of a better chance of success. It is expected that nonghetto minority entrepreneurs will attempt to hire a higher proportion of nonwhites than the white entrepreneurs in the same geographic area. It is, of course, probable that the success of this change in emphasis will require programs which assist unemployed nonwhites in commuting to the new business enterprise.

The high salaries paid by ghetto firms for some occupations suggest an inadequate supply of such labor from the area in which the firm is located. This information may indicate the occupations which offer the best potential employment for manpower program trainees. Accounting and business machine operation was, for example, an occupation which received a relatively high salary and is a likely candidate for a ghetto training program.

Part II: Employment Distribution in Relation to Residence of Workers

5

Decentralization of Employment Within the City

The decentralization of job opportunities within the metropolitan area is a trend that has been widely discussed recently. Despite this trend a majority of total employment in any region still resides within the city, and yet there is relatively little knowledge on the nature of the geographic distribution of these jobs. Since the low-income residents of the city tend to be clustered close to the core of the city, the citywide distribution of job opportunities has significant employment implication for "disadvantaged" residents. The appropriate public policy response to high unemployment in urban labor markets therefore largely depends on the dispersion pattern of job opportunities within the city.

A relatively uniform geographic distribution of city jobs suggests that it is necessary to attract new job opportunities to the core of the city which experiences the highest unemployment rates. This approach has been described as "gilding the ghetto."[1] One alternative to this policy solution is to improve the transportation network between the inner core and other sectors of the city, so that inner-city residents may be able to expand their normal preference area for employment. In addition public policy may attempt to disperse the urban poor more uniformly within the city by reducing the segregated housing pattern. On the other hand, if most employment opportunities are concentrated within the core of the city and not uniformly dispersed throughout the city, then the major public policy solution to high unemployment should consist of changing the nature of labor supply through retraining the unemployed in the inner city for the potential job opportunities which exist close to their residence. The justification for the concentrated employment program—a major feature of current manpower policy—appears to rest on this assumption.

Employment Distribution Hypotheses

In an attempt to provide the basic information necessary to assess the appropriate balance between manpower retraining and improved transportation facilities as possible solutions to urban unemployment, this chapter discusses the geographic distribution of employment within Philadelphia. It is expected that the geographic distribution of employment will vary by type of industry. A substantial proportion of employment in the service sector, especially business services, obviously will be located in the central business district. Employment in wholesale and retail trade, construction, and other major industry groups are likely to be widely distributed throughout the city.

87

The distribution of manufacturing job opportunities usually varies with type of manufacturing. In most cities there is a tendency for printing and some types of textile firms to locate near the central core, while manufacturing firms which require a large proportion of space per unit of output, such as light engineering, chemical firms, and so forth, are more likely to be located towards the perimeter of the city. These tendencies are of course only generalizations and many factors peculiar to a specific urban area may result in a different geographic pattern of employment distribution.

Measurement of Decentralization

The distribution of employment may be estimated on the basis of air-mile distance from the central business district displayed as a series of concentric circles radiating to the city boundary. The proportion or density of employment within each distance category may be depicted graphically. For purposes of studying the employment potential of businesses for residents of low-income areas it is, however, more meaningful to use travel time rather than air mile as the distance criterion.

Data on travel time from the center of the city to various areas of the city, perhaps postal zones, normally involves a special large-scale commuting study. Fortunately, the results of such a study of the Philadelphia metropolitan area have recently been published, and with certain adjustments to the data it was possible to construct estimates of travel time for each zip area in the city to the center of the city.

In the city, the Delaware Valley Regional Planning Commission study identified forty-seven data collection districts which were surveyed to estimate various types of commuting information. The base year of the study was 1960 and projections on travel time to center city were made for 1985. The forty-seven collection districts did not coincide exactly with the forty-three postal zones within the city, but the boundaries of the two sets of geographic subdivisions were close enough to estimate the 1960 travel time from each postal zone to the center of the city.[2]

From the city wage tax it was possible to estimate the total 1968 employment by industry for each zip code and classify each zip by travel time in minutes. Travel time was an average daily travel time for commuting to the center of the city by highway in automobile or truck. From these data the cumulative distribution 1968 city employment by 1960 travel time was calculated for broad industrial groups and by two digit manufacturing industry. Obviously, it is preferable to have 1968 travel time but this is not regarded as a problem. Although citywide traffic density has undoubtedly increased over the past decade, there have also been highway improvements, such as coordinated traffic light timing and one-way street networks, which offset the effect of increased traffic load.

This method of studying the potential job opportunities available to low-income residents has the advantage of concentrating on the large number of jobs within the city compared to the marginal opportunities available in the suburban ring. The approach also has several inadequacies. For example, the existence of a large proportion of jobs within the core does not necessarily mean that ghetto residents will find employment at these locations. Most individuals employed in these jobs may commute to the central core from the perimeter of the city, and possible employment opportunities for the poor may not be extensive, though this will vary by type of industry. The data would be improved if the travel time criterion were also based on public transit as well as on automobile travel, since it would be more meaningful for analyzing the problem of increasing employment opportunities for low-income residents. For similar reasons it would also be helpful to have data on the cost of commuting. Nevertheless, the concentration of employment within specified levels of auto travel time from the city center provides, in terms of absolute number of jobs, a much more realistic framework for studying high sectoral unemployment in the city than does reliance on the suburban growth in job opportunities which has occurred in recent years.

Dispersion of Urban Employment in Major Industries

Figures 5-1 and 5-2 show the degree of dispersion of jobs in various industries. If the total jobs in a particular industry were equally distributed throughout the city according to travel time to the center of the city, then the dispersion line for that industry would coincide with the 45 degree line in the figure. If an industry's dispersion line is below the 45 degree line, this means that its employment is decentralized and concentrated towards the perimenter of the city. In contrast, the centralization of industry employment is associated with a dispersion line above the 45 degree line.

It is apparent from the findings that in all major industries, with the exception of the primary industries,[a] employment is concentrated close to the center of the city. The primary industry exception is not quantitatively an important consideration since total citywide employment in this industry is only a little over 700 jobs distributed among a large number of small firms.

For discriptive purposes, the travel time axis is divided into three major strata. The first is the central business district. It is possible to travel from any point in this area to center city within 5 minutes. This geographic area is represented on the horizontal axis of the figures by the point A. The second strata, represented by point B, is designated the central core of the city and any point within this area is within 19 minutes of the center. Geographically this

[a]Primary industries include SIC codes 1 through 14. This includes agriculture and related industries, fisheries and mining.

90

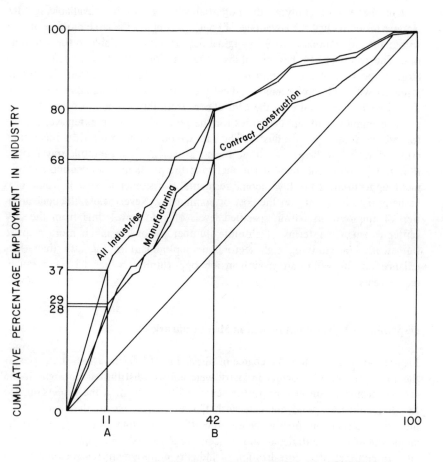

CUMULATIVE PERCENTAGE TRAVEL TIME TO CENTER CITY

LEGEND:

OA REPRESENTS THE CENTRAL BUSINESS DISTRICT. TRAVEL TIME IS 5 MIN. TO CENTER CITY FROM THIS AREA.

OB REPRESENTS THE INNER OR CENTRAL CORE. TRAVEL TIME IS 19 MIN. TO CENTER CITY FROM PERIMETER OF THIS AREA WHICH INCLUDES THE FOLLOWING SUBLABOR MARKETS: NORTH PHILADELPHIA, WEST PHILADELPHIA, SPRING GARDEN AND SOUTH PHILADELPHIA.

Figure 5-1. Dispersion of Employment in Selected Major Industries.

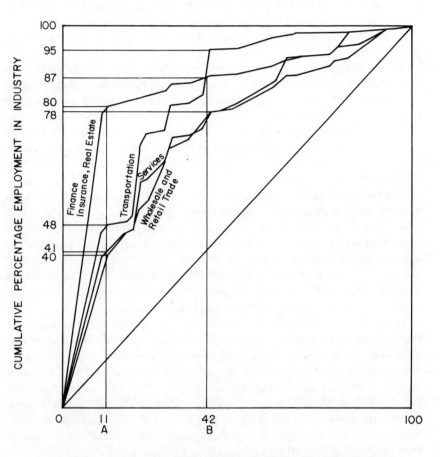

CUMULATIVE PERCENTAGE TRAVEL TIME TO CENTER CITY

LEGEND:

OA REPRESENTS THE CENTRAL BUSINESS DISTRICT. TRAVEL TIME IS 5 MIN. TO CENTER CITY FROM THIS AREA.

OB REPRESENTS THE INNER OR CENTRAL CORE. TRAVEL TIME IS 19 MIN. TO CENTER CITY FROM PERIMETER OF THIS AREA WHICH INCLUDES THE FOLLOWING SUBLABOR MARKETS: NORTH PHILADELPHIA, WEST PHILADELPHIA, SPRING GARDEN AND SOUTH PHILADELPHIA.

Figure 5–2. Dispersion of Employment in Selected Major Industries.

area constitutes the southern half of the city and includes the three ghetto sublabor markets and South Philadelphia as well as the central business district. The third area is the northern half of the city and is defined as the outer region. The travel time from within this area is a maximum of 45 minutes. The geographic demarcation of these areas is shown in Figure 5-6 which appears later in this chapter.

The employment of all industries taken together is highly concentrated, with 37% located in the central business district and some 80% within the central core of the city. A density of employment map of the city would show an even slightly higher degree of concentration, since the increment of land area encompassed increases with each additional minute of travel from the center. As a result, although 37% of employment is within 11% of the total cumulative travel time, the same amount of employment is in a land area of less than 5% of the total land area in the city.

The fact that 80% of employment is located either in or close to the ghetto areas of the city suggests that the manpower policy which adjusts the nature rather than the location of labor supply is the correct priority in any solution to high urban unemployment. The maximum highway travel time to most employment for ghetto residents is about 40 minutes, and this casts some question on the view that better transportation networks to the outer region of the city is required. This implication may of course have to be modified when public transit time is substituted for highway travel time.

There are some important variations among industries in the degree of employment concentration. For example, although about 80% of employment in services, wholesale and retail trade, and manufacturing is within the central core, manufacturing employment is much less concentrated in the central business district than is employment in the other two major industries. Employment in finance, insurance and real estate is the most highly concentrated with almost 80% within the central business district. Contract construction is fairly well dispersed throughout the city with some 29% in the central business district and about 68% within the central core.

The exception for this industry is not unexpected and can be partially explained by size and number of firms in the industry. In contract construction the average size of firms is quite small and there are a large number of these firms making up the 40,000 total employment. As a result, although the large general contractors may be located close to the center of the city, there is a significant geographic distribution of the large number of relatively small firms in the industry. The geographic dispersion of employment in this industry may be even more pronounced than the results suggest. This is because, even though the large construction firms may locate in the central business district, the actual operations may be widely dispersed outside the inner core of the city.

In finance, insurance, and real estate, a relatively small number of large firms probably account for a large share of total employment in the industry, and since these firms rely heavily on white-collar office workers, the central business district, with its excellent rail network to various parts of the region, is an ideal location.

The high degree of concentration of manufacturing industry in the inner core was somewhat unexpected, and perhaps there are some major variations among the industries within manufacturing which explain this finding.

Dispersion of Urban Manufacturing Employment

Figures 5-3, 5-4, and 5-5 show the variation in employment concentration among selected manufacturing industries. Although there is a tendency towards centralization among all industries, the employment in several industries is fairly uniformly distributed throughout the city. This is the case for fabricated metal, machinery (except electrical), stone, clay, glass and concrete, and to a lesser extent paper products manufacturing.

There is an important difference between the apparel and textile mills industries. Almost 50% of the apparel employment is in the central business district, and over 90% of the employment is located within the central core. In contrast, the employment in textile mills (although still mostly (70%) in the central core) is of little importance in the central business district. The most highly concentrated manufacturing industries are petroleum refining, printing and publishing, and chemicals. Transportation and electrical machinery manufacturing both have about 90% of their employment in the central core of the city but have very little within the central business district.

Several factors probably explain some of the differences among manufacturing firms. The existence of several large employers within an industry will dominate its employment distribution. This is likely to explain the pattern in transportation manufacturing. Several physical characteristics of the city influence the high degree of employment concentration. The city's port facilities are geographically quite close to the center of the city; the same is true of region's major railroad yards and the focus of its highway system. These reasons and the dominant influence of several large employers, account for the centralization of petroleum refining and chemicals. In this respect, the industrial land-use pattern in Philadelphia may not be typical of other large cities and the high degree of concentration in manufacturing employment cannot be generalized.

Manpower Policy Implications

The lack of decentralization of industrial employment is an important finding, but even if it is typical of other cities it is not enough information to draw implications for future manpower policy. Additional employment data is

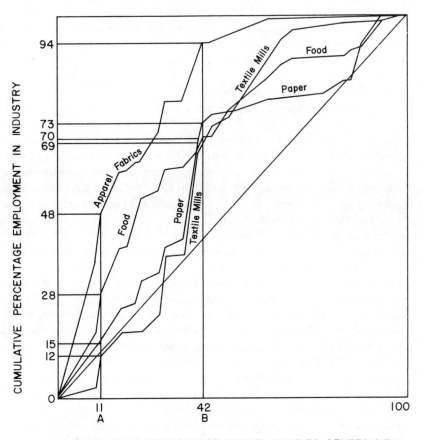

CUMULATIVE PERCENTAGE TRAVEL TIME TO CENTER CITY

LEGEND:

OA REPRESENTS THE CENTRAL BUSINESS DISTRICT. TRAVEL TIME IS 5 MIN. TO CENTER CITY FROM THIS AREA.

OB REPRESENTS THE INNER OR CENTRAL CORE. TRAVEL TIME IS 19 MIN. TO CENTER CITY FROM PERIMETER OF THIS AREA WHICH INCLUDES THE FOLLOWING SUBLABOR MARKETS: NORTH PHILADELPHIA, WEST PHILADELPHIA, SPRING GARDEN AND SOUTH PHILADELPHIA.

Figure 5-3. Dispersion of Employment in Selected Manufacturing Industries.

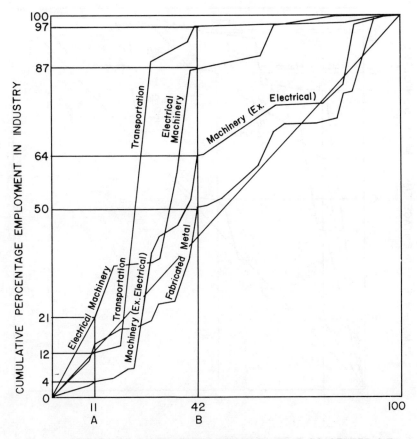

CUMULATIVE PERCENTAGE TRAVEL TIME TO CENTER CITY

LEGEND:

OA REPRESENTS THE CENTRAL BUSINESS DISTRICT. TRAVEL TIME IS 5 MIN. TO CENTER CITY FROM THIS AREA.

OB REPRESENTS THE INNER OR CENTRAL CORE. TRAVEL TIME IS 19 MIN. TO CENTER CITY FROM PERIMETER OF THIS AREA WHICH INCLUDES THE FOLLOWING SUBLABOR MARKETS: NORTH PHILADELPHIA, WEST PHILADELPHIA, SPRING GARDEN AND SOUTH PHILADELPHIA.

Figure 5-4. Dispersion of Employment in Selected Manufacturing Industries.

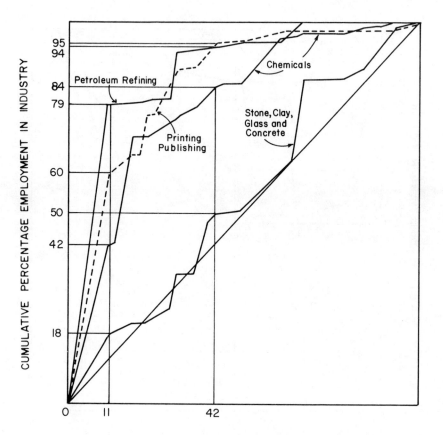

CUMULATIVE PERCENTAGE TRAVEL TIME TO CENTER CITY

LEGEND:

OA REPRESENTS THE CENTRAL BUSINESS DISTRICT. TRAVEL
TIME IS 5 MIN. TO CENTER CITY FROM THIS AREA.

OB REPRESENTS THE INNER OR CENTRAL CORE. TRAVEL TIME
IS 19 MIN. TO CENTER CITY FROM PERIMETER OF THIS AREA
WHICH INCLUDES THE FOLLOWING SUBLABOR MARKETS:
NORTH PHILADELPHIA, WEST PHILADELPHIA, SPRING GARDEN
AND SOUTH PHILADELPHIA.

Figure 5–5. Dispersion of Employment in Selected Manufacturing Industries.

required. It is necessary to have estimates of the absolute number of jobs in each industry if the significance of a centralized or decentralized industry is to have any meaning for policy. In order to plan future policy, it is also preferable to have information on the industrial employment trend, otherwise one may decide to retrain ghetto residents for jobs in a centralized industry with a large number of jobs but whose total employment is declining. This problem raises the issue of whether short-run or long-run solutions to urban unemployment should be given priority. Finally, policy decisions affecting labor supply are more meaningful if the trend in the geographic location of demand by occupational as well as industrial group is available. Unfortunately, since this study is based on cross-sectional rather than time-series data, and since the city wage-tax data does not provide occupational information, it is necessary to adopt data from other sources to provide the data necessary for policy decisions.

Table 5-1 shows estimates of total employment by industry and the absolute number of jobs by travel region of the city. The ghetto residents who are all within the central core are in close proximity to the industries, with large numbers of employees concentrated close to the center of the city. Relatively, they are not in a particularly favorable location for jobs in the primary industries or contract construction. Fortunately, in terms of the absolute number of jobs, these industries are a small proportion of city wide employment; construction for example, according to the data, accounts for about 41,000 jobs which is about 4.6% of city employment. The remaining industry groups—in particular transportation, finance, real estate and insurance—therefore appear to be the industries which, on the criterion of job accessibility, provide potential opportunities to ghetto residents.

In most of the manufacturing industries which employ a large absolute number of employees, the criterion of geographic accessibility also favors training of ghetto residents for jobs in these industries. This is the case for printing and publishing, apparel, chemicals, and transportation manufacturing.

Table 5-1 also shows the importance of the employment trend in industrial employment as a criterion influencing the choice of industries which are likely to provide job opportunities for ghetto residents. The employment trend during the 1960s is based on data from *County Business Patterns*,[3] and it is assumed that the same trend is applicable to the employment estimates obtained from the city wage tax. If a similar trend continues during the next decade, the potential job opportunities for ghetto residents which, according to the accessibility criterion, are available in several manufacturing industries employing large numbers of workers are likely to be more apparent than real. This is likely to be the case for chemical manufacturing which has shown a steady decline in number of employees.

The chemical industry may also be rejected as an attractive industry for employing ghetto residents because of the occupational distribution of jobs by skill level within the industry; the proportion of low or semiskilled jobs in this

Table 5-1
Distribution of Employment by Industry and Highway Travel Time to Center City

	City Employment (1968)	Estimated % Change 1959-68a	Central Business District 5 Min. Travel to C.C.		Central Core 19 Min. Travel to C.C.		Outer Region 45 Min. Travel to C.C.	
			%	Employment	%	Employment	%	Employment
City	866,068	+6.3	37	320,445	80	692,854	20	173,214
Primary industries	721	−22	12	87	33	238	67	483
Contract construction	40,806	11	29	11,834	68	27,748	32	13,058
Transportation	76,903	39	48	36,913	95	73,058	5	3,845
Wholesale & retail	213,249	−5	40	85,300	78	166,334	22	46,915
Finance, insurance & real estate	68,363	22	80	54,690	87	59,476	13	8,887
Services	188,435	39	41	77,258	78	146,979	22	41,456
Manufacturing	277,591	−7	28	77,725	80	222,073	20	55,518
Ordinance & acces.	14	–	5	1	67	9	33	5
Food	27,850	−11	28	7,798	70	19,495	30	8,355
Tobacco	220	–	46	101	100	220	0	0
Textile mills	20,510	−30	12	2,461	69	14,152	31	6,358
Apparel	40,132	0	48	19,263	94	37,724	6	2,408
Lumber & wood	1,511	25	21	317	95	1,435	5	76
Furniture & fixtures	3,665	0	12	440	70	2,566	30	1,099
Paper	10,651	4	15	1,598	73	7,775	27	2,876
Printing, publishing	28,760	3	60	17,256	95	27,322	5	1,438
Chemicals	16,069	−22	42	6,749	84	13,498	16	2,571
Petroleum refining	5,025	−30	79	3,970	94	4,724	6	301
Rubber, plastics	1,992	−15	2	40	64	1,275	36	717

Leather	2,157	−53	35	755	95	2,049	5	108
Stone, clay, glass, concrete	3,325	−10	18	599	50	1,663	50	1,662
Primary metal	3,866	11	4	155	52	2,010	48	1,856
Fabricated metal	26,377	−8	12	3,165	50	13,189	50	13,188
Machinery	16,209	−5	4	648	64	10,374	36	5,835
Electrical machinery	40,225	29	21	8,447	87	34,996	13	5,229
Transportation	14,195	−17	12	1,703	97	13,769	3	426
Instruments	1,899	−15	31	589	69	1,310	31	589
Misc.	12,939	−26	20	2,588	70	9,057	30	3,882

aThe percentage change is based on estimates published data in *Country Business Patterns*, 1959 and 1968. The 1968 employment estimates obtained from the city wage tax and the estimates in *County Business Patterns* are similar in magnitude in most industrial categories. It is therefore assumed that the percentage change is also similar.

industry is likely to be small compared to many other manufacturing industries. However, even in industries with a high proportion of semiskilled jobs and which are readily accessible to ghetto residents, the trend in employment suggests that the future job potential in the industry is not high.

In an industry such as textile manufacturing, with the characteristic of good geographic accessibility to the ghetto and representative of a large number of semiskilled jobs, the employment has declined some 30% during the past decade. Consequently, it is unlikely to provide jobs to the unemployed residents of the urban core. In contrast, the apparel industry is by all relevant criteria likely to continue to be an important source of job opportunities, provided its past employment trend continues.

Table 5-1 suggests that the greatest growth in job opportunities is in the service and finance, insurance and real estate sectors, and that in manufacturing the future opportunities are likely to vary widely among type of manufacturing. In wholesale and retail trade, employment growth within the city has not occurred and this may reflect a decentralization trend within the city. This is not an encouraging trend for inner-city residents, although the net impact of this tendency may not be serious since at the same time there has been an outmigration of city residents, especially white residents. Many segments of the wholesale and retail industry are likely to employ a high proportion of low-skilled and low-cost labor from the immediate environment of the firm. As a result, many of the 166,000 jobs in the inner city, while not expanding, may become available to ghetto residents through a "queue effect" brought about by the residential migration pattern within the metropolitan area.

The employment opportunities for ghetto residents are greatest in industries employing large numbers of semiskilled workers. Obviously industries with a high proportion of managerial, professional-technical and highly skilled craftsmen are not expected to provide many opportunities for the hard core unemployed. Those industries which hire a large number of operatives, service workers, and sales personnel are the ones most likely to provide the necessary jobs. Consequently, from a policy point of view, it is more desirable to have firms in wholesale and retail trade and the service industries located close to the inner city than some manufacturing, such as firms in petroleum products and the chemical industry.

Appendix B presents estimates of selected occupational employment by industry for firms located within the central core of the city. These estimates give some indication of the importance of some skilled, semiskilled, and unskilled job opportunities which are expected to be available within the inner city during the next few years. The data suggest the types of jobs for which ghetto residents should be trained and shows the difference in employment impact among industries. It is, of course, not known whether the estimated job opportunities are adequate to employ all the labor force within the central core, but it is clear that the quantity of accessible relatively low-skilled job opportunities is substantial.

Conclusions

The major finding which emerges from the analysis of the distribution of jobs within the city is that a substantial portion of job opportunities are within the central core of the city. As previously pointed out, in some industries in which there are a number of firms with many branches throughout the city it is possible that there is an overestimate in the concentration of employment close to the center of the city. This is because the head office, or the reporting unit, frequently located in the central business district, reports the total employment of the firm including the information from all branch operations without specifying the employment at each individual branch. This is most likely to occur in retail trade where firms such as dairies, local supermarket chains, and so forth, have several branches in Philadelphia. In banking, and to some extent in real estate operations, a similar tendency can be expected.

In the opinion of the researchers, the magnitude of this bias in the data is not large. Many multiestablishment firms do report employment separately by branch, and in some cases where citywide employment is reported from one address the reporting unit is not in the central core of the city. This appears to offset the magnitude of the bias. In addition, since the tendency towards geographic concentration is consistent among most industries, many of which are not organized in a system of branch operations, the degree of concentration is probably reasonably accurate.

The labor market implications of this result are that ghetto residents are in close proximity to the location of a substantial portion of city jobs. If ghetto residents have the skill and experience necessary to compete with nonghetto and suburban residents, and discrimination in hiring is not present, there does not appear to be a serious commuting problem for ghetto residents who have access to automobile transportation. However, the conclusion that most potential jobs are located near the residences of low-income families, where high sectoral unemployment exists, assumes that most ghetto residents have access to automobile for travel to work. The travel time within the inner city increases significantly when public transit is used as the means of travel.

Figure 5-6 shows a comparison of highway and public transit travel time for zip code areas of the central core of the city.[4] The public transit travel time for each data collection unit is an average time for all sections of the area. For this reason it is possible for regions at the perimeter of the central core to have a lower average travel time than an area close to the central business district.

The figure highlights the importance of the north-south subway line and the east-west elevated transit line. The existence of elongated normal preference areas of employment and the possibility of some ghetto residents being "isolated" from the major public transit routes within the central core is clearly demonstrated. The comparison between public and auto transit is quite striking. The maximum average daily travel time by auto from the perimeter of the inner city to center city is 19 minutes, while the maximum for public transit is some

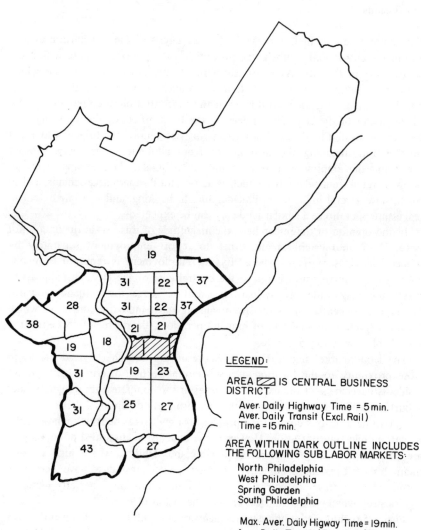

Figure 5-6. Travel Time to Center City from Selected Areas of Philadelphia.

43 minutes. For the ghetto resident in some parts of North Philadelphia, it may take about 70 minutes to travel to a job in the southwestern part of the city by public transit while it will probably take less than half that time to travel by car. The conclusion about relative ease of commuting to potential job opportunities within the central core has to be modified somewhat depending on the distribution of employment by public transit time. This is an important area for further analysis, and it is recommended that this research be completed to substantiate or modify the conclusions on the concentration of employment.

The logical implication drawn from the apparent high degree of geographic concentration of city jobs is that public policy should give the highest priority to preparing the unemployed for the job opportunities close to their residences. It is appropriate to allocate resources to change the nature of ghetto labor supply to increase its ability to compete for inner city jobs. It is, of course, clear that the disadvantaged will never be able to compete for many jobs in the city, especially those in the central business district which employ a high proportion of high level manpower. Nevertheless, the analysis of available job opportunities by occupation (Appendix B) shows that if the unemployed are given some basic skills there are many semiskilled and low-skilled jobs within the central core. The Concentrated Employment Program approach receives strong justification from the findings and should continue to be the basic feature of a manpower policy which seeks to reduce high sectoral unemployment.

Since city jobs are not widely dispersed geographically, the policy of encouraging new business enterprises within the ghetto should, according to the results, be given a lower priority than retraining the unemployed. The mere development of new businesses does not necessarily mean that the entrepreneur will hire the unemployed ghetto residents. In fact, in order to reduce the high risk involved during the development stage of a new business the entrepreneur is unlikely to employ labor which lacks skill and because of their labor force status, has had little work experience in the recent past. It is therefore concluded that new ghetto businesses or black capitalism type programs do not appear to have a high payoff in reducing high sectoral unemployment. It seems that the problem is not so much the lack of available jobs as the inability of ghetto residents to compete effectively for these jobs. Their inability to compete is the result of many factors, including the residents' low-labor productivity, discrimination in hiring and, for a majority of ghetto families, lack of an automobile.

The results of this chapter also indirectly call into question the policy which places a high priority on improving the transportation network between the inner city and other sectors of the city. Such a policy appears appropriate only if the labor turnover and job vacancy statistics suggest higher rates in the outlying areas of the city compared to the core of the city. Reasons other than the reduction of high ghetto unemployment may of course necessitate the improvement of intracity transportation; if all future expansion in employment occurs outside the inner city, this policy has a high priority as a long-run solution. As a solution to the pressing problem of unemployment, the most appropriate policy seems, however, to be changing the labor supply so that ghetto residents become more competitive in the search for jobs and secondly, improving the public transit system *within* the core of the city.

6

Employment Concentration
in Sublabor Markets

In Philadelphia, as in many of the nation's cities, a high proportion of city jobs in most industries is concentrated in the inner city. The extent of this concentration has already been estimated by travel time from the center of the city, but this does not describe the industrial employment structure of the various sublabor markets identified in the study. The purpose of this chapter is to treat each area of the city as a subsystem of the city's economy. The absolute number of jobs in each area are not compared since the areas vary considerably in population, geographic area as well as total employment. The focus of the analysis is a comparison of the employment structure of the sublabor markets within the city. This approach is useful in forecasting the economic outlook for each area by examining the dependence of each area on particular industries for employment opportunities. If, for example, a ghetto area's economy tends to specialize heavily in manufacturing compared to other types of industry, then a secular decline in manufacturing within the city will acutely affect the local ghetto economy to a much greater extent than the more diversified areas or those which specialize in other industries.

The industrial structure of a local economy depends on its degree of specialization which is a function of many variables. Included among them are the location of transportation lines and terminals, the site of public buildings (city hall, courts, government offices, and so forth), the pattern of residential housing, and proximity to raw materials. Moreover, once an area develops into a center of certain activities, there is a tendency for further specialization if agglomerative economies are present.

Given the approximate importance of these factors in Philadelphia, a certain pattern of industrial development could be expected. Center city, with its concentration in public facilities, its role as a transportation center, and its past history of development would suggest a high concentration in business services, trade, and finance-insurance-real estate. Areas surrounding center city with their transportation access and their role in the city's development would probably be major concentrations of manufacturing; these might include Spring Garden, Frankford-Richmond, and North Philadelphia.

Since retail trade tends to follow population and income movements, rapidly growing areas like the Northeast should have a relatively large concentration of trade. Lower-income areas should be less important in trade and services—particularly where there is a relatively small residential population compared to the job population. Examples of such areas in Philadelphia are expected to include

Spring Garden and Frankford-Richmond. Some industries like construction are much more "foot loose" in the sense that the location of the direct economic activity varies with each building project. Consequently, the concentration of employment in particular sublabor market areas due to the location of the firm's administrative office has much less labor market significance than is the case for other industries. In addition, no easy prediction, based on economic rationale, can be made concerning the concentration of construction firms' main offices.

Comparative Economic Structure of Sublabor Markets

The comparison of the economic structure of the various sublabor markets is shown by indices of employment concentration based on the location quotient concept.[1] This is a device for comparing an area's percentage share of employment in an industry with its percentage share of some aggregate base. For example, if a sublabor market accounts for 20% of construction employment in the city and the sublabor market's total employment is 10% of total city employment, the sublabor markets construction location quotient is 2.

The location quotient, with 1968 estimated employment as the base, was calculated for each major industry in the various sublabor markets. The results are shown graphically in Figure 6-1. The bar graphs are purely descriptive statistics, and variations in the value of the location quotient in themselves carry no direct labor market implications. In the instances where the value of the quotient for a given industry is more than 1, it simply means that, on the basis of an area's share of city employment, the area has more than its proportionate share of employment in that industry. Considered as a "separate" local economy within the city, it therefore tends to concentrate on this industry proportionately more than the other areas of the city.

The results shown on the bar charts indicate the following differences among the areas of the city. The low-income areas of the city (Spring Garden, West and North Philadelphia) are heavily involved in manufacturing, transportation, and construction. Further, these segments of the economy are strong in trade but are deficient in finance and real estate and services. Within these particular areas, however, substantial differences emerge. A larger share of Spring Garden's total employment is in manufacturing than is the case for the industrial employment distribution in West Philadelphia. West Philadelphia has, of course, a much larger total employment and consequently has more manufacturing jobs, even though its degree of concentration in manufacturing is less than in the local economy in Spring Garden. Spring Garden has a very low proportion of its employment in transportation when compared with all other sublabor markets. West Philadelphia has a surprisingly high proportion of its employment in service jobs.

Center City is an area of unique characteristics. Like most other central business districts, it specializes in nonmanufacturing activities, particularly finance-insurance-real estate; it is also a transportation center. The industrial employment structure of the other nonghetto areas is of course quite different than the structure in Center City. South Philadelphia has a well-balanced employment structure but is proportionately low in employment in finance and general services. By contrast, Frankford-Richmond has a rather unbalanced local economy. Manufacturing appears to dominate the industrial structure of the area. Primary industries and contract construction are concentrated in the Northwest and Northeast. In addition, the Northwest is a major repository of service employment, while the Northeast has substantial employment in trade.

Concentration of Industrial Employment in the City

The previous discussion has compared the economy of geographic areas of the city by focusing on the employment structure of each separate area. The location quotient can also be used to compare the extent to which industry employment is concentrated without identifying the specific geographic areas in which each industry is concentrated. This is done by constructing localization curves for each industry. Figures 6-2 and 6-3 illustrate these curves for the major industrial categories.

The curves are constructed as follows: for each industry the location quotients calculated for each area of the city are ranked highest to lowest. For the area with the highest location quotient, the percentage of an industry's employment located in this area is plotted against the percentage of total (all industry) employment in the city. This procedure is continued cumulatively by taking the next highest location quotient so that the final curve is composed of straight line segments equal in number to the number of areas of the city.[2]

The localization curve thus ranks city areas by location quotient, and the slopes of their straight line segments measure the location quotients of the individual city areas. If a given industry's employment is distributed equally among the areas of the city in exactly the same way as total employment, the location quotients will all be unity and the localization curve will be a 45° diagnoal from the origin. Any divergence in the two employment distributions will be reflected in a deviation of the curve above and to the left of the 45° line. The extent of the deviation is a measure of concentration of the industry's employment compared to overall employment. Several localization curves have been superimposed on each graph and this provides a means of comparing employment specialization within Philadelphia.

The localization curves shown in the figures generally confirm the expected degree of industrial concentration among the local areas of the city. Finance, insurance and real estate is one of the most concentrated industries and obviously agglomeration economies are extremely important to location decisions for this industry. In urban areas these economies are available in the central

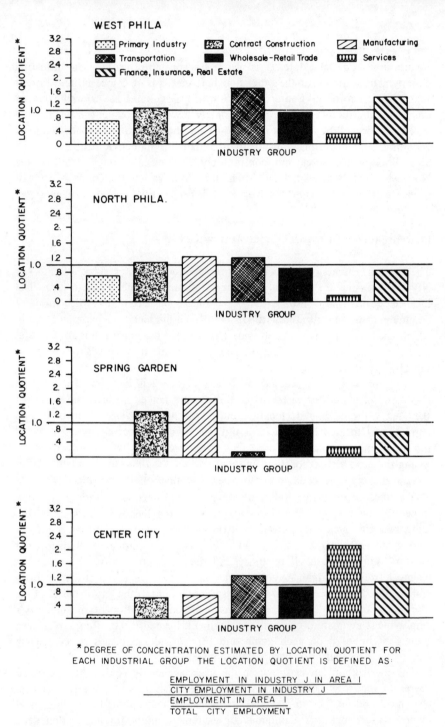

Figure 6-1. Concentration of Employment in Major Industries by Sub-labor Markets.

108

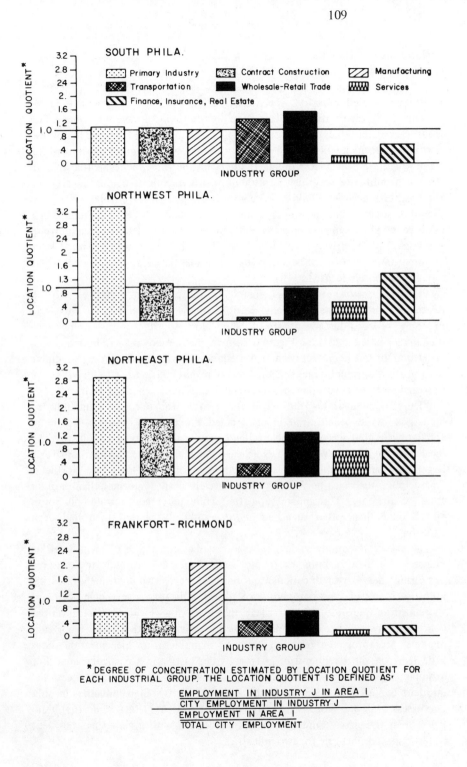

* DEGREE OF CONCENTRATION ESTIMATED BY LOCATION QUOTIENT FOR EACH INDUSTRIAL GROUP. THE LOCATION QUOTIENT IS DEFINED AS:

$$\frac{\dfrac{\text{EMPLOYMENT IN INDUSTRY J IN AREA I}}{\text{CITY EMPLOYMENT IN INDUSTRY J}}}{\dfrac{\text{EMPLOYMENT IN AREA I}}{\text{TOTAL CITY EMPLOYMENT}}}$$

business district, and the findings show that in Center City this industry has a very large location quotient.

At the other end of the spectrum, wholesale and retail trade is the most widely distributed industry. Specifically, this means that employment in the industry has a distribution similar to the distribution of total employment. This is not completely unexpected, but it does differ somewhat from the hypothesis that employment in this industry is proportionately very important in the local areas which are heavily residential. If this were the case, the residential areas of the city would have very high location quotients for this particular industry and the localization curve would show considerable diversion from the 45° line. It therefore appears that the employment in this industry is of similar importance in all geographic segments of the city's economy. A more detailed breakdown of wholesale and retail trade may, of course, show that some types of retail trade are more important in the economy of the residential areas than in areas where industry is densely located.

Figure 6-3 shows that employment in transportation and in services is relatively more important in some sections of the city than others. This again probably reflects the advantages of being close to other firms in the same industry or allied industries. Figure 6-2 shows that employment in both contract construction and manufacturing is not equally distributed with the geographic pattern of total employment in the city. If manufacturing is considered at the two digit level, however, there is considerable difference among industries.

Figure 6-4 illustrates the localization curve for selected manufacturing industries. As expected, the more detailed the industry analysis, the more apparent it is that sectors of the city tend to specialize by type of industry. The local areas of North, West, and Northeast Philadelphia are the locations for a large share of the rubber industry. In the economy of North and Northeast Philadelphia, the machinery industry is relatively more important than in other areas of the city. The apparel industry, while more concentrated in South Philadelphia than other areas, is more evenly distributed than had been expected.

The variations among sublabor markets in the importance of manufacturing industries in their economies is shown in Table 6-1. It indicates the area possessing the largest locational quotient of each two-digit manufacturing industry. Many of these quotients exceed 3.0, indicating a very high degree of specialization indeed. It seems clear that particular locational forces effect concentrations of specialized manufacturing activities within given labor submarkets. Moreover, the overall pattern of manufacturing specialization sheds little light on the likelihood of given activities resting in a particular area. For example, for all manufacturing Frankford-Richmond has the largest locational quotient by far, but it has the largest quotient for two-digit industries in only two cases, while the Northeast—with a median quotient (1.08)—ranks first in no fewer than five cases. Similarly, West Philadelphia with a very small quotient (0.66) ranks number one for two industries.

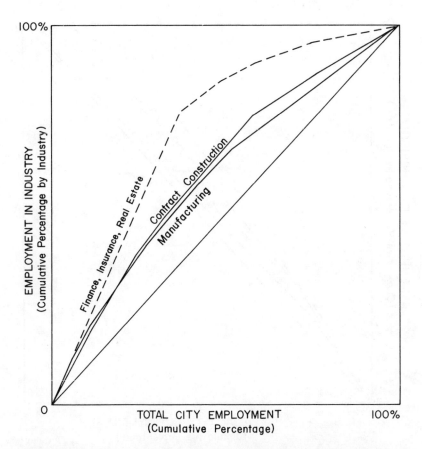

Figure 6-2. Localization Curves for Selected Industries. Note: Primary industries are excluded because of the small number of firms and law employment in this category.

The total employment impact of location of industry produces a diversified pattern of industrial employment throughout the city. For example, the largest number of manufacturing jobs are in the apparel industry which is extremely important in South Philadelphia. However, out of the next five largest industries only one (food) is of prime importance in South Philadelphia, with the others scattered over the city. The local economic units of the city represent employment centers which not only vary in absolute number of jobs but also in the nature and extent of diversification of industrial employment. The degree of specialization in each geographic section of the city increases the more specific the industry designation. As a result, although a wide variety of different types of jobs are available throughout the entire labor market, the relative importance of specific types of job varies from one local area to another.

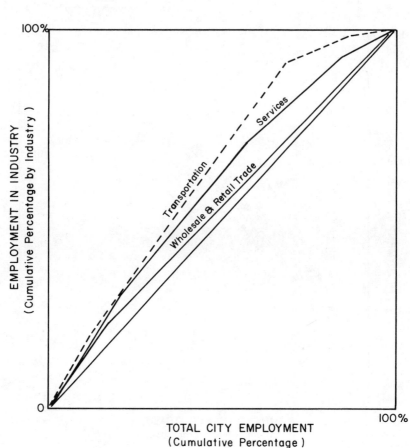

Figure 6–3. Localization Curves for Selected Industries.

Conclusions

The application of localization indices to very small geographic areas may emphasize weaknesses inherent in the use of these measures in concentration of industrial employment when applied to any size of geographic area. It is possible, for example, in defining sublabor markets that a shift in the geographic boundary by a very short distance, perhaps one or two city blocks, may change the value of a location quotient substantially. This is especially the case where the density of employment per square block is high. Nevertheless, the focus on sublabor markets as the units of analysis has many advantages since it identified the areas of the city which are important in generating, through a multiplier effect, employment for the local sublabor market, the city, and (in some industries) a much larger geographic area.

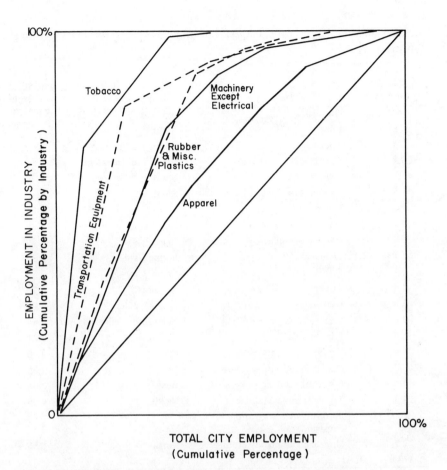

Figure 6-4. Localization Curves for Selected Industries.

The employment implications of the concentration of industrial employment in the sublabor markets depends on an estimate of the urban employment multiplier in each local area. This concept is based on the difference between "base" and "nonbase" industries. A base industry exports a considerable share of its output outside the metropolitan area. A nonbase industry is oriented towards supplying service to the residents of an area. It is expected that changes in income flows in exporting sublabor markets (those which have a high proportion of base industries) after a period of time also produce a series of income changes in other local areas, including those which are not exporting sectors. The final outcome of the expansion or contraction process produces an increase or decrease in income greater than the original change.

The level of employment is also affected by the change in income. This

Table 6-1

Sublabor Market Areas with Largest Location Quotients for Manufacturing Industries

Employment (in 000's) 1968	Industry	Area of Largest Quotient	Location Quotient
0.01	Ordinance	Northeast	5.67
27.8	Food	South	2.39
0.3	Tobacco	Spring Garden	8.40
20.5	Textile mill	Frankford-Richmond	2.13
40.1	Apparel	South	2.25
1.5	Lumber & wood	South	6.17
3.6	Furniture & fixtures	South	2.27
10.7	Paper	Northeast	1.89
28.7	Printing & publishing	Center City	2.39
16.1	Chemicals	Spring Garden	3.35
5.1	Petroleum	Center City	3.17
2.0	Rubber	Northeast	2.73
2.2	Leather	Spring Garden	1.90
3.3	Stone, clay & glass	Frankford-Richmond	2.64
3.9	Primary metal	Northeast	3.21
26.4	Fabricated metal	Northeast	2.90
16.2	Machinery except electrical	North	2.35
40.2	Electrical machinery	West	2.96
14.2	Transportation equipment	North	4.06
1.9	Professional & scientific instruments	West	2.32
12.9	Miscellaneous manufacturing	North	1.51
277.6 TOTAL			

impact in number of jobs varies among industries depending on the nature of the production function. The size of the multiplier (the multiple of the original change) is likely to be quite large for large metropolitan areas.[3] When the concept is applied to very small areas, however, the multiplier is expected to be small since much of the additional expansion occurring because of the original expansion is likely to "leak" to other geographic areas, some of which will be located outside the metropolitan area entirely.

In view of the expected role of the employment multiplier in small areas, the findings on the concentration of employment in the sublabor markets suggest the following conclusions. It is clear that the direct employment effect of a base industry is of considerable benefit to a local area. This applies to both ghetto and nonghetto areas, though the benefit to the residents of a ghetto from having a manufacturing base industry is less certain. Ghetto residents will only benefit if the base industry employs a high proportion of low and semiskilled workers and if the industry has future growth potential. The view that a base industry with high skilled labor requirements is equally attractive because a large urban multiplier will generate many indirect jobs is not necessarily a valid solution to the unemployment problems of ghetto residents. In small areas, such as those designated in this study, leakages from the local area are likely to result in most of the additional indirect jobs being located some distance from the ghetto. Since ghetto residents apparently have a relatively small normal preference area of employment, they are unable to take advantage of the indirect employment effect.

If the policy goal is to reduce high sectoral unemployment in ghetto areas, then these areas should specialize in base industries which generate a high proportion of direct employment per unit of investment. For example, if the skill level and growth potential criteria are assumed constant among industries, the apparel, lumber and wood, and furniture and fixtures industries are high priority industries for ghetto areas because they generate a higher absolute number of jobs than most other industries.[4]

The results of the industrial employment concentration show that the relative strength of the ghetto economies in manufacturing is encouraging. In addition, the heavy concentration of manufacturing in a local area close to the core of the city is also an advantage. However, the national trend which suggests that in most metropolitan areas the city has failed to match the suburban counties in the growth of manufacturing job opportunities makes it more difficult to reduce high sectoral unemployment in cities. Also, the net employment loss due to firm entry-exit behavior found in some Philadelphia ghetto areas raises some apprehension concerning future job opportunities for ghetto residents.

It is of course possible that an increase in "nonbase" industries within the ghetto will provide employment opportunities for ghetto residents. However, many "nonbase" industries are not particularly attracted to ghetto areas, especially if their development depends primarily on the demand of local residents. If the "nonbase" industry depends primarily on the indirect jobs created by a base industry located outside the local area, the development of this type of nonbase industry in the ghetto may offset any future weakness in manufacturing. In Philadelphia the structure of industrial employment varies among local areas. The implications of this finding is that the increasing tendency for the expansion of some types of manufacturing to occur outside the city affects some local areas more than others. The policy response to this trend is to encourage "nonbase" industries in the city which will perform services to the expanding base industries in the suburbs. It may, of course, be difficult to achieve this type of linkage between expanding suburban manufacturing operations and industries in ghetto areas. Unless the linkage is achieved or there is some other appropriate local response to the national trend in growth of manufacturing jobs, than the economic viability of the ghetto areas will diminish. If this occurs, then skill training alone will not solve high unemployment of ghetto residents, and other policies which assist workers to find employment in other areas of the city or the suburbs may be required.

Part III:
Plant Location Decisions

7

Size of Firms and the Location of Employment Opportunities

As urban areas become more densely populated and land values increase, it is possible that expanding businesses will move farther from the center of the city where land values are likely to be higher than at the perimeter of the metropolitan area. As a result, for some industries the average size of firm will tend to be larger the farther its location from the center of the city. The trend may, of course, be in the opposite direction for industries which require close proximity to the central business district and are able to expand facilities by utilizing a given land area more intensely. Some types of retail trade and financial services may be able to expand in this manner. Consequently, it is expected that in these industries the size of firms near the center of the city will be larger than firms located on the outskirts of the city.

The national trend in the growth of manufacturing employment which has been more rapid in the counties outside the city than within the city is believed to be a function of the space requirements of manufacturing industries. It is argued that in industries which are either capital intensive or which have production techniques requiring a high level of output to realize the maximum economies of scale, it is likely that the farther the distance from the center of the city, the larger the size of firms.

In this chapter the relationship between size of firm and distance from the core of the city is analyzed for manufacturing industries. The employment implications of this trend depend on the residential distribution within the city. Since the ghetto areas are usually close to the center of the city, the geographic distribution of firms by size will influence the job search process for unemployed ghetto residents. For example, the approach used to train and place unemployed residents in jobs through "job development" procedures is likely to be different depending on whether small or large manufacturing firms in an industry are located near the core of the city. Large firms usually have a more formal recruitment and placement procedures than do small firms. Small firms are likely to rely heavily on personal contacts through friends and current employees in the search for new workers. In contrast, large firms rely more heavily on public and private employment agencies and newspaper advertising. The industrial size distribution of firms is therefore an important factor in any program which aims at placing the disadvantaged ghetto residents in gainful employment.

119

Size of Firm Hypothesis and Method of Analysis

It is expected that if production techniques do not have substantial space requirements in industries which employ a high proportion of low-skilled labor, the firm size will be inversely related to distance from the center of the city. Conversely, if the availability of low-skilled labor is not important and space requirements are crucial, the size of firm is expected to vary directly with distance from the center of the city.

There are several conceptual difficulties in the approach which expresses location of firms vis à vis the center of the city as a function of the firm's size.[1] First, it assumes that land values decrease with distance. It is preferable to have information on the specific cost of land by census tract or zip code. Such data are not readily available and distance from the central business district is only a proxy for the level of land values. Since firms vary considerably in the number of years they have been located in the city, it is possible that for cities which have experienced slow growth over the past decade the correlation between size and distance may be much lower than in cities which have experienced a higher rate of growth. Similarly, the most rapidly growing industries are more likely to expand near . the city boundary where room for expansion exists than are industries having a slow growth rate. Finally, the available data only permit a cross-sectional study of firm size in one year. A comparison of the change in the size distribution of firms over a decade would give a much clearer indication of the influence of size of firm and the geographic trend in employment opportunities.

The correlation between size of firm and distance from city center was calculated for all two digit manufacturing industries. The data on size of firm for this analysis is based on the number of employees indicated in city wage-tax returns and includes all firms reporting in 1968. Distance is measured by the average daily highway travel time from various locations throughout the city. (For a detailed discussion of the travel time data, see Chapter 5.) The following procedure was used to organize the data for each industry. The average size of firm in each distance zone was calculated by summing the number of employees in each firm and dividing by the number of firms. The result was therefore an average size of firm in a geographic section of the city. This geographic section was similar to a postal zip code zone, though in some instances two zip codes were merged to conform to a distance zone. The maximum number of observations was twenty-four since this is the number of distance zones in the city. For many industries there are fewer than twenty-four observations. This occurs when there are no firms in a particular industry located in some distance zones of the city.

The correlation of the average size of firm for a geographic area with distance from city center is, of course, less desirable than the correlation of the size of each firm with its distance from the city center. This latter procedure would have substantially increased the number of observations. Unfortunately, in order not to divulge the identity of individual firms it was necessary to aggregate the firms within a geographic area of the city. Nevertheless, the aggregate approach does give an indication of the differences among industries in the size distribution of firms throughout the city.

Geographic Trend of Firm Size within the City

The relationship between size of firm and distance from center city varies among industries. The extent of the variation is illustrated in Figures 7-1 through 7-8, which represent the linear correlation results for selected manufacturing industries.

For each industry the simple linear correlation coefficients were calculated for three groups of firms. The coefficient was calculated for all firms in the industry, and in addition separate calculations were made for the large firms (reporting employment monthly) and the small firms (reporting employment quarterly) in the industry. For almost all industries, the separate results by size of firm did not substantially change the value of the total industry coefficient. The electrical machinery industry was an exception where there was a substantial difference in value of the coefficient for large and small firms. In fact, the direction of the relationship was different for the two firm-size categories. The coefficient for small firms was negative, and the scatter diagram (Figure 7-8) suggests that there was no definite relationship between the number of employees in the firm and its proximity to the central business district.

The scatter diagrams indicate that for most industries the relationship between size of firm and distance from center city is not strong and in some instances it appears that a curvilinear, rather than a linear, relationship exists. However, since the results represent a cross-sectional analysis of firms of widely different "ages," the findings do indicate that the locational pattern of firm size does vary considerably among industries. For some manufacturing industries, the firm size increases directly with distance from the center of the city. This is the result for stone, clay, glass, and concrete, or fabricated metal, textiles, and the larger firms in electrical machinery. A negative correlation was found for apparel, lumber and wood, printing and publishing, and small firms in the electrical machinery. The results shown in the scatter diagrams are illustrative of the variations found among manufacturing industries.

In those industries where there was a positive correlation between average number of employees and distance from the center of the city, it appears that, because of the nature of the production process, they used more land per unit of output than in industries with a negative correlation. This is clearly the explanation for the positive correlation in fabricated metal and the larger firms (17 or more employees) in the electrical machinery industries. In addition, the

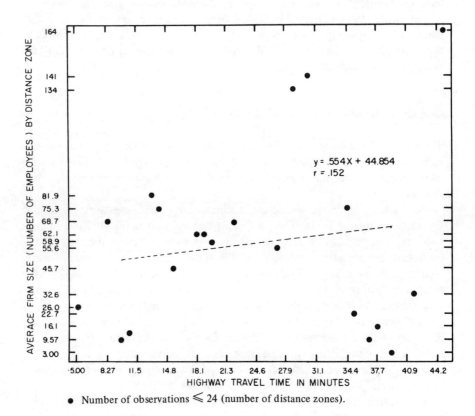

Figure 7-1. Average Firm Size by Distance from Center City, Textile Mill.

average size of firm in these industries is larger than in most other industries, and this probably increases the need for more land per unit.

In the stone, clay, glass, and concrete industry the average size of firm is slightly smaller than in the other industries which show a positive correlation between size and distance. The strong positive correlation therefore suggests that in the production of stone, clay, glass, and concrete products it is not feasible to use a given land space intensely. Consequently, for firms with large outputs (and number of employees), it is necessary to have a relatively large amount of land which is more readily available the farther the location from the center of the city. The textile mill industry appears to contrast quite sharply with the production of stone, clay, glass, and concrete. The average size of textile mill firms is quite large but the correlation between size and distance, though

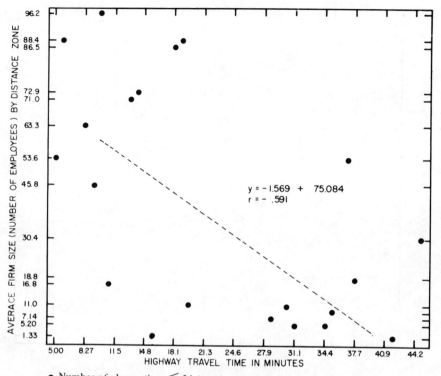

Figure 7-2. Average Firm Size by Distance from Center City, Apparel Fabrics.

positive, is not strong. In fact, as the scatter diagram (Figure 7-1) shows there is virtually no relationship between size and distance. The nature of production in many segments of this industry may make it feasible to utilize space intensely, and consequently the pressure for more land as the firm size increases is less pronounced than in many other industries. In addition, the labor-intensive nature of this industry requires large firms to locate near or remain close to the source of supply of semiskilled labor and this discourages large textile mills from locating near the perimeter of the city.

A negative relationship between size and distance exists in the apparel, lumber and wood, printing and publishing, and small firms in the electrical machinery industry. The apparel industry like the textile industry has an occupational structure in which semiskilled jobs predominate. In the apparel

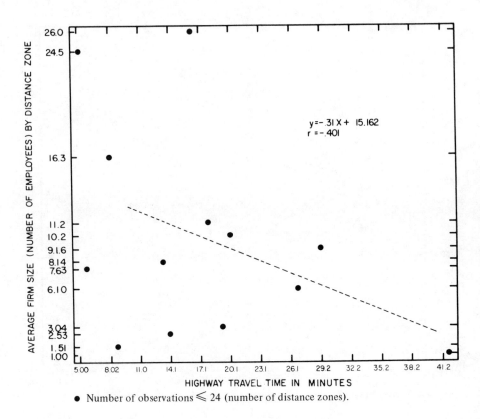

Figure 7–3. Average Firm Size by Distance from Center City, Lumber and Wood.

industry the nature of the operation also makes it possible to utilize land space intensely by organizing production on a multifloor basis. It is for these reasons that it is possible for the large apparel firms to locate close to city center. An additional reason for the concentration of this industry close to the central business district is the requirement of face-to-face contact with the retail industry which it supplies.

The printing and publishing industry requires close proximity to the central business district since a large proportion of its sales are made to the head offices and major branches of the large corporations which usually locate in the financial district. Governmental institutions located in the downtown area are also potential customers for the printing industry. Traditionally, the newspaper industry with its need for quick access to information also tends to choose a location close to the business and government center of the city.

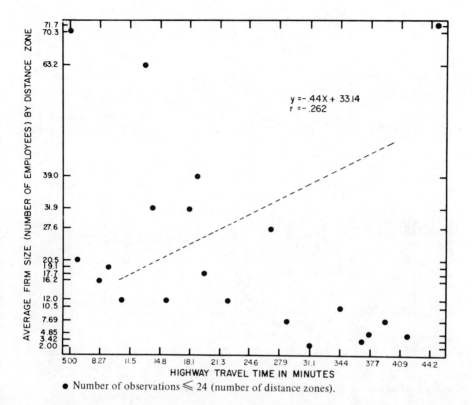

Figure 7-4. Average Firm Size by Distance from Center City. Printing and Publishing.

The fairly strong negative correlation between size and distance in the lumber and wood industry is somewhat surprising. Two factors may explain the tendency for the larger firms in the industry to be concentrated close to the central business district. The average size of firms in this industry is relatively small, with the largest average size of firms in any distance zone being only twenty-six employees while, as shown in Figure 7-3, almost all distance zones had average firm sizes of fewer than twelve employees. This suggests that even large firms in this industry are relatively small operations compared to firms in other industries. Consequently, the amount of land space required for a large firm in this industry is not likely to be great. The reason why the large firms in the industry tend to locate closer to the center of the city than the small firms is probably attributable to the demand for a low-skilled labor which is more readily available in the core of the city.

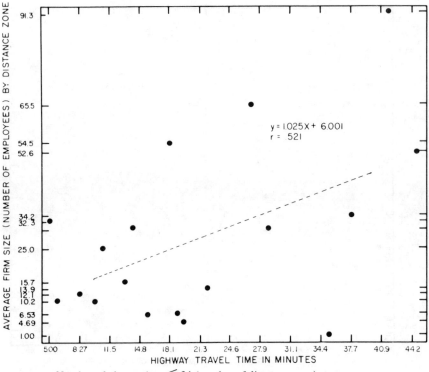

● Number of observations ≤ 24 (number of distance zones).

Figure 7–5. Average Firm Size by Distance from Center City, Stone, Clay, Glass and Concrete.

Locational Requirements and the
Geographic Trend of Firm Size

The impact of the economic factors influencing the size dispersion of firms by geographic location has already been discussed for several industries. A more extensive summary of the role of locational factors is shown in Table 7-1. If the availability of low-skilled labor and the advantages of agglomeration are important to an industry and the availability of space is of low importance, it is expected that the large firms in an industry will tend to locate near the central business district. The apparel industry has these requirements and the results in Table 7-1 show that for this industry there is a high negative correlation between firm size and distance from the city center.

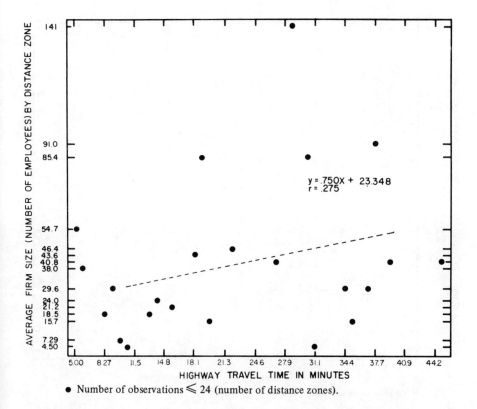

Figure 7-6. Average Firm Size by Distance from Center City, Fabricated Metal.

If the importance of the locational factors is completely reversed—that is, space requirements are highly important while the availability of low-skilled labor and the need for the advantages of agglomeration are relatively unimportant—then the large firms are expected to locate farther from the center than the small firms in the same industry. The petroleum industry which has a high positive correlation coefficient for the size-distance relationship is an example of this type of industry.

If the locational requirements of an industry do not conform to a pattern associated with either of these two industries, then it becomes more difficult to predict the magnitude and direction of the trend in the firm size-distance relationship. In most industries which showed a negative correlation between size and distance from the center, the locational requirements of the industry

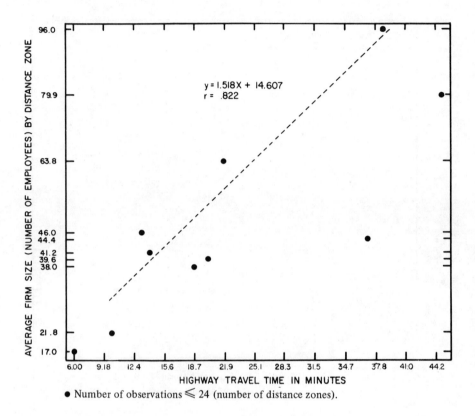

Figure 7-7. Average Firm Size by Distance from Center City, Electrical Machinery (Large Firms).

provide an explanation for the results. In the manufacture of transportation equipment, the economic characteristics of the production process suggest a positive correlation coefficient. The weak negative coefficient (−0.05) found in the study is perhaps attributable to the fact that several large long-established firms in the industry are located close to the core of the city and this probably influences the findings so that there is apparently little relationship between size and distance in this industry.

Some of the results are not easily explained by the factors influencing the locational pattern of the industries. For example, it is rather surprising that the coefficient of correlation for the chemical industry is only 0.18 given the capital-intensive nature of this industry. The coefficient for the food industry is also much lower than expected. It is emphasized, however, that since the

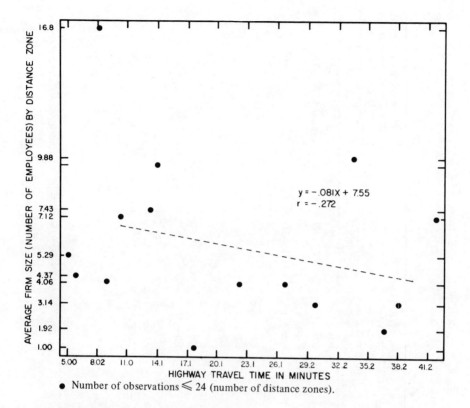

Figure 7-8. Average Firm Size by Distance from Center City, Electrical Machinery (Small Firms).

analysis is based on two-digit manufacturing, it is unlikely that the locational requirements are capable of explaining accurately the relationship between size of firm and distance from the city center. The coefficients of correlation are likely to be larger if the analysis is conducted at the three-digit level of manufacturing industry. Data at this level are currently not readily available.

Conclusions

The cross-sectional analysis of firms in the aggregate provides an estimate of the size distribution of manufacturing firms by distance from the central business district.

Table 7-1
Factors Affecting Dispersion of Firms within the City

Industry	Locational Requirements of Firms[a] (Degree of Importance)			Relationship Between Size of Firm and Distance from Center City (Simple Linear Correlation Coefficient)
	Space (Capital Intensive Economies of Scale)	Agglomeration (Concentration Dependence)	Avail. of Low Skilled Labor	
Food	High	Low	Medium	.15
Textile Mills	Low	Low	High	.15
Apparel	Low	High	High	−.59
Lumber	Low	Low	High	−.40
Furniture & fixtures	Medium	Medium	High	.07
Paper	High	Low	High	.23
Printing & publishing	Low	High	Low	−.26
Chemicals	High	Low	Low	.18
Petroleum refining	High	Low	Low	.62
Rubber & plastics	High	High	Low	.21
Leather	Low	High	High	−.11
Stone, clay & glass	Medium	Medium	High	.52
Primary metal	High	Medium	Low	.24
Fabricated metal	Low	Medium	High	.28
Machinery	Low	Low	Low	.22
Electrical machinery	High	Low	High	.41
Transportation	High	Low	Low	−.05
Instruments	Medium	Medium	Low	.15

aThe degree of importance of factors affecting locational decisions was adapted from Federal Reserve Bank of Philadelphia, *Mainsprings of Growth* (Philadelphia, Federal Reserve Bank of Philadelphia 1967), p. 100-109.

This distribution of firms has several important policy implications. In many cities the ghetto areas surround the central business district. The lack of adequate public transit in these areas, its cost, and car ownership status of ghetto residents tend to restrict the distance the unemployed central city resident can travel to work. Consequently, if the large firms in an industry tend to locate near the center of the city, this type of industry provides ghetto residents with attractive potential employment opportunities. For this reason the apparel, lumber, printing and publishing, leather, and transportation manufacturing industries are, on the basis of accessibility, most likely to provide job opportunities to disadvantaged workers.

A second employment implication of the findings concerns the "job development" activities associated with many manpower programs. Experience with the Job Opportunities in the Business Sector (JOBS) program suggests that the "development" or the "pledge" of a job in the suburban ring will be extremely difficult to fill because disadvantaged workers do not have easy access to jobs outside the core of the city. In terms of long-term employment of the disadvantaged, the most successful contracts under JOBS are likely to be with firms within the central core of the city. In addition, the payoff for job development effort is likely to be greater with large rather than small firms. It is normally much easier for a firm with 500 employees to pledge ten jobs than it is for a small one with only 50 employees. The importance of size of firm was recognized early in the administration of the program and the consortium type of contract was introduced to try to handle this problem. The manufacturing industries with large firms close to city center therefore have more potential for the placement of workers in the JOBS program as well as many other manpower programs.

These employment implications may have to be qualified substantially if a time-series analysis of firm size showed that the size of firms was increasing more rapidly at the periphery of the city than at the core. Such a finding would suggest that the lack of space for expansion was inhibiting growth of firms at the center of the city. Consequently, it may actually be economically desirable to encourage growth outside the core. The long-run manpower implications of this possibility are quite different than the short-run implications discussed above. In this case, the analysis suggests that the long-run policy solution for reducing unemployment in in the ghettos may involve the different task of assisting manufacturing firms which are experieencing space difficulties in their inner-city location. This may involve either some industrial land redevelopment in the core of the city or, if this proves too costly, it may be necessary to assist firms to relocate in other sections of the city. If this latter policy is adopted, it may also be necessary to develop programs to enable ghetto residents to move from the ghetto.

8

Locational Choices Within the Metropolitan Area

The changing distribution of employment and establishments within the city and the differential distribution of new businesses among sections of the city has been described in earlier parts of this study. This chapter attempts to explain the shifts in the distribution of employment opportunities by briefly reviewing intrametropolitan location theory and testing some specific hypotheses which appear relevant to locational choices in Philadelphia, especially for new businesses. The factors influencing the choice of region and site decisions have been studied for the New York metropolitan region[1] and the Pittsburgh area.[2] These studies suggest that the major variables affecting location include proximity to market, relative transportation costs of inputs and products, availability of appropriate labor supply, proximity to other establishments, socioeconomic environment, tax structure, availability of space and quantity, quality of public facilities, and so forth. The relative importance of each of these variables will, of course, vary from industry to industry. The extent to which each of these factors exist varies among regions as well as within regions. The data in this study refer mainly to the role of these factors within the Philadelphia metropolitan area.

The characteristics of the Philadelphia area and the importance of the locational factors[3] along with the evidence presented in the studies of other metropolitan areas suggest the following three hypotheses.

First, the mix and relative importance of locational factors is based upon such characteristics as type of product, type of production technique, labor requirements, linkage requirements, transportation costs and requirements, and market size.

Manufacturing establishments tend to emphasize the importance of spatial considerations, access to transportation networks and, to a lesser extent, labor market characteristics. In particular, the relatively heavy capital investment in plant and equipment which characterizes many manufacturing industries puts a premium on the availability of existing facilities or new building sites which will permit large-scale operations.

Also in manufacturing, access to transportation facilities is of major concern. This is because a large share of their total cost of operation involves the acquisition of inputs and the distribution of final products. Similarly, if labor costs are a high percentage of total costs, the residential location of the potential source of labor supply becomes an important consideration. If the labor required is mainly low-skilled, the firm may have to locate in close geographic proximity to low income residential areas. If, on the other hand, a high proportion of the labor costs are attributable to hiring high skilled manpower, the firm is less restricted in its geographic choice of site.

Nonmanufacturing establishments place more stress on market factors and agglomerative economies than do manufacturing firms. Since nonmanufacturing is a category embracing a large and diversified group of industries, it is difficult to generalize. It is preferable to consider wholesale and retail trade separately from services.

A primary cause of differences in locational preference within nonmanufacturing is the size and type of the market to be served. Industries whose market is regional or national in scope would tend to prefer the advantages of the central business district. This permits them to take advantage of being near their competitors and to take advantage of the other economies of agglomeration at the core of the metropolitan area. This pattern of location is likely to be found among banks, insurance companies, hospitals, and so forth. For those nonmanufacturing industries which rely on the local market for demand for their product or service, a much more diverse locational pattern is expected.

Second, the locational factors noted above have tended to concentrate particular types of industries in different geographical subdivisions of the metropolitan area. That is, firms with similar locational requirements will locate together in that part of the urban area which satisfies their requirements. Perhaps the most widely accepted geographic subdivisions are the central business district, the central city, and the suburban ring. Another geographic subdivision of importance to manpower policy is the ghetto-nonghetto difference.

Predicting from the experience of studies done in other cities like New York and San Francisco, one can argue that nonmanufacturing establishments emphasizing agglomerative economics would be located in the central business district; these would include financial institutions, corporate headquarters, general office activities, firms offering specialized services where close communications with customers is desirable, and so on. The central city would contain the older manufacturing and trade areas where those activities were important when older modes of transport and higher population densities existed. In the suburban ring, the newest manufacturing establishments are likely to be found. This is because space and better access to the newer modes of transportation suit the needs of many manufacturers. Moreover, durable goods producers might find a slightly lower wage level for certain kinds of semiskilled workers.

As the population of the suburban ring expands, retail trade and certain consumer services are expected to follow. Other advantages include easier consumer access and parking—often at highway shopping centers—in automobile-oriented suburbia.

Third, just as industry and geographic section of the region shape the configuration of locational factors considered by enterprises, so too does size of establishment. As a broad generalization, large establishments clearly attach more importance to space as a factor than do firms with few employees. Large operators also are more likely to make a careful analysis of sites and place far less weight on such personal factors as access to home of owner or familiarity with the neighborhood.

Reasons for Choice of Location

As previously indicated, the firm's choice of location is a complex decision involving many factors. This study attempts to assess the relative importance of these factors for firms which have recently selected a site for their business activity. In interviews with a sample of city entrant firms and a sample of firms which had recently located in the suburban ring, the respondent entrepreneurs were asked to rank in order of importance the factors which were considered in the firm's location decision. In addition, a sample of city entrants was surveyed by mail and a similar ranking procedure followed.

Table 8-1 shows the relative importance of location factors for all firms surveyed by means of a frequency distribution indicating how often each of the factors listed appeared among the two most important reasons for the firm's choice of location. In all cases, factors relating to the availability and price of space were the predominant reasons for choosing the particular location. Market factors followed closely in importance. When the specific reasons within the major factors were considered, close proximity to customers ranked first, followed by the price or availability of facilities and close proximity to the owner's residence. Labor supply factors were only moderately important for the larger city respondents.

Suburban entrants differed from city ones in several respects. Many more of the establishments in the outer ring emphasized space factors, particularly reasonable rental. On the other hand, labor supply factors and environmental issues were weighted less. At the same time a somewhat greater emphasis on characteristics of access and entrepreneurial attachment was found in suburbia.

The influence of size within the city is most apparent in the role assigned to entrepreneurial factors. The firms in the mail survey had a substantially smaller average number of employees than did the firms in the interview sample. As shown in the results, the smaller firms place substantially greater weight on nearness to owner's residence or the area where the owner spent his growing years.

These overall figures, although pointing up some differences among entrants by geographical area, ignore the impact of industry affiliation. Tables 8-2 and 8-3 show interindustry differences by geographic area. Within the city, manufacturing establishments place great importance upon space factors, especially availability of facilities, and to a lesser extent, upon labor factors—both

Table 8-1
Percentage Distribution of the Two Most Important Reasons for Choice of Location for All Entrants Surveyed

Market Factors	Entrant (Interview)	Entrant (Mail Survey)	Suburban Entrant
Close proximity to customers	19	22	19
Adequate parking	2	3	1
Expanding local market	4	4	1
	25	29	21
Labor Factors			
Close proximity to low priced labor supply	5	1	3
Close proximity to skilled labor source	7	0	4
	12	1	7
Space Factors			
Reasonable rental or price of property	9	12	17
Incentive of government subsidized urban renewal	1	0	0
Availability of facilities when started	14	12	17
Ample space for future expansion	5	1	5
	29	25	39
Environment			
Legal problems	2	7	0
Avoidance of risks of theft and vandalism	1	2	0
Little traffic congestion	1	1	0
	4	10	0
Access			
Good access	8	6	12
	8	6	12

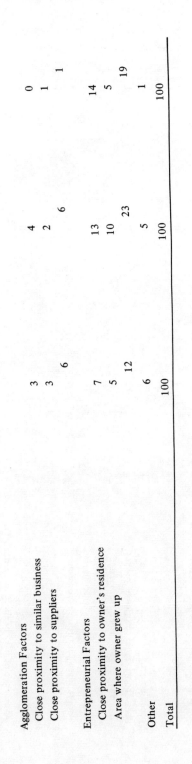

Agglomeration Factors	6	6	1
Close proximity to similar business	3	4	0
Close proximity to suppliers	3	2	1
Entrepreneurial Factors	12	23	19
Close proximity to owner's residence	7	13	14
Area where owner grew up	5	10	5
Other	6	5	1
Total	100	100	100

Table 8-2

Percentage Distribution of the Two Most Important Reasons for Choice of Location by Manufacturing Entrants Surveyed

	City Entrant (Interview)	City Entrant (Mail Survey)	Suburban Entrant
Market Factors			
Close proximity to customers	13	20	14
Adequate parking	0	10	0
Expanding local market	2	10	0
	15	40	14
Labor Factors			
Close proximity to low-priced labor supply	7	0	5
Close proximity to skilled labor source	11	0	2
	18	0	7
Space Factors			
Reasonable rental or price of property	12	20	21
Incentive of government subsidized urban renewal	0	0	0
Availability of facilities when started	19	30	25
Ample space for future expansion	5	0	2
	36	50	48
Environment			
Legal problems	2	0	0
Avoidance of risks of theft and vandalism	0	0	0
Little traffic congestion	1	0	0
	3	0	0
Access			
Good access	7	0	9

Agglomeration Factors			
Close proximity to similar business	3	0	0
Close proximity to suppliers	4	0	2
	7	0	2
Entrepreneurial Factors			
Close proximity to owner's residence	7	10	14
Area where owner grew up	4	0	5
	11	10	19
Other	4	0	2
Total	100	100	100

Table 8-3

Percentage Distribution of the Two Most Important Reasons for Choice of Location by Non-manufacturing Entrants Surveyed

	City Entrant (Interview)			City Entrant (Mail Survey)			Suburban Entrant		
	All Nonmfg.	Wholesale & Retail	Services	All Nonmfg.	Wholesale & Retail	Services	All Nonmfg.	Wholesale & Retail	Services
Market Factors									
Close proximity	25	24	29	22	26	21	24	17	33
Adequate parking	9	13	8	1	0	2	3	0	0
Expanding local market	6	8	0	3	2	2	2	6	0
	40	45	37	26	28	25	30	23	33
Labor Factors									
Close proximity to low priced labor supply	2	3	4	1	0	2	0	0	0
Close proximity labor source	2	0	8	0	0	0	5	0	17
	4	3	12	1	0	2	5	0	17
Space Factors									
Reasonable rental or price of property	6	8	4	11	14	13	14	11	17
Incentive of government subsidized urban renewal	1	3	0	0	0	0	0	0	0
Availability of facilities when started	8	3	13	10	9	11	8	17	0
Ample space for future expansion	5	5	4	1	0	2	8	11	8
	20	19	21	22	23	26	30	39	25

	C1	C2	C3	C4	C5	C6	C7	C8	C9	C10	Total
Environment											
Legal problems	1	0	3	0	7	12	4	0	0	0	100
Avoidance of risks of theft and vandalism	2	5	0	7	0	4	0	0	0	0	100
Little traffic congestion	0	0	1	0	15	8	0	0	0	0	100
Access											
Good access	9	11	13	6	6	0	11	16	6	17	100
Agglomerations Factors											
Close proximity to similar business	0	0	4	2	5	0	0	0	0	0	100
Close proximity to suppliers	1	0	2	2	7	0	0	0	0	0	100
Entrepreneurial Factors											
Close proximity to owner's residence	8	3	8	13	9	11	14	17	8	8	100
Area where owner grew up	7	3	4	10	16	7	5	6	23	0	100
Other	8	13	4	6	7	5	0	0	0	0	100
Total	100	100	100	100	100	100	100	100	100	100	

low-priced and low-skilled—and the importance of highly skilled manpower. In contrast, nonmanufacturing firms stress market factors with special attention given to close proximity to customers. The fact that there are major differences in reasons for choice of location by type of industry is illustrated by a rank correlation coefficient of less than 50% between manufacturing and nonmanufacturing city entrants.[a]

The size of firm also seems to affect the relative importance of factors in locational preferences for manufacturing establishments. Within the city, as shown in Table 8-2, the entrants responding to the mail survey, whose average size was considerably smaller than that of those interviewed, stressed space and market factors with 90% of the responses citing factors in these categories. In contrast, only about 60% of the responses from the larger entrants, those surveyed by interview, emphasized space and market factors.

The suburban manufacturing entities when compared to city entrants also place considerable emphasis on space, especially reasonable rental or property price but much less stress on labor supply elements. Suburban manufacturing is not too dissimilar from nonmanufacturing as measured by a rank correlation.[b]

Table 8-3 further shows differences within the large and complex nonmanufacturing sector. Among city entrants, wholesale and retail establishments reflect their strong affinity toward locating closer to the market and less stress on proximity to a labor supply. Service firms are also concerned about market factors, especially close proximity to customers. In fact, the proximity to customers was even more important to service firms than it was to those in wholesale and retail trade. The importance of labor supply was also relatively important to service firms, especially when the market for skilled labor was considered. The importance of space factors is given similar stress in both the wholesale and retail trade and service sectors. The availability of facilities is, however, afforded greater weight by service establishments than the trading entities. Perhaps the service firms are more able to make use of existing facilities than most other types of new business.

Suburban nonmanufacturing entrants differ from their city counterparts especially when trade and service firms are considered. The stronger emphasis on market factors, especially close proximity to customers, by suburban service establishments is noteworthy. The heavy stress on space factors by suburban trade establishments contrasts with the somewhat lower importance of this factor among trade firms in the city. In the suburbs, the availability of facilities for firms in trade is a large factor in their locational calculus, while suburban service businesses place greater stress on good access than their wholesale-retail neighbors. Entrepreneurial factors are relatively important for trade firms— particularly close proximity to owner's residence—compared to service firms.

---

[a]R_s = 0.46 for manufacturing vs. nonmanufacturing at the 0.90 level of significance.

[b]R_s = 0.81 at 99% significance level.

Smaller city entrants are less concerned with parking and more concerned with legal and other environmental problems than the larger city entrant firms.

Criteria for the Location Decisions
of Ghetto and Nonghetto Firms

Clear differences emerge between city and suburban entrants and among industry groups across geographical lines. Even within the city, sharp differences exist as between firms in low-income or "ghetto" areas and those locating in the rest of the central city. According to the results in Table 8-4, the ghetto establishments are less concerned than nonghetto firms about market factors, particularly proximity to customers, the expansion of local markets, and the proximity to skilled labor. On the other hand, space advantages within the ghetto are apparently a major attractive force for certain entrants (the larger firms) since facilities are available and rentals are relatively low.

The elements influencing the locational choice of ghetto entrants may reflect the industrial and occupational characteristics of the firms. Certain manufacturing activities which require relatively low-skilled labor appear to describe many entrants to the ghetto. These firms seek low-cost space and facilities and require low-cost labor. Sometimes the advantage of low cost and available space outweighs many disadvantages—including the lack of a nearby skilled labor supply. Many marginal enterprises no doubt locate in the ghetto in the hope of surviving in the low-cost, low-price segment of an industry. There are, of course, environmental disadvantages associated with the ghetto location and these can be inferred from the slightly greater concern shown by ghetto firms for vandalism and general legal problems. Nevertheless in Philadelphia, like many other cities, the ghetto areas are close to center city and this proximity allows some firms, as in the printing industry, to avail themselves of the economies of agglomeration which offset the disadvantages of this type of area.

There were only a few differences between large firm (interviewed city entrants) and small firm (mail survey city entrants) responses when comparing the ghetto-nonghetto results. An example of these differences is that the smaller entrants in the ghetto stress proximity to customers more than do their nonghetto counterparts. Overall, however, there is a close similarity in locational requirements (as measured by rank correlation) between the ghetto and nonghetto firms irrespective of size.[c]

The major contrast is among ghetto firms of different size. The larger ones put less stress on market, environmental, and entrepreneurial factors but much more on labor and space elements. It would seem natural to expect larger units to worry more about facilities and their price.

[c]For interview entrants, R_s = 0.61 at 95% confidence level, for mail entrants, R_s = 0.77 at 98% confidence level.

Table 8-4

Percentage Distribution of the Two Most Important Reasons for Choice of Entrant's Location by Geographic Location

	Entrant (Interview)			Entrant (Mail Survey)		
	All Firms	Ghetto	Nonghetto	All Firms	Ghetto	Nonghetto
Market Factors						
Close proximity to customers	19	14	20	22	29	19
Adequate parking	2	4	1	2	0	2
Expanding local market	4	0	5	4	0	5
	25	18	26	28	29	26
Labor Factors						
Close proximity to low-priced labor supply	5	6	4	1	3	0
Close proximity to skilled labor source	7	2	9	0	0	0
	12	8	13	1	3	0
Space Factors						
Reasonable rental or price of property	9	14	8	12	8	13
Incentive of government subsidized urban renewal	1	0	1	0	0	0
Availability of facilities when started	14	18	13	12	11	12
Ample space for future expansion	5	2	6	1	0	1
	29	34	28	25	19	26
Environment						
Legal problems	2	2	1	7	8	6
Avoidance of risks of theft and vandalism	1	2	1	1	3	0
Little traffic congestion	1	2	1	1	3	0
	4	6	3	9	14	6

Access						
Good access	8	8	8	6	5	6
Agglomeration Factors	9	8	9	8	11	9
Close proximity to similar business	3	2	3	3	3	4
Close proximity to suppliers	6	6	6	5	8	5
Entrepreneurial Factors	12	10	13	29	24	21
Close proximity to owner's residence	7	4	8	13	11	13
Area where owner grew up	5	6	5	16	13	8
Other	6	8	5	5	3	6
Total	100	100	100	100	100	100

Locational Disadvantages

Another way of analyzing the "locational package" of an area within the region is to ascertain its major locational disadvantages. Of course, entrants expressing discontent concerning their present site may simply have underestimated these factors or, more likely, were unaware of them when entering but rated the advantages more important on balance.

Table 8-5 shows the results of surveys asking for the single major disadvantage of a firm's current location. City and suburban entrants and existing city establishments were included in the sample. City and suburban entrants were in dispute as to the relative importance of locational disadvantages, but in some respects older establishments in the city (the existing firms) responded quite like the suburban entrants concerning current locational problems. This suggests that the existing firm in the city may not find the solution to its problems in the suburbs.

From the standpoint of all respondents, the threat of theft and vandalism was the major disadvantage cited. This disadvantage was particularly important to city entrants with some 28% of the respondents mentioning this as a major disadvantage. It was much less important to suburban entrants and existing city firms, though still one of the most significant disadvantages. Space and market factors were generally listed as other major problems. Room for expansion and adequate parking were major issues for some firms, especially among city firms.

Variations in disadvantages become more pronounced when the industrial differences are considered. In both the city and the suburbs, manufacturing establishments put major weight on space problems—especially for expansion. However, the suburban firms were twice as concerned with this factor as a disadvantage, with about one-third of them placing it at the top of their list of disadvantages.

Although all city entrants showed a much greater concern for environmental problems than did suburban entrants and existing city firms, this difference was especially great in manufacturing. About a quarter of new suburban manufacturers cited environment disadvantages compared to nearly one-half of city entrants who stressed environmental disadvantages. The most prominent disadvantage within the environment groups was, of course, fear of theft and vandalism. Labor supply factors were not viewed as a major disadvantage by any group of firms, though the suburban entrants did consider it a problem and appeared to be concerned with their proximity to low-priced labor. In those instances where the city entrants mentioned labor supply disadvantages, the problem was proximity to skilled labor.

The results suggest a significant city-suburban contrast on locational disadvantages. For suburban firms in many industrial categories, the general absence of major locational problems resulted in 40% of the responses falling in the "other" category which included a wide variety of individualized disadvantages.

Of those that did mention one of the disadvantages listed, one out of every six cited lack of close proximity to a lower-priced labor supply. The other major disadvantages were absence of reasonable rentals or property prices and good accessibility.

The city entrant responses reflected the varied problems that are usually associated with central city locations. The risk of theft or vandalism was noted as the single most significant disadvantage with 21% of all nonmanufacturing entrants putting it at the top of their list. Second in importance were market factors with the foremost among them being adequate customer parking; city entrants in wholesale and retail trade ranked this disadvantage much more significant than nonmanufacturing firms as a group.

This disparity between sectors of the nonmanufacturing group shows up in other ways, particularly among entrants. For example, space problems in terms of room for expansion represents 18% of the disadvantages for all nonmanufacturing, but one-third of trade establishments list it as a significant problem. Similarly, access has double the importance among trade respondents as other nonmanufacturing firms. By contrast, as would be expected among smaller organizations, the trade establishments are less concerned about labor factors, many kinds of special legal problems, and distance separating them from similar businesses.

Variations by Type of Firm and Geographic Location

Another view of locational disadvantages is expressed by existing business firms in Table 8-6. From a citywide standpoint, new establishments are most concerned with the problems of the immediate environment, especially of theft and vandalism threats; some 35% of entrants rate environmental factors the major disadvantage as compared with 16% of the existing firms. Theft and vandalism represented the bulk of this major locational discontent. Existing firms differ from their newer counterparts in few other aspects of locational disadvantages. The exceptions are a slightly greater emphasis on space factors by existing units and more stress on the problem of labor supply, especially close proximity to skilled labor by new firms.

Categorizing the city into "ghetto" and "nonghetto" areas reveals some major variations in respect to disadvantages. The major differences seem to stem from geography rather than from establishment industry or size. For example, market factors—especially adequate parking—is a much more pressing problem in nonghetto areas; the influence of center city (when considered as a nonghetto area) is undoubtedly involved in this response.

The really deep felt problem in the ghetto is that of theft and vandalism. Forty-three percent of ghetto entrants and over one-fourth of the established firms rate it as the chief disadvantage of their location. The difference between

Table 8-5
Percentage Distribution of the Major Disadvantage of Firms' Current Location by Type of Firm and Industry

	City								Suburban Entrant		
	Entrant (Interview) Nonmanufacturing				Existing (Mail Survey) Nonmanufacturing						
	All	Mfg.	All Nonmfg.	Wholesale & Retail	All	All Nonmfg.	Wholesale & Retail	Services	All	Mfg.	Nonmfg.
Market Factors	17	12	25	42	19	19	29	13	11	5	15
Close proximity to customers	4	2	7	17	10	10	15	8	3	0	5
Adequate parking	12	10	14	25	8	8	12	5	5	5	5
Expanding local market	1	0	4	0	1	1	2	0	3	0	5
Labor Factors	6	6	8	0	1	1	0	3	8	5	10
Close proximity to low priced labor supply	1	0	4	0	1	1	0	0	8	5	10
Close proximity to skilled labor source	5	6	4	0	0	0	0	3	0	0	0
Space Factors	18	16	18	33	23	20	27	13	24	37	15
Reasonable rental or price of property	3	4	0	0	3	3	2	5	8	5	10
Incentive of government subsidized urban renewal	3	4	0	0	1	0	0	0	0	0	0
Availability of facilities when started	0	0	0	0	11	10	15	3	0	0	0
Ample space for future expansion	12	8	18	33	8	7	10	5	16	32	5

Environment											
Legal problems	4	2	7	0	1	1	0	3	3	5	0
Avoidance of risks of theft and vandalism	28	43	21	17	14	14	12	16	10	16	5
Little traffic congestion	3	4	0	0	1	1	2	0	3	5	0
	35	48	28	17	16	16	14	19	16	26	5
Access											
Good access	3	2	4	8	9	9	5	11	8	5	10
Agglomeration Factors											
Close proximity to similar business	4	4	4	0	3	3	5	3	3	0	5
Close proximity to suppliers	1	2	0	0	3	3	3	3	0	0	0
	5	6	4	0	6	6	8	6	3	0	5
Entrepreneurial Factors											
Close proximity to owner's residence	1	0	4	0	5	6	5	5	0	0	0
Area where owner grew up	0	0	0	4	7	7	5	8	0	0	0
	1	0	4	4	12	13	10	13	0	0	0
Other	16	19	11	0	15	16	7	24	31	21	40
Total	100	100	100	100	100	100	100	100	100	100	100
Number of Businesses	76	48	12	93	89	41	38				

Table 8-6
Percentage Distribution of the Major Disadvantage of Firms' Current Location by Type of Firm and Geographical Location

	Entrant (Interview)			All Firms	Existing	
	All Firms	Ghetto	Nonghetto		Ghetto	Nonghetto
Market Factors						
Close proximity to customers	4	5	4	10	5	13
Adequate parking	12	5	15	8	0	13
Expanding local market	1	0	2	1	3	0
	17	10	21	19	8	26
Labor Factors						
Close proximity to low-priced labor supply	1	0	2	1	3	0
Close proximity to skilled labor source	5	5	6	0	0	0
	6	5	8	1	3	0
Space Factors						
Reasonable rental or price of property	3	5	2	3	5	2
Incentive of government subsidized urban renewal	3	0	4	1	3	0
Availability of facilities when started	0	0	0	11	8	13
Ample space for future expansion	12	14	11	8	8	7
	18	19	17	23	24	22
Environment						
Legal Problems	4	5	4	1	0	2
Avoidance of risks of theft and vandalism	28	43	22	14	27	5
Little traffic congestion	3	0	4	1	0	2
	35	48	30	16	27	9

Access						
Good access	3	0	4	9	3	13
Agglomeration Factors	5	10	4	6	3	9
Close proximity to similar business	4	5	4	3	0	5
Close proximity to suppliers	1	5	0	3	3	4
Entrepreneurial Factors	4	0	2	12	19	8
Close proximity to owner's residence	1	0	2	5	8	4
Area where owner grew up	3	0	0	7	11	4
Other	16	10	18	15	14	16
Total	100	100	100	100	100	100

the two groups of establishments is probably related to the industrial composition and the rather broad range of locations lumped together under the nonghetto headings. Since manufacturing is somewhat more heavily represented in the established firms, they are not as sensitive to "crime problems" as the direct consumer servicing establishments. The diversity of the nonghetto area can be somewhat misleading. For example, the locational disadvantages in center city are quite different from those in the Northeast section of the city.

Desirability of Relocation

Another way of judging the locational disadvantages of areas is to ask already established enterprises as to whether they would be willing to move. Even though stated willingness to relocate does not mean that actual movement will occur, it does reflect the feeling of managers about their present site.

Tables 8-7 and 8-8 pose the choice in terms of no significant moving costs to the firm. As Table 8-7 shows, almost one-half of all sampled establishments (ninety-four in all) felt the urge to move. However, about two-thirds of the ghetto firms were so disposed compared to only 38% of all other city establishments. Moreover, it was mainly the nonmanufacturing establishments which indicated a tendency to move, with 50% of them wishing to move compared to only 25% of the manufacturing firms. Within the nonmanufacturing sector, trade and service units were the major respondents.

Along with the "push" to move, the locational decision also involves a "pull" toward particular areas as shown in Table 8-8. There was a clear trend in favor of the newer, developing areas of the region which include industrial parks, a growing population, and rising purchasing power. One-half of the establishments desiring to move would prefer the suburbs as a new location and another fifth would seek a site in Northeast Philadelphia. Another 14% wanted to leave this region altogether, while 9% had their sights on center city.

The ghetto and nonghetto establishments as before, differed somewhat in their appraisal of preferred location. Ghetto firms were more likely to seek out the Northeast or the suburbs, while nonghetto firms had much more orientation toward center city or toward leaving the region.

Part of the explanation for these differences was no doubt the effect of industrial composition of the respondents. The manufacturing units either sought the Northeast or wanted to move outside the region. Even though they represent a small sample, it is of interest that none mentioned the suburbs or anywhere else in the city.

The nonmanufacturing firms particularly in the service sector, put great stress on the advantages of the suburbs and to a lessor extent, the Northeast. Wholesale-retail units liked city center as well as the Northeast-suburbia complex. However, many were willing to go to the far reaches of the region or outside of it altogether.

Table 8-7

Percentage of Existing Firms Willing to Relocate if No Significant Moving Costs Were Involved (by Firm's Industry and Geographic Location)

	Proportion of Firms
All Firms	47
Ghetto firms	65
Nonghetto firms	38
All Manufacturing Firms	25
All Nonmanufacturing Firms	50
Wholesale and retail trade[a]	49
Services[a]	50
Contract construction[a]	33

[a]These categories do not exhaust the set "All Nonmanufacturing Firms."

Conclusions

The locational survey of new establishments in the city, in suburbia and of well-established enterprises in Philadelphia is a cross-sectional view of a long-term process of locational change in the region. A series of interrelated forces produce a complex weave of job and establishment movements, some aspects of which are discussed in an earlier part of this study. The forces influencing this dynamic change include the aging of central cities, the development of new transportation arteries, the shift of population, the changing mix of purchasing power, the growth and decline of demand in various types of industries, and continuous revisions in governmental policies relating to land use.

The analysis focuses on three major parameters of intrametropolitan location: industry composition, characteristics of the geographic segments of the region, and size of establishments. The findings substantiate the importance of these variables in locational choice as measured by questioning reasons for location, advantages and disadvantages of current sites, and the willingness to move.

Among entrants, space and market factors assume primary importance. Smaller establishments and some of the suburban ones rank entrepreneurial preferences high.

The availability of space and facilities, their price, and the ability to expand are major forces "pulling" manufacturing entrants both within and outside of Philadelphia. Nonmanufacturing units are more marked-oriented and some stress economies of agglomeration in the city.

Ironically, space advantages which pull firms to suburbia also attract them to the city's ghettos, as availability of cheap facilities and close proximity to the central business district provide a "hot house" for newer establishments, especially the older areas outside the central business district.

The city clearly has problems in supplying the locational characteristics

Table 8-8
Preferred Choice of Location of Existing Firms Interested in Relocating Outside the Geographic Location in which Presently Located

Type of Firm	Number of Firms	North Phila.	Spring Garden	West Phila.	Center City	South Phila.	N.W. Phila.	Frankford Richmond	N.E. Phila.	Suburbs	Outside Phila. Region
					Percentage Distribution of Preferred Geographic Area for New Location						
All Firms	44	2	0	2	9	0	0	2	21	50	14
Ghetto Firms	21	5	0	5	0	0	0	0	21	52	10
Nonghetto Firms	23	0	0	0	17	0	0	4	13	48	18
All Manufacturing Firms	4	0	0	0	0	0	0	0	50	0	50
All Nonmanufacturing Firms	40	3	0	3	10	0	0	3	18	55	10
Wholesale & Retail Firms	17	0	0	0	18	0	0	6	18	35	24
Services	17	6	0	6	6	0	0	0	24	59	0

preferred by new firms. This is shown by a very strong desire on the part of establishment to leave if the opportunity arises, a desire especially pronounced among the newer firms. Although room for expansion, availability of customer parking, and problems of transportation access are viewed as important disadvantages of a city location, the overriding issue especially in the ghetto and among smaller nonmanufacturing enterprises is the fear of theft and vandalism.

This interwoven picture of locational pulls and pushes has public policy implications. To achieve the goal of making the city more attractive to business will probably require adjustments in land use, building codes, and tax policy to make sites cheaper and to provide low-cost means of expanding existing facilities. A more rational automobile parking policy outside the CBD might help some firms. The nature and quality of the urban labor force does not seem to be a major disadvantage to locating in the city. Consequently, improving the quality of labor supply in itself is not expected to change locational patterns.

Most important from the standpoint of keeping and/or attracting jobs to the ghetto would be to arrest or reduce the fear of theft and vandalism. Unless this is done, the ghetto might not only continue to lose manufacturing jobs but might even experience a loss of nonmanufacturing jobs. The desire to move out of the ghetto by new business is so strong and so widespread that the threat of increasing outmigration is a possibility in a central city like Philadelphia.

Location of Business and the Employment of Local Residents

The industrial and geographic distribution of employment within a city describes the pattern of labor demand and consequently identifies where potential employment opportunities are located. To fully evaluate the employment impact of new business formations, however, it is important to know not only the geographic location of firms with job openings, but also to what extent a firm which locates within a particular section of the city actually provides jobs for the residents of that area. This question is, of course, equally important for all job opportunities including those created by existing firms. For example, new businesses, the expansion of existing firms, and normal labor turnover may create a substantial number of employment opportunities in ghetto areas, while at the same time the direct employment impact on ghetto residents may be small. This occurs if most of the job openings are filled by persons living outside the ghetto. Such an effect could be the result of skill requirements associated with the occupational structure in the firms with the job vacancies, racial discrimination, or perhaps because of lack of transportation facilities within and among ghetto areas compared to the facilities that link the core of the city with the outlying residential areas.

In order to study such possibilities and to give a more complete picture of the pattern of labor demand, the mail survey included several broad questions on the distance of employee's residences from the firm's location and how their employees traveled to work.

Patterns of Residential Proximity of Employees

The distances between a firm's location and its employees' residences is determined by the interaction of its industrial characteristics, its occupational structure, and its geographic location within the metropolitan area interacting with the commuting preferences and geographic location of the labor force from which it hires. In the short run, a period in which workers are not able to change their place of residence, this interaction is essentially a supply-demand relationship in which commuting distances are determined rather than the wage rate which is assumed fixed. In the longer run it would be expected that residential patterns would change, although the direction this change would take is uncertain. Many employees would seek to economize on transportation costs by moving closer to their place of employment. Others, however, might be induced to seek residential amenities farther from the location of their plant by higher incomes resulting from continued employment and job tenure. Furthermore, the short run is most relevant to designing most types of demand-oriented manpower programs for two very important reasons. First, the purpose of these programs is to create new jobs, and thus the residential location of the employees hired initially will be of greatest concern. Secondly, residential segregation limits the geographic mobility of many of the persons in the target population of such manpower programs.

The supply side of the equation determining residential proximity of a firm's employees describes the commuting preferences of labor. At any given level of unemployment and rate of compensation, there exists a maximum commuting effort each worker will make to get to his place of employment. The distance which will be traveled from the worker's home as a result of this commuting effort will be determined by his alternative evaluations of commuting costs, in time and expense, and leisure. At high rates of unemployment, higher wages or quicker means of transportation he will be willing to commute farther.

The geographic area that can be reached from the worker's residence by that commuting effort he is willing to make at the existing rates of unemployment, wages, and so on, has been called his "normal preference area" by Goldner.[1] Demand-oriented manpower programs must locate new jobs within the normal preference area of persons living in areas of high sectoral unemployment. Of the several factors affecting the size and shape of this preference, one of the most important is the available transportation network. It will be elongated along the major arteries and, for the worker who has no automobile, it will be restricted to those areas served by the public transportation system. The size of the normal preference area is likely to increase with income since the worker will be willing to travel farther because of higher wages and his ability to afford more comfortable and less geographically restricted modes of transportation such as the automobile. In addition, there are probably significant variations in the size and shape of the preference by age and sex of the worker.

Another factor which affects the geographic portion of the labor market in which a worker will consider employment is the distribution system of labor-market information. It has been found that the geographic scope of information dissemination will vary with the skill and pay level of the job in a manner similar to the variation between pay level and commuting preferences. Formal advertising and specialized private employment agencies will reach the entire metropolitan area for high level manpower. Personal contacts with friends and relatives, on the other hand, which limit information to jobs in a more restricted area, are the dominant channels for many occupations, especially those of lower skill and pay.

The demand side of the equation determining the residential proximity of a firm's employees is described by the firm's industrial type, its occupational structure, and its geographic location in relation to residential areas. An understanding of the effect of these factors is one of the more important prerequisites to planning effective job creation programs. If businesses are to be created within the ghetto, it will be important to know the types of firms which hire a large proportion of their employees from the local area. If such firms are not found suitable for meeting policy objectives, then the effects of industrial type and location on the distances from which employees are hired will provide information on the obstacles which need to be overcome.

The firm's industry type is the most important variable in the demand equation since it largely determines the firms occupation and salary structure, its intrametropolitan location, and the level of external costs it imposes on its immediate neighborhood. The occupation and wage structure determine levels of employee compensation which are so important in the individual's normal preference area decision. There is a theoretical relationship between the geographic labor market in which the firm hires labor for specific types of jobs and the worker's normal preference area of employment. Assuming that there is perfect competition in the labor market, equal pay and equal commuting preferences for workers in particular job types then the firm will be located at the boundary of the normal preference area of the last employee hired in that job. Thus the hiring radius for a given job will equal the radius of the normal preference areas of persons hired for that job.

The last major consideration in the determination of the residential proximity of employees is the effects of residential amenities and firm location. All employees, no matter what their income, would be expected to economize on travel time and expense, but in previous studies it has been shown that workers tend to do so only when their expected levels of residential amenities—such as open space, safe streets and clean air—are met.[2] An individual's demand for a quality living environment appears to be income elastic. Therefore the higher an individual's income, the more likely he is to choose a residential location which provides greater space and an attractive neighborhood. For numerous reasons the quality of living environments tends to increase farther from the location of business activity. This is partly because business operations impose costs on the immediate neighborhood environment. Another reason is the tendency observed in this study of all major industry groups to be highly concentrated at the core of the city. Perhaps because of this and the lower intensity of land use and the lower average age of structures as one moves away from the central core, the residential environment is likely to improve as one moves out toward the suburban ring. It is therefore expected that in general employees in managerial, professional-technical and other high-paying occupations will commute farther due to both their larger normal preference areas and the fact that their expected level of residential amenities is likely to be met farther from the place of business activity.

Industry type, in addition to determining the income of its employees, also influences the location of the firm within the metropolitan area and in relation to residential neighborhoods of varying socioeconomic characteristics. A large number of finance, insurance, and real estate firms, for example, locate in the central business district. This makes it necessary for their higher income employees who live in the suburbs to commute farther on the average than employees of equal pay in other industries. Similarly, many manufacturing industries impose heavy costs on their immediate neighborhood in the form of odors, smoke, noise, and unsightly structure. Employees of a given pay level will seek to live farther away from such operations. Conversely, retail establishments, which impose fewer costs on the community and tend to locate as close to residential areas, would have a larger number of employees living nearby.

On the basis of this analysis, several observable patterns were expected in the relation between a firm's industry type and whether it is located in ghetto, nonghetto, or central business district sections of the city of Philadelphia. In general, those industries with higher average wages will have a longer average commuting radius for their employees. For this reason employees in manufacturing are likely to commute farther distances than employees in nonmanufacturing firms. Since the occupational and salary structure within wholesale and retail trade firms includes a high proportion of semiskilled, low-paying jobs, many of the employees are likely to live close to the place of operations. Retail trade firms would also tend to locate close to residential areas.

There are, of course, exceptions to this general tendency, especially when more specific types of industries are concerned. For example, the wage and salary structure in textile manufacturing is lower than that of the insurance industry, and therefore the general manufacturing-nonmanufacturing differences do not apply. In addition, the nature of operations in some industries is quite unique and this will dominate the commuting pattern of its employees. For some contract construction firms, especially nonunion and noncommercial enterprises, it would be expected that employees would travel a considerable distance to the place of work.

Differences in the residential proximity of employees of firms located in ghetto and nonghetto areas were expected to be influenced in part by racial factors. If a ghetto firm employs, for whatever reason, a high proportion of white workers, the existing segregated housing patterns in urban areas will necessarily mean longer commuting distances for its employees. If the racial composition of the ghetto firm's work force is mainly nonwhite, most of its employees will live a shorter distance away. The location of ghetto areas close to the center of the city will also affect ghetto-nonghetto differences in commuting patterns. Since the distance from more desirable residential areas decreases as one moves away from the central business district, the proportion of employees living close to the firm's location would be expected to increase the closer that location is to the suburban ring. Since the nonghetto sections of Philadelphia are generally closer to the suburban ring, a larger proportion of the employees of firms locating there would live nearby than for firms in ghetto sections. This does not imply, however, that ghetto residents would travel farther, only that the majority of persons employed in ghetto-located firms do not also live there.

Another factor affecting the ghetto-nonghetto-central business differences in employee residence patterns is the difference in transportation services available to these sectors. Most public transportation and automobile arteries connect the central core with outlying areas, thus reducing the travel time and expense incurred by persons living farther away from firms located where these converge—in the ghetto sections and central business district. The relative scarcity of public transportation in nonghetto areas is expected to result in a larger proportion of employees who will need to work for a firm within walking distance of their homes. The lower density of work places per unit of land characteristic of nonghetto areas may offset such a tendency, however, by reducing the probability that a worker will find a job that close.

Work-Residence Relationship for Industrial Groups

In the mail survey of both entrant and existing firms, the entrepreneurs or senior executives were asked the number of their employees who resided in each of the following distance zones: near the plant (within a two-mile radius of the plant), the remainder of Philadelphia, or in the suburbs. The results for the proportion of the firms' employees living within two miles of the plant are shown in Table 9-1. The data are presented by type of industry and geographic location of the firm so that the hypotheses previously discussed may be analyzed.

A fairly high proportion (slightly more than one-third) of entrepreneurs in entrant firms said that none of their employees lived within the two-mile radius while about one-fifth said that all employees lived close to the firm's location. It is interesting that the existing firms' employees appear to reside somewhat farther from the plant than is the case for entrant firm employees. Almost one-half of existing firms indicated that all their employees were outside the two-mile geographic area. Apparently the new business hired a substantial proportion of its employees from the immediate locality, but when the firm is well established, some of its original employees have moved to more distant residential locations and/or the firm's recruitment efforts are directed towards a more extensive geographic population of manpower for its labor supply.

The hypothesis that a lower proportion of manufacturing firms' employees live closer to the plant is partially supported by the entrant responses. The results show that manufacturing firms tended to have a lower proportion of their work force within the two-mile radius. About one-third of the nonmanufacturing firms, compared to only 14% of manufacturing firms, indicated that more than two-thirds of their employees were in close proximity to the plant. However, since manufacturing firms had a lower proportion of firms with no employees close to the establishment, the results do not permit the hypothesis

Table 9-1
Proportion of Firms' Employees Residing within Two Miles of Establishment (Percentage Distribution of Firms)

Proportion of Employees within Two Miles	All Firms %	Type of Industry					Geographic Location		
		Manufacturing %	Nonmanufacturing %	Wholesale & Retail Trade %	Services %	Contract Construction %	Ghetto %	Nonghetto %	Central Business District %
Entrant Firms[a]									
No Employees	36	29	37	21	47	40	21	40	58
1-33%	17	14	18	11	23	0	21	16	34
34-66%	16	43	13	11	7	40	21	14	8
67-99%	10	0	11	16	7	0	11	10	0
All Employees	21	14	21	41	16	20	26	20	0
Total	100	100	100	100	100	100	100	100	100
Existing Firms[b]									
No Employees	46	46	46	42	53	17	59	39	55
1-33%	16	9	17	18	16	17	14	18	23
34-66%	12	18	12	11	12	17	7	15	10
67-99%	6	9	5	4	5	33	2	8	0
All Employees	20	18	20	25	14	16	18	20	12
Total	100	100	100	100	100	100	100	100	100

aBased on mail survey of returns from 91 city firms with usable responses from about 80% of the firms. The average size of firm was small with some 5.2 employees as of June 1969.

bBased on mail survey of returns from 141 firms with usable responses from some 88% of the firms. The average size of firm was 17.3 employees as of June 1969.

to be accepted with certainty. The issue is also not clear when the existing firms are considered, since there is apparently no significant difference between the results for existing manufacturing and nonmanufacturing firms; about 50% of both types of firms said that none of their employees lived within the vicinity of the establishment.

As anticipated there was considerable variation within the nonmanufacturing sector. Over 40% of firms in wholesale and retail trade indicated that all of their employees lived in the vicinity of the establishment and an additional 16% said that more than two-thirds of their employees were within the two-mile radius. The information obtained from existing firms did not reveal a similar finding. A much lower proportion of their wholesale and retail trade employees lived close to the firms.

The residential pattern for employees in new firms in the service sector was in marked contrast to the pattern for new firms in wholesale and retail trade. Almost half of the service section entrants had none of their employees close to the establishment. This was also the case in existing service firms. This pattern seems contrary to the expected one since the average wage in the service sector is lower than that in manufacturing. The concentration of service establishments in the central business district, relatively isolated from most residential areas and close to a large number of economical public transit routes, is probably the best explanation. Service sector employees in existing firms apparently have a similar preference.

Due to the nature of the construction industry in which a firm would be expected to accept numerous projects from a large geographic area and to hire a large part of its work force specifically for a given job from the trade unions, it appeared likely that many of the persons employed by construction firms would reside quite far from those firms' locations. The results for the entrant firms support this presumption. The findings for construction workers in existing firms showed a surprisingly high proportion living close to the place of operations. Almost half of these firms said that over two-thirds of their employees lived within the two-mile radius. It is not possible to make confident predictions about the behavior of construction workers in existing firms because of the small number of construction firms responding to the mail survey. It is possible, however, that new construction firms are more likely to accept contracts within a much larger geographic area than existing firms since the new firm has fewer business contacts. Another possibility is that more established firms will hire certain tradesmen on a regular basis, especially those living near the firm's location which would tend to be at the center of the firm's area of operation.

The employees of city firms who do not live within the two-mile area usually reside in the remaining area of Philadelphia. Few firms had substantial portions of their labor force living in the suburbs. The results showed that about one-third of city firms had less than 33% of their employees residing in the suburbs.[a] The suburban areas were most important among manufacturing employees, with 43% of the firms indicating up to one-third of their employees living in the suburbs; an additional 14% reported that between one- and two-thirds lived outside of the city. For nonmanufacturing firms the data showed that the suburbs were proportionately much less important as a place of residence for employees. This finding provides some additional weight to the conclusion that a higher proportion of employees in manufacturing firms live a substantial distance from the plant.

The suburban residential location was found to be moderately important to employees in construction and in the service sector. This finding is consistent with the results in Table 9-1 which showed a higher proportion of employees in these industries did not live close to the work site. The suburban data for existing firms suggested similar conclusions from responses by type of industry.

Work-Residence Relationship by Location of the Firm

The city entrant firm responses do not appear to support the hypothesis that a high proportion of employees in nonghetto firms and a low proportion of ghetto firm employees reside in close proximity to the plant. The data actually suggests the opposite relationship. Over one-third of ghetto firms said that over two-thirds of their employees lived within two miles of the plant, and only about 20% of the firms had no employees living close to the work site. Among the nonghetto firms, 40% had none of their employees in the vicinity of the plant and apparently commute a longer distance than employees in ghetto firms. Most employees of firms in the central business district did not live within the two-mile area. Over 90% of the firms indicated that either none or less than one-third of their employees resided close to the firm. Most of these employees live in the remaining part of the city. The same is true for both ghetto and nonghetto firm employees who do not reside near their employer's place of business. The suburbs are, however, a more frequent choice for ghetto and central business district firms' employees who do not live close to the firm. About half the firms in the central business district and about one-third of ghetto firms estimated that up to one-third of their employees resided in the suburbs. For the ghetto entrant firm, therefore, a high proportion of employees live close to the establishment, and of those who do not, the suburbs are almost as important a residential location as the remainder of the city. One factor affecting this result may be the existence of a good transportation network between the core of the city and the suburbs.

The hypothesis that a high proportion of nonghetto firm employees and a low proportion of ghetto firm employees are residentially close to their place of

---

[a]The data showing the proportion of employees is not reported in detail since the findings are related to the results in Table 9-1.

work is supported by the data on existing firms, shown in Table 9-1. Almost three-quarters of the ghetto firms said that either none or less than one-third of their employees lived within two miles of their work. The other more distant residential areas within the city were most important to ghetto firm employees. A similar finding was obtained for existing firms in the central business district, except that the suburbs were relatively a more important residential choice for employees of firms in this location. The employees of existing firms in nonghetto areas were more likely to live close to their work, and of those who did not reside within the two mile area, most were in the city rather than the suburbs.

The previously discussed tendency for new businesses to hire employees close to the plant is particularly true of new firms in the ghetto. Consequently, the hypothesis that a high proportion of new ghetto firm employees commute some distance to their work is not supported. In time, however, once the new firm is established and presumably increases in size, the residential pattern of the ghetto firm's employees may change. If this occurs the proportion of employees living in the vicinity of the firm will decline substantially and become lower than the proportion of employees in nonghetto firms residing near the firm.

Patterns in Means of Journey to Work

The mode of travel for employees is likely to be a function of the density of work places (per unit of land) and the proportion of the firm's work force which lives close to the plant. A low density of work places is likely to be poorly serviced by public transportation and a high proportion of workers will have to use private automobiles.[3] Consequently it is expected that in suburban areas and nonghetto areas of the city other than the central business district, the automobile will be the major means of transportation. In addition, the relatively high proportion of employees living close to the plant in nonghetto areas indicates that a larger proportion of employees will walk to work compared to employees in firms located in either the ghetto or central business district areas.

Public transportation will be utilized proportionately more by employees working in the high work-place density areas of the central business district and, to a lesser extent, ghetto areas, provided of course that a relatively high proportion of employees in ghetto firms live close to the work site.

The modal method of transportation for various industries depends on both residential proximity of employees and the location of firms in relation to the public and highway transit system. Since the proportion of employees living close to the plant is lower for manufacturing than for nonmanufacturing, and because wholesale and retail trade firms are likely to locate close to public transit, a larger proportion of manufacturing employees will use automobiles. Nonmanufacturing employees will have a better opportunity to use public transit and walk to work.

Entrant Employees' Means of Transportation

The data in Table 9-2 were compiled from the interviews conducted with the sample of 113 firms which started business in the city during 1967. The entrepreneur was asked to identify the number of his employees who used each of the three major means of transportation. The results for all firms show that the automobile is clearly the most important method used by employees. Only 12% of the firms said that none of their employees traveled to work by auto and in about half the firms, over two-thirds of the employees drove their private car to work. Public transportation was the next most important means of travel, with walking only important to a small proportion of employees in a few firms. In fact, nearly three-quarters of the firms said that none of their employees walked to work.

The relative importance of each of these means of transportation varies with the geographic location of the firm. Employees who work in new businesses in the central business district walk less and use the automobile less for journey to work than employees of new firms in other areas. The major means of transportation for this group of employees is public transportation. The remarkably high proportion of one-half of central business district entrepreneurs said that more than two-thirds of their employees traveled to work by public transportation.

Although walking to work was not frequently used by employees, it was relatively more important to employees in nonghetto firms than for firms in other geographic areas. The nonghetto firm employees also used the public transportation more frequently than ghetto firm employees. Almost one-third of the nonghetto firms indicated that more than two-thirds of their employees journeyed to work on the public transit system. Employees of ghetto firms relied heavily on the automobile with one-half of the ghetto firms estimating that over two-thirds of their employees used this mode of travel.

These findings are not entirely consistent with the expected pattern of means of travel to work. The hypothesis that the areas of high work-place density are well serviced by the public transportation system appears justified on the experience of the new business in the central business district. It was expected that the nonghetto firms would rely more on walking to work than other groups of firms and this view was substantiated. However, it was not expected that the nonghetto firms would have less reliance on the automobile than the ghetto area. This heavy reliance on the automobile clearly indicates lack of commuter services between the ghetto and the residential areas of ghetto employees. Perhaps the lack of "corridor patterns" to the ghetto means that large parts of the ghetto areas are isolated from the public transportation system servicing both nonghetto and ghetto residential locations. Apparently, not only does the ghetto resident require an automobile to get employment in a nonghetto area, but for those living in nonghetto areas and working in the ghetto the automobile is also an important means of transportation.

Table 9-2
Proportion of City Entrant Firms' Employees Using Major Means of Transportation

Proportion of Employees Using Means of Transportation %	All Firms %	Type of Industry					Geographic Location		
		Manufacturing %	Nonmanufacturing %	Wholesale & Retail Trade %	Services %	Contract Construction %	Ghetto %	Nonghetto %	Central Business District %
Walk									
No Employees	72	72	72	66	67	100	80	69	75
1-33%	17	20	14	15	33	0	4	21	13
34-66%	3	2	4	5	0	0	4	3	0
67-100%	8	6	10	14	0	0	12	7	13
Total	100	100	100	100	100	100	100	100	100
Automobile									
No Employees	12	9	14	30	8	0	16	10	20
1-33%	29	36	24	20	42	0	12	35	60
34-66%	10	6	14	15	25	0	16	8	13
67-100%	49	49	48	35	25	100	56	47	7
Total	100	100	100	100	100	100	100	100	100
Public Transportation									
No Employees	43	42	44		25	100	56	38	18
1-33%	19	17	22		8	0	16	20	19
34-66%	13	13	12		25	0	16	12	13
67-100%	25	28	22		42	0	12	30	50
Total	100	100	100		100	100	100	100	100

Note: Based on interviews of a sample of 113 firms of which some 92% responded with usable data. The average size of firm as of June 1969 was 26.7 employees.

There is not much difference in means of travel used by employees in the various industries. The employees in the service and wholesale and retail trade industries have a slightly different pattern than employees in other industries. The employees in wholesale and retail trade walk to work more frequently than most other groups, and in the service sector the public transportation system is used more than in other industries. These variations are interpreted to be more a function of locational bias of the industries rather than the nature of the industry. However, the relatively low wages in wholesale and retail trade occupations may prevent some employees from accepting a job unless the transportation costs are not high. Consequently, job seekers will prefer to live near their work location so that they can walk to work. The frequently changing nature of the work site in the construction industry makes the automobile an essential asset for almost all employees.

The results of the suburban interviews in Table 9-3 are, with a few exceptions, consistent with the analysis of the city entrant firms. Suburban employees rely even more heavily on the automobile than do those employed in city firms. This is especially the case for employees in manufacturing, where almost all the firms indicated that more than two-thirds of their employees traveled to work by car. This was a much greater proportion than in nonmanufacturing. As for the city firms, the only sector where public transportation is important is in the service industries. Presumably, business and personal services are located in nodes of population concentration in suburban towns, and this makes it feasible for public transit to provide service. In many cases, this service may be part of suburban central business district corridors and may even involve reverse commuting. However, apart from this industry, public transit as a means of journey to work is much less important to employees in suburban entrant firms than it is for new businesses in the city.

Conclusions

The results of this chapter provide some indirect evidence on the impact of new business formations on the employment opportunities for residents in the core of the city. The employment possibilities for ghetto residents are, of course, increased if the new businesses are located in the ghetto area, since new firms recruit a higher proportion of their employees from the immediate environment than do existing firms in the same geographic area.

The important question for public policy is which type of new businesses generate the greatest amount of local employment. This study suggests that the nonmanufacturing firms, especially in wholesale and retail trade and in the nonbusiness service sector, hire a larger proportion of their employees from the firm's immediate environment than do manufacturing firms. New construc-

Table 9-3
Proportion of Suburban Entrant Firms' Employees Using Major Means of Transportation

Proportion of Employees Using Means of Transportation	All Firms %	Manufacturing %	Type of Industry			
			Nonmanufacturing %	Wholesale & Retail Trade %	Services %	Contract Construction %
Walk						
No Employees	80	96	62	55	50	100
1-33%	16	4	28	27	50	0
34-66%	2	0	5	9	0	0
67-100%	2	0	5	9	0	0
Total	100	100	100	100	100	100
Automobile						
No Employees	0	0	0	0	0	0
1-33%	8	0	19	27	17	0
34-66%	14	4	24	10	66	0
67-100%	78	96	57	63	17	100
Total	100	100	100	100	100	100
Public						
No Employees	66	74	57	64	16	100
1-33%	18	22	14	18	17	0
34-66%	14	4	24	18	50	0
67-100%	2	0	5	0	17	0
Total	100	100	100	100	100	100

Note: Based on interviews of a sample of 44 firms. The average size of firm as of June 1969 was 29.3 employees.

tion firms located in the ghetto are not likely to generate much employment among ghetto residents since most of their employees require a car for commuting to the work site and, perhaps related to this finding, most workers appear to live some distance from the firm's location.

There are, however, several findings which suggest that any public policy which seeks to attract new businesses to the ghetto will have a low payoff for ghetto residents. It appears that once the new firm is established, the proportion of the labor force from the ghetto declines. This may, of course, occur because employees who once lived in the ghetto have moved to a nonghetto area. The impression gained in conducting the study is that the reason is simply that once the firm is established, it enlarges the geographic dimensions of its search for employees and this extends beyond the boundaries of the ghetto area. It was also found that the rate of expansion in employment during the development stage of the new firm's life was much slower for ghetto than for nonghetto firms. This suggests that it may be difficult to achieve a high degree of economic success from any policy which concentrates on aiding new ghetto firms.

The journey-to-work section of the study shows the high reliance of employees on the automobile. The lack of utilization of public transport and walking by employees in ghetto firms suggests that some ghetto area firms and residential areas may be somewhat isolated from the public transit network. It therefore appears that the contribution of new businesses to solving the high unemployment rate among ghetto residents is not expected to be great unless public policy is able to rapidly increase the size of these new firms and induce employers to hire a larger proportion of ghetto residents.

10

172

The Entrepreneur and the Manager in Urban Enterprises

The supply of entrepreneurs in a particular industry and location depends directly on the investment opportunities available at any point in time. These opportunities in a local area are affected by the expected return to the investment which is dependent on demand pressure created by consumer preference and the level of per capita income, both within the local area and its larger economic environment. The entrepreneurial response to the investment opportunities is also influenced by the level of per capita income since this affects ability to raise initial funds and the cost involved in acquiring the basic skill and knowledge necessary to embark on the new enterprise.[1]

The personal characteristics of the individual who decides to establish a new business in an urban environment are also likely to influence the supply function of entrepreneurs. The exact role which the characteristics of age, education, and experience play in determining the nature and location of business is, of course, probably indeterminate, but a comparative analysis of the businessman's personal characteristics in different types of firms does provide an insight into the "managerial background" associated with new businesses.

In this chapter the comparative analysis involves sample data collected from the entrant firms, the suburban entrants, and the existing establishments. The data for the entrant firms are reported separately for the mail questionnaire and the interview survey. Respondents from new entrant firms and existing firms in many cases do not perform the same precise functions within their respective organizations. In the entrant firms, the respondent businessman is mainly an entrepreneur whose function is:

To reform or revolutionize the pattern of production by exploiting an invention or, more generally, an untried technological possibility . . . [or] by opening up a new source of supply of materials or a new outlet for products.[2]

The new businessman also has to perform an administrative function and in many instances may be actually involved in the direct production of the firm's output. In contrast, the respondent from the existing firm, a senior executive, is unlikely to participate directly in producing the firm's output, and the "entrepreneurial" type of decisions he is required to make may be made in conjunction with other senior officials including members of a board of directors. Consequently, these differences in functions performed may be

171

associated with slightly different personal characteristics among the groups of respondents.

Variations in Entrepreneurial Characteristics

Variations in the nature and geographic location of new industries suggest the existence of several regularities in the characteristics of entrepreneurs and top level managers. The precise formulation of some of these expected regularities are as follows:

1. Entrepreneurs (and managers) in manufacturing firms have had more formal education and more experience in the same industry than non-manufacturing entrepreneurs.

   Since the nature of production is usually more technical in manufacturing than in nonmanufacturing, it is more difficult to begin operations in a manufacturing enterprise unless the entrepreneur has had previous experience in a similar type of production. In addition, entry into many nonmanufacturing industries probably requires little formal educational training. As a result, it is likely that on the average nonmanufacturing entrepreneurs will have less formal education than their counterparts in manufacturing.

2. Entrant entrepreneurs are younger than top managers from existing firms in similar industries. The age differential between the new entrepreneur and the top manager in the established firm is related to the size of the organization. Firms which have been established for some time are usually larger in size and have a more complex management hierarchy. Progress to the top of this type of organization usually takes many years and as a result it is likely that the average age of top-level decision makers in existing firms will be quite high compared to the entrepreneur who establishes a new business.

   It is expected that the black entrepreneur is older than his white counterpart. The reason for this differential is probably attributable to the lower per capita income among blacks compared to whites. Consequently, the lack of financial resources and other barriers restrict business opportunities for young blacks.

3. A comparison of the ghetto and nonghetto entrepreneur is likely to reveal that blacks tend to establish businesses in the ghetto, and that the ghetto entrepreneur is older, has less formal education, and has had less previous experience in the same industry.

   Studies have shown that black businesses are not widely distributed throughout all geographic sections of the city. They are usually concentrated in a few areas where a relatively high proportion of the black population resides. For example, in one city in 1964 some 77% of black businesses were located in three of the city's twenty business areas and about 40% of all black business was located in one area which accounted for about one-third of the city's black population.[3]

It is also expected that the ghetto entrepreneur will be somewhat older than the nonghetto entrepreneur since the black entrepreneurs who tend to be restricted (because of discrimination and by individual choice) to ghetto locations are expected to be older than whites. In recent years there has been considerable change in the ownership and structure of businesses within ghetto areas. Many white businessmen are apparently moving out of the inner city and indigenous black entrepreneurs are increasingly becoming more important in the ghetto business structure. This development is being encouraged by current public policy, and as a result it is likely that many ghetto entrepreneurs are entering business with little previous business experience.

4. New businesses require start-up capital and it is expected that the entrepreneur will provide a large part of these funds. Furthermore, ghetto entrepreneurs will tend to provide a larger share of the total funds required than the nonghetto entrepreneur. An additional factor influencing the type of business started by entrepreneurs of different socioeconomic groups is differences in capital requirements by type of industry. In general it is expected that a larger amount of funds is required to establish a new firm in manufacturing than in nonmanufacturing.

The capital requirements of manufacturing usually involve larger funding than nonmanufacturing activities. Differences in scale of operations (number of employees) could, of course, affect this hypothesis, but since all new entrants are relatively small in size, it is expected that the data will support the hypothesis. It is alleged that the ghetto entrant has difficulty in obtaining credit either because of discrimination and/or a host of ghetto market factors, such as fluctuating income base, poor transportation, and so forth, and consequently the ghetto entrepreneur is likely to contribute a sizable proportion of the original capital from his own savings.

The foregoing expected regularities in the characteristics of the entrepreneur are explored in the present study. The size of the sample in some categories of the firms studied restricts the testing of the hypothesis in a definitive manner. The data are, however, sufficient either to provide some substantive support or to question some of the generalizations made about entrepreneurs in urban areas.

Entrepreneurial Characteristics and Type of Industry

The job requirements necessary to initiate and direct a new business are likely to require many skills and knowledge which are quite similar. On the other hand, entry into the construction industry as an entrepreneur is likely to involve quite different past experience than is the case in wholesale and retail trade. The demographic and educational background of entrepreneurs may be an important factor in determining the type of business chosen as the new business activity.

Demographic Characteristics

Table 10-1 shows the distribution of the entrepreneurs' racial and age characteristics by type of industry for three categories of entrant firms and for a sample of existing firms. One of the most striking results is the relatively low proportion of nonwhite entrepreneurs. Given the residential pattern of whites and nonwhites in metropolitan areas, it is expected that most black businesses will be concentrated in the central city and few in the suburban ring. In the sample of 1967 suburban entrants, none of the entrepreneurs was nonwhite. The proportion of nonwhites in the three categories of city firms varied from 4% of the respondents from the existing firms to 14% among the entrant firms in the mail survey. The difference in the racial characteristics between city entrants and suburban entrants was statistically significant at the 90% level for the entrant interviews and the suburban firms.[a]

These findings may be a reflection of the socioeconomic changes which have been occurring in urban areas during the past decade. As already discussed, there has been a movement of whites from their residences in the central city. This, coupled with the deteriorating business climate for many owners of small firms—and especially white owners—has apparently motivated white entrepreneurs to look to the suburban ring and selected nonghetto areas of the city as potential location sites. In the interviews with white entrepreneurs and sometimes in additional comments to the mail questionnaires, the difficulties accompanying the central core location were frequently mentioned and the criticism of the surrounding physical environment such as the high crime rate was often expressed in racial terms.

Several possibilities may explain the difference between the proportion of nonwhites as top level managers in existing firms and the proportion among the entrant (mail) firms. The influx of nonwhites to the central city has created a substantial nonwhite consumer market. The goods which are supplied in this market are mostly imports to the geographic area, but a large

[a]The Chi Square test was used to test the level of significance of differences in results throughout this chapter.

part of the distribution of these goods and other local services is likely to be provided from within the boundaries of the central core. However, the movement of white businessmen to other parts of the metropolis has resulted in opportunities for new businesses in this section of the city. The social pressure from within the black community to improve their economic status by relying on their own resources, and a public policy which encourages black capitalism may partially explain why a much larger proportion of nonwhite entrepreneurs were found among city entrants than the proportion of nonwhite top level managers in the existing firms which have been established for many years.

The nonwhite entrepreneurs and top level managers are not uniformly distributed throughout all major types of industry. None of the respondent firms in contract construction were headed by nonwhites. Similarly, among manufacturing, wholesale, and retail trade firms which had been established for some time, there were no nonwhite top level managers. This was not true of both samples of city entrants. Nonwhite entrepreneurs were directing between 7 and 14% of the new enterprises, depending on the specific entrant sample. Similarly, depending on the industry group, between 5% of the interview entrants and 25% of the mail entrants were headed by nonwhites. This difference between the existing and entrant firms may also be a reflection of the overall growing participation of blacks in the organization and management of business activity.[b] Nevertheless, despite the apparent increasing importance of blacks in manufacturing, the wholesale and retail trade and the service sectors continue to offer most entrepreneurial opportunity to nonwhites.[c]

The variation in the mean age of respondents in each category of firms confirms the hypothesis that entrant entrepreneurs are younger than managers from existing firms, and this differential is significant at the 99% level. The average age of managers in existing firms is some seven years higher than the average age of entrepreneurs in the entrant firms. This differential in age is present when entrant firms and existing firms are compared for each broad industry group.

City entrant entrepreneurs tend to be younger than suburban entrepreneurs, and this difference is significant at the 80% level. The difference in age between manufacturing and nonmanufacturing managers was significant in existing firms (80% level) but not significant in the entrant firms. However, among the entrant firms the entrepreneurs in the manufacturing and service

---

[b]The racial difference between city entrants and established firms is statistically significant but only at the 75% level for the city interview and existing firm samples.

[c]There was no significant racial difference between manufacturing and nonmanufacturing city entrepreneurs. The difference between manufacturing and sectors within nonmanufacturing probably was significant, but the size of the sample restricted a meaningful Chi Square test.

Table 10-1
Personal Characteristics of Entrepreneurs and Managers by Category of Firm and Type of Industry

Type of Firm	Race (% Distribution)			Age (% Distribution)				Age (Mean No. of Years)
	White	Nonwhite	Total	<40 Yrs.	40-54 Yrs.	>54 Yrs.	Total	
Entrant (Mail)								
All Firms (n = 91)	86	14	100	47	41	13	100	41.6
Manufacturing	86	14	100	57	29	14	100	—
Nonmanufacturing	86	14	100	46	42	12	100	—
Wholesale & retail	75	25	100	38	41	21	100	—
Services	89	11	100	58	42	0	100	—
Contract construction	100	0	100	29	43	29	100	—
Entrant (Interview)								
All Firms (n = 113)	93	7	100	42	45	14	100	42.4
Manufacturing	93	7	100	38	48	14	100	—
Nonmanufacturing	93	7	100	46	41	13	100	—
Wholesale & retail	95	5	100	30	50	20	100	—
Services	86	14	100	71	21	7	100	—
Contract construction	100	0	100	50	25	25	100	—
Suburban Entrant								
All Firms (n = 44)	100	0	100	39	57	5	100	
Manufacturing	100	0	100	43	57	0	100	
Nonmanufacturing	100	0	100	33	57	10	100	
Wholesale & retail	100	0	100	27	64	9	100	
Services	100	0	100	33	67	0	100	
Contract construction	100	0	100	0	50	50	100	

Existing Firms								
All Firms (n = 141)	96	100	4	100	18	49	33	100	49.6
Manufacturing	100	100	0	100	0	62	39	100	—
Nonmanufacturing	96	100	4	100	20	48	33	100	—
Wholesale & retail	100	100	0	100	23	44	33	100	—
Services	89	100	11	100	13	53	33	100	—
Contract construction	100	100	0	100	25	38	38	100	—

sectors tend to the younger than in other types of industry. In contrast, in the existing firms the youngest managers tend to be in wholesale and retail trade.

Level of Formal Education

Table 10-2 shows that about one-third of all entrepreneurs and managers are college graduates. As expected, however, there are differences in the formal educational attainment level of respondents in different industry groups. For all groups of firms, the entrepreneurs in the service sector had received the most formal education before establishing a business enterprise. A large number of the respondents from this group of firms provided business services rather than personal services, and to some extent this is likely to account for the overall service sector being directed by a highly educated group of individuals. Among all groups of entrant firms, except the interview sample, manufacturing entrepreneurs are also a highly educated group. This is particularly true among the entrant (mail survey) firms where the educational difference between manufacturing and nonmanufacturing entrepreneurs is significant at the 90% level. This finding may be partially explained by a bias among those responding to mail questionnaires. However, even though the bias may be present, the same high educational level was not found among manufacturing managers in existing firms who also responded by mail. Within the existing firms, the managers in contract construction and services had more formal education than the manufacturing managers. The relatively low overall educational attainment in this category of firms may be a reflection of the high average age of these managers, especially for those in manufacturing firms.

The relatively lower level of education among city entrant interviewees may be partially explained by the presence of ghetto entrepreneurs and black entrepreneurs who are likely to have had less opportunity to acquire higher education.

The results of the analysis of formal education confirm that manufacturing entrepreneurs have more formal education than most groups of nonmanufacturing entrepreneurs. The service sector is a possible exception where the presence of business service entrepreneurs tends to raise the educational level of all entrepreneurs in the sector.

Nature of Previous Experience

Experience in the same industry is likely to be a prerequisite for entry into most industries. Most entrepreneurs and managers did indicate this type of prior experience, but between one-quarter and one-third of all respondents said they had no such experience.

From Table 10-3, which illustrates the variations by type of industry, it is apparent that in some industries entrepreneurs have had less prior experience in the same industry than in others. There is no significant difference between manufacturing and nonmanufacturing respondents in the city mail entrant survey or in the survey of existing firms. Significant differences were found between these industrial categories for the city entrant interviews (at the 90% level) and the suburban firms (at the 85% level). In both cases a higher proportion (between 13 to 20% higher) of manufacturing respondents said they had some experiences in the same industry than did the nonmanufacturing respondents.

The importance of experience in the same industry varies among respondents within the nonmanufacturing category. Among most samples of firms, it was found that in the construction industry a very high proportion of the entrepreneurs had previous experience. In contrast, among those in wholesale and retail trade a very high proportion (between one-third and one-half) of the respondents said they had no experience in this industry before starting operations. It is therefore not surprising that potential black entrepreneurs, who for various reasons have usually been unable to acquire the basic skill and experience necessary in industries in which the production process is technical in nature, have frequently established their new business in wholesale and retail trade.

It is interesting to know something about the nature of the respondents' previous job experience. Do most entrepreneurs have a substantial amount of managerial experience before embarking on their own venture? Table 10-3 presents an index of the importance of several types of experience which provides an insight into this type of question.

For entrant entrepreneurs, managerial experience is generally the most important prerequisite, at least in terms of exposure before starting the business. This is followed by nonsupervisory experience with exposure to beginning level management jobs, such as first line foreman, being the least mentioned.

Among existing firms, all managers tend to have been exposed to all three types of occupational experience, although when the mean number of years in each type of position is calculated, a pattern similar to the entrant entrepreneurs emerges. This suggests that the entrepreneur or top level manager in the existing firm receives diverse training experience but only spends a short time in the nonmanagerial ranks and moves quickly into the managerial hierarchy where he receives most of his experience. Although managerial experience is generally most important for entrant entrepreneurs, it is likely that a considerable amount of experience will also have been acquired in nonmanagerial and beginning supervisory positions. In some industry categories, there was a deviation from this general pattern of type of previous experience. For example, in the service, contract construction, and wholesale and retail trade sectors nonsupervisory experience was of greater importance

Table 10-2
Formal Education of Entrepreneurs and Managers by Category of Firm and Type of Industry (Percentage Distribution)

Type of Firm	Level of Formal Education					
	Less than H.S. Grad.	H.S. Grad.	Post H.S. Experience (Nongrad.)	Tech. or Bus. School Grad.	College or Univ. Grad.	Total
Entrant (Mail)						
All Firms (n = 91)	16	24	14	5	40	100
Manufacturing	0	29	14	0	57	100
Nonmanufacturing	18	24	14	6	39	100
Wholesale & Retail	27	35	12	8	19	100
Services	8	19	8	8	57	100
Contract Construction	43	29	14	0	14	100
Entrant (Interview)						
All Firms (n = 113)	20	25	27	6	22	100
Manufacturing	21	27	21	11	20	100
Nonmanufacturing	18	24	33	0	25	100
Wholesale & Retail	21	32	26	0	21	100
Services	7	14	50	0	29	100
Contract Construction	33	67	0	0	0	100
Suburban Entrant						
All Firms (n = 44)	21	12	35	2	30	100
Manufacturing	18	14	32	5	32	100
Nonmanufacturing	24	10	38	0	29	100
Wholesale & Retail	27	9	64	0	0	100
Services	17	0	17	0	67	100
Contract Construction	50	50	0	0	0	100

Existing Firms

All Firms (n = 141)	24	18	19	7	32	100
Manufacturing	39	8	23	0	31	100
Nonmanufacturing	22	19	19	8	32	100
Wholesale & Retail	33	21	13	10	23	100
Services	19	19	21	4	38	100
Contract Construction	13	13	13	25	38	100

Note: Detail may not add to 100 percent due to rounding.

Table 10-3

Previous Experience of Entrepreneurs and Managers by Category of Firm and Type of Industry

Type of Firm	Experience in Same Industry (% Distribution)				Type of Experience (Index of Importance)[a]			Amount of Experience (Mean Number of Years)		
	Some	None	NA	Total	Manager	Other Sprvsry.	Non Sprvsry	Manager	Other Sprvsry.	Non Sprvsry.
Entrant (Mail)										
All Firms (n = 91)	73	25	2	100	111	87	102	8.3	5.5	5.4
Manufacturing	71	29	0	100	99	133	67	—	—	—
Nonmanufacturing		21			114	84	105	—	—	—
Wholesale & Retail	64	36	0	100	108	84	108	—	—	—
Services	79	16	5		138	66	105	—	—	—
Contract Construction	86	14	0	100	69	117	117	—	—	—
Entrant (Interview) (n = 113)										
All Firms	68	27	5	100	111	96	93	10.2	4.9	6.6
Manufacturing	76	19	5	100	114	90	93	—	—	—
Nonmanufacturing	63	32	5	100	105	102	93	—	—	—
Wholesale & Retail	62	38	0	100	114	93	93	—	—	—
Services	71	29	0	100	96	108	96	—	—	—
Contract Construction	50	25	25	100	150	75	75	—	—	—
Suburban Entrant										
All Firms (n = 44)	68	32	0	100	130	84	91	—	—	—
Manufacturing	78	22	0	100	133	84	84	—	—	—
Nonmanufacturing	57	43	0	100	124	82	97	—	—	—
Wholesale & Retail	46	54	0	100	132	67	100	—	—	—
Services	50	50	0	100	88	88	130	—	—	—
Contract Construction	100	0	0	100	152	76	76	—	—	—

Existing Firms									
All Firms (n =141)	68	28	4	100	101	99	101	12.1	2.0
Manufacturing	69	31	0	100	100	100	100	—	—
Nonmanufacturing	68	27	5	100	101	99	101	—	—
Wholesale & Retail	58	37	5	100	99	99	101	—	—
Services	69	18	6	100	101	99	99	—	—
Contract Construction	88	12	0	100	100	100	100	—	—

aThis index represents the extent to which each group of managers was exposed to each type of experience. If all managers in each group indicate an exposure to each type of experience, the index is 100 for each experience. To the extent that managers are increasingly directing their own economic activity, the index rises above 100. The proportion of blacks in both ghetto and nonghetto firms is greater than the proportion in existing firms.

than in manufacturing firms among the city (mail survey) and suburban entrants.

Characteristics of Ghetto and Nonghetto Entrepreneurs

Studies of black businesses have found that such enterprises are concentrated in particular geographic areas of the city. The data from this particular study can be used to confirm or question this hypothesis by analyzing the racial characteristics of the ghetto and nonghetto entrepreneurs in the samples of firms surveyed. In addition, the age, education, and previous experience in industry is compared by geographic location of the business.

Demographic Characteristics

The racial distribution of entrepreneurs by geographic location, shown in Table 10-4, clearly supports the hypothesis that proportionately, black entrepreneurs tend to locate in ghetto areas. Between one-quarter and one-third of all entrants to geographic areas which contain a significant ghetto are headed by blacks. In contrast, only about 4% of entrants to areas without any ghetto are organized by black entrepreneurs. Similar racial differences exist among the sample of existing firms. The differences in racial distribution of entrepreneurs and managers in all samples of firms is statistically significant above the 95% level. Since the proportion of blacks in both ghetto and nonghetto firms is greater than the proportion in existing firms, the suggestion that nonwhites are increasingly directing their own economic activity is again illustrated.

There was no significant age differential between managers in ghetto and nonghetto firms which had been in existence for some time. For the sample of city entrant (interview) firms, there was also no significant difference in age differential. In the city entrant (mail) sample, it appears that the ghetto respondents tend to be younger, although the age differential was only significant at the 60% level. This finding does not support the hypothesis that ghetto entrepreneurs tend to be older than their counterparts in nonghetto geographic areas. This result should, however, be treated with considerable caution since it probably reflects a nonrespondent bias in that the younger nonwhite entrepreneurs were apparently more enthusiastic in their participation in a study of ghetto business. On the other hand, a trend towards more younger blacks starting businesses in the ghetto may be emerging. If true, this is certainly a break with tradition.

Table 10-4

Personal Characteristics of Entrepreneurs and Managers by Category of Firm and Geographical Location

Type of Firm	Race (% Distribution)			Age (% Distribution)			
	White	Nonwhite	Total	<40 Yrs.	40-54 Yrs.	>54 Yrs.	Total
Entrant (Mail)							
All Firms (n = 91)	84	14	100	47	41	12	100
Ghetto firms	63	38	100	46	50	4	100
Nonghetto firms	96	4	100	47	38	15	100
Entrant (Interview)							
All Firms (n = 113)	93	7	100	42	45	14	100
Ghetto firms	79	21	100	36	54	11	100
Nonghetto firms	96	4	100	43	43	15	100
Suburban Entrant							
All Firms (n = 44)	100	0	100	39	57	5	100
Existing Firms							
All Firms (n = 141)	96	4	100	18	49	33	100
Ghetto firms	92	8	100	16	38	46	100
Nonghetto firms	99	1	100	19	30	51	100

Level of Formal Education

The distribution of level of education between ghetto and nonghetto entre-preneurs neither definitively confirms or supports the contention that in new ghetto firms entrepreneurs have less education than entrepreneurs in the nonghetto section of the city. The results in Table 10-5 suggest that in the mail entrant survey the ghetto entrepreneur has more formal education, but the difference is significant at a very low level of confidence. On the other hand, nonghetto entrepreneurs in the interview sample and managers in existing firms have more education than their counterparts in ghetto firms. Since it is believed that the better educated were more prone to participate in the study, the nonrespondent bias in the mail entrant survey may partially explain this apparent conflict in results. The levels of confidence in the educational differentials in the city interview study and the existing firm survey were relatively high (80% and 75% respectively). On balance it is therefore concluded that entrepreneurs and managers in nonghetto firms have generally more formal education than those in ghetto enterprises.

Table 10-5
Formal Education of Entrepreneurs and Managers by Category of Firm and Type of Industry (% Distribution)

Type of Firm	Less than H.S. Grad.	H.S. Grad.	Post H.S. Experience (Nongrad.)	Tech or Bus. School Grad.	College or Univ. Grad.	Total
Entrant (Mail)						
All Firms (n = 91)	16	22	14	6	42	100
Ghetto firms	14	18	18	0	50	100
Nonghetto firms	17	24	13	8	38	100
Entrant (Interview)						
All Firms (n = 113)	20	25	27	6	22	100
Ghetto firms	30	33	15	7	15	100
Nonghetto firms	16	23	31	5	25	100
Suburban Entrant						
All Firms (n = 44)	21	12	35	2	30	100
Existing Firms						
All Firms (n = 141)	24	18	19	7	32	100
Ghetto firms	31	18	20	2	29	100
Nonghetto firms	19	18	19	11	33	100

Nature of Previous Experience

Table 10-6 presents the data on the proportion of respondents who had experience in the same industry before embarking on their own operations. The findings are fairly consistent for both the entrant and existing firms. Nonghetto entrepreneurs and managers have had more experience in the same industry than the entrepreneurs and managers in ghetto firms. The differences between ghetto and nonghetto are not statistically significant for respondents in the interview entrant sample but significant for the entrant mail survey (at the 90% level) and the survey of existing firms (at the 95% level). This is a rather important finding since it suggests that there are more entrepreneurs and managers in ghetto areas who enter with the disadvantage of unfamiliarity with some of the operations of their particular type of firm. The importance of this disadvantage, of course, may be less significant in some types of industries, but it is likely to increase the probability of failure among ghetto enterprises.

The results on the importance of several types of previous experience are somewhat conflicting. In the mail survey of entrants, the ghetto respondents stressed previous managerial experience as most important, followed by non-supervisory and finally lower level supervisory experience. The nonghetto respondents, on the other hand, stressed managerial and nonsupervisory experience as about equal in importance. In contrast, the interview entrant results showed that managerial experience was more important to nonghetto entrepreneurs than it was to ghetto entrepreneurs. It is difficult to be sure of the reason for this difference, and any conclusion from this particular result is fairly speculative.

The Entrepreneur and Financing the New Business

Financing a new business puts considerable demands on the entrepreneur's financial resources. It is likely that a fairly high proportion of the initial funding is borne by the individual, despite the possible assistance from relatives, friends, and financial institutions. Most new businesses are small as measured by the number of employees, and it is expected that the initial amount of funds invested is also quite small. Is there a difference in the amount of initial funding by type of industry and geographic location of the new business? It is also interesting to know whether some groups of entrepreneurs contribute a higher proportion of the funds than other groups. For example, do ghetto entrepreneurs have more difficulty in receiving external financing and therefore have to finance the initial investment out of their personal resources?

Financing by Type of Firm and Type of Industry

Table 10-7 shows that the initial financial investment in most new businesses is relatively small. Among the city entrant firms surveyed, about one-half said the

Table 10-6
Previous Experience of Entrepreneurs and Managers by Category of Firm and Geographic Location

Type of Firm	Experience in Same Industry (% Distribution)				Type of Experience (Index of Importance)[a]			Amount of Experience (Mean Number of Years)		
	Some	None	NA	Total	Manager	Other Sprvsry.	Non Sprvsry.	Manager	Other Sprvsry.	Non Sprvsry.
Entrant (Mail)										
All Firms (n = 91)	73	25	2	100	112	89	103	8.3	5.5	5.4
Ghetto firms	63	38	0	100	136	79	88	–	–	–
Nonghetto firms	76	21	3	100	105	90	108	–	–	–
Entrant (Interview)										
All Firms (n = 113)	68	27	5	100	112	97	94	10.2	4.9	6.6
Ghetto firms	69	28	4	100	97	103	103	–	–	–
Nonghetto firms	71	25	4	100	118	94	91	–	–	–
Suburban Entrant										
All Firms (n = 44)	68	32	0	100	130	84	91			
Existing Firms										
All Firms (n = 141)	68	28	4	100	101	99	101	12.1	2.0	2.7
Ghetto firms	60	39	2	100	100	100	100	–	–	–
Nonghetto firms	73	21	6	100	101	99	101	–	–	–

[a]This index represents the extent to which each group of managers was exposed to each type of experience before becoming an entrepreneur or senior executive. If all managers in each group indicate an exposure to each type of experience, the index is 100 for each experience.

Table 10-7
Financing of New Business by Type of Entrant and Type of Industry

	Initial Funds Invested (% Distribution)					Proportion of Funds Contributed by Entrepreneur (% Distribution)					
	⩽$10,000	10-25,000	25-100,000	>100,000	Total	0%	1-24	25-49	50-74	75-100	Total
Entrant (Interviews)											
All Firms (n = 113)	53	20	22	6	100	15	11	6	10	59	100
Manufacturing	47	23	21	9	100	10	12	2	15	61	100
Nonmanufacturing	59	16	23	2	100	19	10	10	5	57	100
Wholesale & retail	50	13	38	0	100	–	–	–	–	–	100
Services	57	21	14	7	100	–	–	–	–	–	100
Contract construction	100	0	0	0	100	–	–	–	–	–	100
Suburban Entrant											
All Firms (n = 44)	45	18	18	18	100	32	11	9	11	36	100
Manufacturing	60	20	5	15	100	26	22	13	13	26	100
Nonmanufacturing	28	17	33	22	100	38	0	5	10	48	100
Wholesale & retail	25	25	38	13	100	27	0	9	9	55	100
Services	0	17	50	33	100	50	0	0	17	33	100
Contract construction	50	0	0	50	100	0	0	0	0	100	100

funds put into the business were less than $10,000. The suburban entrants tended to involve a somewhat larger financial investment with almost one-fifth of the firms exceeding the $100,000 amount compared to about one-seventh of the city entrants with this size of investment. The difference in size of investment between city and suburban entrants was statistically significant at the 85% level.

There is apparent variation in initial funds invested by type of industry. Manufacturing city entrants invested more than did nonmanufacturing entrants in the city. This difference was significant, but only at the 50% level. It is, of course, not possible to attribute this difference solely to the nature of the industry. Obviously, the scale of operations has a great deal to do with the funds necessary to the business. In contrast, among the suburban entrants, nonmanufacturing firms involved a larger financial outlay than the manufacturing businesses (significant at the 90% level). In the suburbs, the firms in wholesale and retail trade, services, and even in the few construction firms studied received higher initial financing than manufacturing firms in the suburbs. This is a rather surprising result since, if it were possible to standardize for scale of operations, one would expect more funds necessary in manufacturing. It must therefore be tentatively concluded that the nonmanufacturing entrants in the suburbs were larger in average size than any other industrial group of entrants.

The proportion of funds actually contributed by the entrepreneur also varied by type of entrant. It is clear from Table 10-7 that in city entrants the entrepreneur contributed a higher proportion of the total funding than was the case for suburban entrants (significant difference at the 90% level). In almost two-thirds of new businesses in the city, the entrepreneur supplied more than three-quarters of the initial funds. This occurred in only about one-third of the suburban new businesses.

In the city, manufacturing entrepreneurs tended to contribute a higher proportion of initial funds than did the nonmanufacturing managers (significant difference at the 75% level). There was a significantly different result in the reverse direction among suburban entrepreneurs. These differences are difficult to explain on any theoretical grounds since manufacturing firms in the city required absolutely more funds than did manufacturing firms, while the opposite occurred in the suburbs. It was expected that as the absolute amount of funds increased the entrepreneurs contribution would decline.

Financing by Geographic Area of the City

Table 10-8 categorizes the responses by ghetto and nonghetto area of the city. The results show that ghetto firms have, generally, invested a larger amount of initial funds than have the nonghetto firms. It also shows that there is no significant difference in the proportion of funds invested by the ghetto

Table 10-8
Financing of New Business by Type of Entrant and Geographical Location

Type of Firm	Initial Funds Invested (% Distribution)					Proportion of Funds Contributed by Entrepreneur (% Distribution)					
	<$10,000	10-25,000	25-100,000	>100,000	Total	0%	1-24	25-49	50-74	75-100	Total
Entrant (interview)											
All Firms (n=113)	53	20	22	6	100	15	11	6	0	59	100
Ghetto	54	21	17	8	100	11	16	5	11	58	100
Nonghetto	52	19	23	5	100	16	9	6	9	59	100
Suburban Entrant											
All Firms (n=44)	45	18	18	18	100	32	12	9	12	36	100

entrepreneur compared to his counterpart who locates in a nonghetto area. The results provide no direct evidence that it is more difficult to finance a new enterprise in the ghetto than in other areas of the city. It is, of course, possible that black entrepreneurs in the ghetto have to contribute a higher proportion of funds than white entrepreneurs in the ghetto. This does not seem likely based on the evidence of this study since the relatively high proportion of nonwhite entrepreneurs in ghetto areas would surely have increased the proportion of all entrepreneurs in these areas who contribute a high proportion of total funds.

It is rather surprising to find that a fairly large proportion of all entrepreneurs did not contribute any of the inital funds to start their businesses. The proportion was especially high among suburban entrants with about 30% saying they contributed none of the initial financing. This practice was much less prevalent among city entrants. It is apparent that in some instances a substantial amount of funding was contributed by relatives of the entrepreneur. This finding also suggests that the franchise may be an important means of establishing a new business in the suburbs.

Conclusions

The results of the analysis of this chapter provide many insights into the regularities in entrepreneurial characteristics which are expected to be related to the nature of the industry and the location of the firm. The number of firms in each sample selected is not large enough to test hypotheses in a definitive way, but the results do provide useful information for public policy decisions.

It seems clear that potential nonwhite entrepreneurs are most likely to enter business in low-income areas of the city. Although this is probably a matter of choice as well as opportunity, it is questionable whether it is desirable for this tendency to occur. It seems likely that there are opportunities for nonwhite entrepreneurs in the suburbs and nonghetto areas of the city, and public policy should encourage blacks to locate their businesses outside as well as within the ghetto areas.

The nonwhite entrepreneur is still most likely to enter the wholesale and retail trade and service sectors, and have less previous experience in industry before starting business. In addition, the ghetto entrepreneur tends to have somewhat less education than the nonghetto entrepreneur. If the nonwhite entrepreneur is to have an equal opportunity of being successful, it may be necessary to develop an entrepreneurial training program as part of the nation's manpower program. Such a program should be something more than a business management education program; it should include practical experience in the management and operations of the industry the entrepreneur intends to enter. Perhaps a cooperative program between schools of business and on-the-job training in industry would be an appropriate format to follow.

The finding supported most of the other expected regularities discussed at the outset of the chapter. Entrepreneurs in manufacturing firms were found to have more formal education and more experience in the same industry than entrepreneurs in most nonmanufacturing industries. Entrant entrepreneurs were younger than top level managers in existing firms. However, the hypothesis that black entrepreneurs are older than white entrepreneurs was not supported. This finding may be partly attributable to public policy over the past several years which has tended to encourage increased black participation in business ownership.

In the financing of new businesses, the city entrepreneurs consistently contributed a higher proportion of the initial funds than the suburban entrepreneurs who apparently utilized external financing to a greater extent. There was no significant difference between ghetto and nonghetto entrepreneurs in the proportion of funds personally contributed to the original investment. There was no evidence from these data that ghetto entrepreneurs had to use larger or less outside funding. No doubt, entrepreneurs, ghetto and nonghetto, white and nonwhite, would benefit significantly from government programs to give financial assistance to new businesses, but the results of this study suggest that programs which give potential entrepreneurs training and experience in management probably should be given a higher priority.

Part IV:
Implications for Public Policy

11

Public Policy and Urban Labor Markets

A successful strategy for reducing the high sectoral unemployment which exists in many segments of urban labor markets probably depends on a more complete examination of the nature of labor demand and supply than contained in this study. For example, the socioeconomic environment of the local areas within the city will affect both the supply and demand for labor within the city. Consequently, the overall strategy for improving the employment potential within the ghetto should consider the influence of the level of crime, poor housing, inadequacies in the educational system, the incidence of poverty, and so forth, as well as other factors which have a more direct impact on high unemployment. The present study was not intended to deal with all the socioeconomic characteristics of the inner city, and it is therefore not possible to present here an overall solution to urban employment problems. The results of the study do, however, make it feasible to examine several possible policy options which are aimed at increasing the potential employment opportunities available to inner city residents.

Direct Assistance to Industry

Most economic evidence suggests that low-income areas of the city are not attractive geographic locations for new or expanding firms in most industries. The locational factors important to business include tax policies, the transportation costs of inputs and outputs, the local labor market, the existence of external economies, and the availability and cost of sites. The quality of these factors is usually less desirable in ghetto areas compared to other potential locations in nonghetto areas.

While nonghetto areas within metropolitan areas usually present a much more favorable combination of these factors than do the ghetto areas, there are some exceptions which do make the ghetto areas attractive to some new businesses. For example, it is relatively easy for small firms to acquire space at reasonable cost, and this may be enough to offset some of the disadvantages usually associated with ghetto areas. If, however, new firms in these areas of the city experience some initial success, their long-run expansion may prove extremely difficult because of the physical constraints of limited space or the high cost of expansion. Unless expressly induced by public policy, it is unlikely that the ghetto areas will ever become attractive locations for businesses which are

197

expected to experience long-run expansion in the scale of their operations.

Aid to Ghetto Businesses

The principle argument for assisting new business involves classifying the ghetto as an undeveloped area which can be developed through investment in its economic base. It is expected that the initial investment will generate, through a multiplier effect, a whole array of secondary effects on income and employment.

This expectation may be quite valid when discussing the relationship between developed and undeveloped national economies or even the economies of large regions of the country. The relationship between geographic areas within a city is an entirely different problem.

As pointed out earlier in the study, the size of the urban multiplier in ghetto areas is likely to be quite small,[1] and much of the indirect employment resulting from the initial investment is likely to occur in nonghetto sections of the metropolitan region. The lack of a "closed" region, similar to a national economy, results in large "leakages" of the new investment in ghetto business to other sections of the region.

The results also confirm the view that the employment multiplier is especially small in the ghetto areas of the city. A comparatively high proportion of the new businesses to ghetto residents. It is clear that, although a higher proportion of services. In addition, the predominance of family businesses which have negligible multiplier impact illustrates the inherent weakness of new businesses in reducing high unemployment in the inner core of many of the nation's cities.

The findings on the location of new businesses and the employment of local residents also cause some apprehension concerning the benefit of new ghetto businesses to ghetto residents. It is clear that, although a high proportion of employees in ghetto firms live close to the firm than is the case for nonghetto firms, many of the employees (perhaps a majority) of new ghetto firms are likely to reside outside the ghetto. This is expected especially among construction and manufacturing firms.

In addition, once the new ghetto firm becomes established, the findings suggest that the proportion of its employees living in the surrounding area declines substantially. This, of course, may not be a disadvantage provided the employees were formerly unemployed ghetto residents who were able to move out of the ghetto. The study provided no information to either confirm or reject this explanation. It therefore appears that any direct assistance to firms in urban areas should be highly selective.

A policy of direct assistance which encourages new business to move to the central core of the city or attempts to retain those already in this area is operating against powerful economic forces, and unless some conditions are attached to assistance program there is no assurance that the goal of reduced unemployment of ghetto residents will be achieved. On grounds of efficiency, the policy of direct assistance raises serious questions concerning the allocation of resources. It may therefore be necessary to justify direct assistance on the basis of equity. If this rationale is adopted, it emphasizes the need for a selective assistance program which will ensure that high urban unemployment will be reduced.

Aid to Business through Investment in Ghetto Human Resources

The criteria for selecting firms for location assistance should be based on the employment impact on ghetto residents. This may be achieved by concentrating on specific firms which employ "disadvantaged" workers. This policy is based on the notion of a tax credit for investment in human resources which is not necessarily restricted to new businesses. There are, of course, difficult administrative problems associated with the human investment tax credit approach. While it is relatively easy to audit a capital investment tax credit plan since the firm's expenditure on physical capital is readily perceivable, the evidence of expenditure of funds on the health, education, and retraining of "disadvantaged" workers is more elusive. Under a tax credit program it is not certain that the number of job opportunities will inevitably increase. There may be a risk of "displacement" of currently employed workers so that employers can receive the tax credit for hiring disadvantaged unemployed persons. It is probably for these reasons that government policy currently favors contracting separately with firms in the private sector who are prepared to make this type of investment in human resources.[2] This is the approach followed in the JOBS program where firms are reimbursed for a wide variety of costs involved in the employment of disadvantaged workers. The results of this study show that a substantial proportion of jobs are within the central core of the city. Any assistance to business should therefore concentrate on making it economically attractive to hire ghetto residents. This may be done through the JOBS type of program or any other variation of the human resource investment tax credit. It is of course recognized that the success of this approach depends to a large extent on the general level of economic activity in the urban area and the nation. It should be emphasized that while many of the policy recommendations may result in lower unemployment rates in the central cities the impact on the overall unemployment rate is likely to be marginal.

A policy which discriminates only in favor of new businesses is difficult to justify on economic grounds. There is a higher rate of failure during the early years of operating new businesses than among established firms. There may therefore be an abnormal amount of employment insecurity among the workers who receive jobs in the new enterprise. From the point of view of job development, it is desirable not to exclude established businesses from any human resource investment program designed to aid industry in the depressed sectors of urban areas.

It may be necessary, for reasons of symbolic importance in the community, to restrict aid to new businesses with minority group entrepreneurs. If this is the case, it does not seem appropriate to have geographic restrictions on the location of firms. In fact, the results of the study suggest that new businesses in nonghetto areas are larger and appear to have somewhat faster growth rates than new firms in the ghetto. If the assistance to new firms is restricted to those employing "disadvantaged" residents, the objective of the public policy of reducing high sectoral unemployment has a better chance of being achieved than would be the case if the firm had to be located in the ghetto to receive aid. If an additional feature of public policy is to develop more minority group entrepreneurs, the results of the study suggest that they should be encouraged to start their new businesses in geographic sections of the city which present the greatest opportunities rather than being restricted to ghetto areas.

Indirect Assistance to Industry

Indirect assistance may be given to industry in several forms. Ghetto businesses may receive indirect assistance either by improving the economic position of these industries by a protectionist policy or by improving the socioeconomic environment of the geographic area.

Isolating New Businesses from Competition

The economic rationale for a policy which subsidizes prices or restricts imports to protect the new business from competition is based on the alledged existence of deviations between social and private benefits and costs of production from industry in the depressed area. Such a policy, however, simply results in making products more expensive to consumers and a less than optimal use of resources. Experience suggests that this type of support of ghetto industry is an extremely ineffective solution of socioeconomic problems in the inner city.[3]

Linking the Ghetto with Other Sections of the Region

Another method of providing ghetto businesses with indirect assistance is to improve the linkages between the ghetto and the major transportation arteries in the region. In many metropolitan areas, the peripheral sections of the city are close to major highways which surround the city. In addition, these areas frequently have high-speed road and rail access to the central business district. The ghetto areas, located far from the highways which surround the city, are in most instances bypassed by the high speed arteries to the central business district.

The long-run metropolitan transit development plans typically emphasize further development of highways in the suburban ring. It is recommended that the present plans of transit development authorities be reevaluated so that the needs of ghettos within the central core may be given greater consideration. Ghetto businesses would benefit significantly from better access to the major transit routes, and new transit development plans should give high priority to this form of assistance to ghetto area.

Improving the Socioeconomic Environment of the Ghetto

The environment for attracting and retaining business within the central city would be improved substantially if the crime rate within the ghetto was reduced. Crime statistics for sections of the city reveal significant differences between ghetto and nonghetto areas. Table 11-1 shows that for all crimes, except manslaughter, larceny under $50, and embezzlement, the rates are higher in the ghetto than for the rest of the city. The size of the differential varies by general class of crime with those related to physical violence (murder, aggravated assault, and so forth occurring at a much higher rate in the ghetto than the rest of the city. In addition, crimes reflecting social difficulties, family disintegration, and broad psychological problems (prostitution, narcotics, drunkenness, offenses against the family) are much more prevalent in the ghetto. Crimes related to property are generally high throughout the city but are even higher in the ghetto. Businessmen felt that the inner city presented many locational disadvantages. These included lack of room for expansion and customer parking as well as problems of transportation access. The most serious issue, especially among smaller nonmanufacturing ghetto firms, is the fear of theft and vandalism.

Lack of employment opportunities, poverty, and other factors may be causal factors in explaining the higher crime rate in ghettos, but the high crime rate itself may restrict the growth of job opportunities simply because it raises the cost of operating a business in or near a ghetto area. A reduction in the crime rate is likely to reduce this cost and make the ghetto more attractive to new and existing businesses. If this goal is achieved, it will not only increase job opportunities in the central core but also have the additional advantage of raising the quality of life generally throughout the urban area.[a]

[a]The increase in job opportunities attributable to the reduction of crime may be partially offset by the loss of "jobs" involved in the supply of criminal activity itself. It is, of course, not certain whether or not the net effect will result in an increase in jobs. The importance of the level of crime and the quality of the local environment in influencing business location decisions suggest that the net effect will be positive.

Table 11-1

Crime Rates in Spring Garden–Compared with Philadelphia as a Whole, 1967 (per 100,000 population)

Type of Crime	Philadelphia	Spring Garden	Percentage Difference
Crimes of violence:			
Murder	11	24	118.2
Manslaughter	7	3	−57.1
Rape	22	30	36.4
Aggravated assault	163	239	46.6
Assault	301	351	16.6
Weapons	90	233	158.9
Property crimes:			
Robbery	141	169	19.8
Burglary	603	848	46.0
Larceny, $50 and over	194	230	18.6
Larceny, under $50	788	248	−5.1
Auto theft	332	387	16.6
Arson	12	30	150.0
Forgery and counterfeiting	11	12	9.1
Fraud	27	33	22.2
Embezzlement	1.5		
Stolen property	5	9	80.0
Vandalism	281	290	4.2
Crime reflecting personal psychological problems:			
Prostitution	23	78	239.1
Sex offenses	99	103	4.0
Narcotic drug laws	75	209	178.7
Gambling	273	354	29.7
Offenses against the family	17	36	111.8
Driving while intoxicated	95	103	8.4
Liquor laws	247	354	43.3
Drunkenness	1901	3496	83.9
Disorderly conduct	147	184	25.2
Vagrancy	23	24	4.3
Other:			
Suspicion	3201	3812	19.1
Traffic violations	114	160	40.3
All others	912	1510	65.5

Source: *Crime in Urban Society*, Barbara McLennan, ed. (New York: The Dunellen Press, 1970).

The interviews conducted in this study reveal a widespread and profound fear of theft, vandalism, and risk of bodily harm among businessmen. Unless this fear is reduced there is likely to be an even slower growth in job opportunities in the central city in the future. It is therefore recommended that policies to reduce the general level of crime and especially crimes against property in the central city be strongly supported.[4]

The other environmental disadvantages cited by businessmen (lack of space for expansion, and so on) will also have to be remedied if the inner city is to continue as an economically attractive area for firms. Some of the space problems may be alleviated through more systematic planning of land use in the core of the city. It may be advantageous to change current zoning laws, many of which originated several decades ago. In many cities the building codes are well out of date and not applicable to current building techniques, and therefore the updating of these codes should be an integral part of the effort to improve the city for business activity. Finally, urban renewal funds should to a greater extent be used to improve the environment for new and existing business in the central core of the city.

Indirect Means of Improving Employment
Potential of Ghetto Residents

There are many institutional factors which make it difficult for members of the labor force living in the ghetto to find employment. Racial discrimination, a relatively poor quality of education, and low levels of health services available to ghetto residents are among the basic institutional forces within urban society which, if changed, will increase the employment potential of the unemployed in the ghetto.

Institutional Adjustments and Low Productivity
of Disadvantaged Ghetto Residents

There are a number of other factors which indirectly affect the ghetto resident's ability to compete in the labor market. In order to compete effectively, participants in the market should have adequate information on job vacancies, including job requirements and wage rates. The development of the job bank concept is an institutional adjustment which is likely to increase occupational information; this type of program should be extended to all labor markets. If the job bank approach is to be successful however, it is essential that the vast majority of employers participate in the program and that the ghetto residents themselves are motivated to consult the service. Public policy should take steps to ensure that this occurs.

Another institutional factor which indirectly affects the employment of ghetto residents is the existence of minimum wages. The effect of minimum wage legislation on the employment of low-skilled workers is an issue which has been the subject of intense debate for several decades. Economic theory clearly suggests that a minimum wage level operates like any other entry restriction to employment. The minimum level raises the rate of pay for low-skilled labor. Consequently, the amount of this type of labor demanded is lower than if the rate for low-skilled labor was determined in a free labor market. The low-skilled workers who are employed are better off under the minimum wage system. On the other hand, those who cannot find employment earn no income.[5]

Despite the logic to the argument against maintaining a system of minimum wages, there are several reasons why no recommendation is made here for their abolition. In developing a strategy for solving employment problems in the central city, a distinction has to be made between feasible and acceptable solutions. It may be economically feasible to increase employment opportunities by changing minimum wage laws, but it is doubtful if such a proposal would receive legislative approval.[6]

There is another reason that the abolition of minimum wages is not an appropriate strategy. Even in the absence of wage legislation and unions representing low-skilled workers, there is strong evidence that employers themsleves are likely to develop a social minimum wage structure. Employers do not pay low or "unfair" wages partially because of union substitution techniques. Many employers feel that if they perform some of the functions the union provides workers then the need for the union is largely eliminated and the employer may avoid having his business unionized. In addition, many employers feel that offering relatively high wages of unskilled work will result in a large number of applicants and the choice of employees will be greater. There is also apparently some satisfaction in being known as a "good firm to work for."

The problem of lack of flexibility of the wage structure in adjusting to potential employees whose marginal revenue of labor is below the minimum wage level is recognized for some groups of disadvantaged workers. For example, many nonprofit organizations which operate small workshops designed to train and rehabilitate handicapped workers are permitted by the U.S. Department of Labor to pay less than the minimum wage to their disadvantaged employees. These workshops sell their output to increase the revenue of the nonprofit organization but the major purpose is to provide assistance to the "clients" (workers) who are "disadvantaged."

Many residents of the ghetto are also disadvantaged, and by the criteria established by employers to perform in the work process, many of the long-term unemployed are handicapped. Experience under the JOBS program has shown that many employees enrolled in the program have to receive medical assistance before entering the training phase of the program. It is also necessary in many instances to provide trainees with motivational and other sociopsychological assistance so that they can adjust to the integrated work pattern associated with modern industry. A JOBS program contract specifically recognizes that during the initial training period the trainee's productivity is lower than achieved by the average worker on the job, and the employer is compensated for the production lost through employing a disadvantaged worker.

An alternative method of handling the low productivity of some ghetto residents is to permit nonprofit organizations to set up workshops for employing and training disadvantaged workers and exempt such workers from the minimum wage law until it is shown that their output is similar to the average output for the particular type of work. It is recommended that this approach be tested on an experimental basis since considerable administrative, rehabilitation, and training problems may make such a program impractical.

A major concern with this approach to training and employment is that there is little incentive for the workshop administrator to encourage the trainee to leave the program and enter the regular labor market. Consequently, if a trainee has acquired the ability and experience to work with another firm but is retained by the workshop, it is possible that wage "exploitation" may occur. This may be prevented by making the organization subject to the Taft-Hartley law as amended and permitting labor unions to organize the trainees. Labor unions are also concerned with the competition created by the output of the workshops. This is not likely to be serious unless the growth of workshops is substantial.

The experimental project designed to test the feasibility of workshops for disadvantaged ghetto residents should consider which legal form of organization is most appropriate. It may be that a cooperative organization is more likely to attract the community support which is essential to ensure the success of this type of program.

Reduction of Restrictive Practices in the Labor Market

Restrictive practices are associated with all occupational levels within the labor market. They are not deliberately intended to discriminate against the ghetto resident but since the "qualifications" criteria used to restrict entry into many types of jobs emphasizes formal training and educational achievement, the ghetto resident is usually at a disadvantage. The "qualifications" used in the applicant selection process frequently have little connection with ability to perform the job successfully.

Research and the experience in the placement of graduates of manpower programs reveal that entry level tests and examinations are frequently out of date. In instances where licensing is required, the examinations are given infrequently, at locations which make it difficult for many to attend, and little publicity is given concerning forthcoming examinations.

The justification for licensing is based on the criterion that failure to perform the job (or service) satisfactorily results in considerable economic costs. For this reason, in many professional occupations it is necessary to ensure a minimum standard of competence. The same is true for many nonprofessional occupations such as diamond cutters and skilled craftsmen working on complex products like those produced in the aerospace industry. It is clear, however, that the training and experience required before one is permitted to enter many trades is in excess of the actual skill demanded on the jobs which most tradesmen are required to perform throughout their career.

The divergence between training and job requirements is most widely discussed in relation to the construction industry. There has recently been considerable criticism of union influence in the apprenticeship program and the examination system. It is frequently alleged that the unions in the construction industry have used the apprenticeship system to restrict entry. This restriction on labor supply improves the union's bargaining power and increases their ability to raise wages. This type of labor market restriction makes it difficult for those without the education and experience to compete for all jobs in the industry, even though many of these jobs are not highly skilled. In the construction industry, the union refers workers (through a hiring hall) to employers. This control gives the union additional power to influence the supply of labor to the industry.

In urban areas a high proportion of city jobs are located near the ghettos. It is therefore imperative that ghetto residents are not handicapped in finding employment because of some of the restrictive labor market practices described above. It is recommended that the government introduce policies which give ghetto residents an opportunity to work at jobs equivalent to their skill level. In the construction industry, for example, there is no logical reason why the unions and construction firms with the assistance of government should not consider changing its union hiring hall as a labor market institution.

Reducing or eliminating restrictive practices in the construction industry will increase job opportunities for ghetto residents. Most of these jobs will, of course, be in the less skilled construction occupations. Increasing the ease of entry into construction employment will not result in a substantial reduction in ghetto unemployment since the construction industry only accounts for about 5% of city employment. In order to increase job opportunities for inner-city residents, it is therefore essential that restrictive practices in all industries be examined. The government should attempt to ensure that the tests actually measure the ability to do the job and do not discriminate on any other grounds.

The government has recently introduced various "home town" plans to ensure that minority employees have an opportunity to a larger share of jobs in the construction occupations than they have had in the past. In addition, employers receiving government contracts are required to indicate goals and timetables for hiring minority group members including women. In the decade ahead it is essential that current equal employment legislation be effectively enforced. Unless minority workers and women receive their fair share of job opportunities the sectoral differences in the unemployment rate are likely to persist. Government must work with both labor and management to ensure that increased labor market opportunities for minorities and women means access to job opportunities at all occupational levels.

Improving the Intracity Transit System

Ghetto residents live in close proximity to a large proportion of city jobs. A major feature of the strategy to reduce ghetto unemployment should therefore concentrate on making the ghetto labor supply more competitive in this inner-city geographic labor market. Ghetto residents may be a noncompeting group for reasons such as lack of skill and experience in type of jobs available, lack of information about job opportunities, discrimination in the labor market, and so on. Difficulties in traveling to work may reduce the ghetto resident's ability to compete in the urban labor market.

Despite the fact that on the basis of average daily highway time ghetto residents are within forty minutes of over 75% of all city jobs, lack of access to central city jobs may still be a problem for the unemployed in the inner city.

The analysis of public transit travel time by geographic section of the city revealed that, despite the close air-mile distance of all ghetto areas to the center of the city, many parts of the ghetto were bypassed by the main public transit routes connecting the middle income residential areas with the central business district. These geographic pockets of isolation in the ghetto are especially serious since studies of low-income areas reveal that the proportion of families who own a car is much less for ghetto residents than for those living in other sections of the city. A recent study of families in North Philadelphia showed that approximately 30% owned a car.[7] The commuting time by public transit is much higher than by auto, and it takes some ghetto residents over an hour to travel from their homes to the most distant points within the inner core of the city. This indicates the need to improve the public transit system in the city, especially within the inner city. The data on journey to work suggest that, unless employees have an auto, even ghetto firms may not be easily accessible to many unemployed residents of the central city.

Specific Recommendations for Improvement of Transit System

The improvement of public transit within the inner core is likely to have a more significant impact on high unemployment than improvement in transportation between the central business district and the outlying residential sections of the city. It is for this reason that top priority should be given to improving the transit system in the core of the city.

Most cities have increasingly used a network of one-way streets to increase the rate of traffic flow in the downtown section of the city. It is recommended that this approach be continued and the use of specific one-way streets restricted to public transit vehicles.

These "public transit" streets should radiate from the central business district to the periphery of the *inner core* of the city. In some instances it may be possible to develop some transit routes which link the ghetto with other sections of the inner core which have a large number of jobs. For example, it may be possible to link North Philadelphia (north of the central business district) by surface transit with the southern fringe of the city (south of the central business district) without actually traveling through the central business district. The fastest link between ghetto areas and the sections with job opportunities would, of course, be by subway in this case, and it would be necessary to pass through the central business district. The cost of extending and developing spurs to existing subway lines are probably prohibitive in most central cities, and it is therefore necessary to consider adjustments to the surface transit network.

The speed of surface transit tends to decrease once traffic enters the central business district. It is therefore recommended that private autos be banned from the heart of the central business district and parking facilities be provided around the fringe of the central business district. The main opposition to proposals which ban autos from the center city area usually comes from the downtown department stores, restaurants, theatres, parking lot owners and so forth. The opposition would be much less if the parking areas were within walking distance of the shopping district or if there existed jitney bus service linking the parking lots with various parts of the central business district.

It is recommended that the cost and benefits of using jitney buses in the inner city be studied. These buses may be more economical to operate, and for the same expenditure of funds as used to operate the traditional buses the service can be improved. Jitney buses have the advantage of taking little curb space for bus stops—an important consideration in a congested downtown area.

A major feature of most urban transit development plans is the improvement of the service (usually subway service) between the central business district and the middle-class residential sections of the city. In many instances, this is a response to the need to revitalize the downtown shopping area. In Philadelphia, for example, it is proposed that the subway be extended into the residential Northeast section of the city. Such transit development proposals are important to the future of the entire central city. They are designed to attract middle-income shoppers to the downtown area, and since this indirectly increases the job opportunities for ghetto residents, it should be encouraged. This would facilitate commutation of white-collar workers to the central business district.

Another goal of plans to improve the transit network is to transport middle- and upper-income residents to employment opportunities in the central business district. Perhaps in planning future transit lines, more concern should be given to extending the network to the areas of the city which have a large number of jobs and in which it appears that the demand for labor is expanding. For example, in Philadelphia if the goal of improving the transit system is to serve the outlying sections of the city where the job opportunities are located, the proposed subway extension would probably have been scheduled for the Northwest section of the city. This, of course, assumes that the Northwest will continue to be an area of expanding economic activity. It is, therefore, recommended that in the development of public transit, the linking of areas of labor surplus in the inner city with areas of expanding job opportunities be given *at least* as high a priority as the proposals designed to transport residents of middle-income areas to the central business district.

The more rapid growth of job opportunities outside the central city has resulted in several experimental programs for transporting unemployed ghetto residents to outlying plants which experience a shortage of labor. In some instances, the company operates the busing program; in others the program is run by a community organization. The results of these programs have been disappointing. The participation of ghetto residents was less than expected and the programs proved very expensive.

As a practical matter, such "reverse commuting" programs must be incorporated into the public transit service. The simplest method of achieving this integration is to revise the pricing system in public transit. The details of a new pricing system requires accurate knowledge of the demand for the service according to distance traveled, time of day, and direction of travel. It is possible, however, to outline the general features of a revised pricing system.

Most urban transit systems have a single price fare structure with an additional small charge for one or two distance zones or for transfer from one form of transit to another. The result of this pricing system is that the cost per mile traveled is lower for those commuting from the outlying residential areas compared to cost to the inner-city resident.

One method of increasing the unemployed inner-city resident's normal preference area for employment is to lower the cost of commuting from the ghetto to the outlying areas of the city. For this reason, it is recommended that the public transit fare from the center of the city to the outskirts of the city be reduced by perhaps 50% or more during the morning rush hour (perhaps 7 to 9 A.M.). In the evening rush hour, the fare for traveling towards the center of the city would be reduced by a similar proportion. The additional cost of such a proposal would be small since the crews, vehicles, tracks and so forth, are already available and paid for to handle the rush hour traffic in the dominant direction.

The method used to subsidize the fare of inner-city residents traveling in the reverse direction of the commuting pattern deserves careful study. It may even be preferable to charge zero fare for reverse commuting. There are cost advantages to the zero fare proposal since the fare collection procedure is completely illiminated. Consequently the cost reduction may completely offset the loss of revenue caused by not charging any fare. In order to avoid subsidizing middle-income groups living in the central business district and working in the outskirts of the city, it may be advisable to use a voucher system, perhaps financed by Model Cities' funds. The problem with this proposal is that the additional administrative costs may not be justified.

The reduction of reverse commuting costs would encourage ghetto residents to commute to potential job opportunities outside the inner city. Depending on the elasticity of demand for public transit by direction and time of day, this proposal may actually have little impact on the transit authority's earnings. There is ample precedent for this type of differential pricing. The "shoppers special" fare during offpeak load time, which is commonly used by railroads and bus transit to attract additional customers, is similarly based on variations in elasticity of demand.[8] Since the cost of special programs to transport unemployed ghetto residents to plants outside the inner city is excessive the differential pricing proposal is suggested as an alternative policy which is economically feasible.

Investment in Human Resources in the Ghetto

The entry of new businesses into the central city does cause a small increase in the number of job opportunities and as a result helps reduce the urban unemployment rate. The pattern of the entry-exit behavior of firms does, however, raise some serious questions as to whether encouraging new businesses is the most appropriate means of reducing the high unemployment rates in some sections of the city, especially within the central core of the city.

Investment in Ghetto Businesses or
Investment in Ghetto Human Resources

The geographic pattern of firms entering and leaving the city showed that the ghetto areas gained less jobs than nonghetto areas. This difference between ghetto and nonghetto areas was consistent for both absolute number of jobs and the relative increase in employment as a proportion of the total employment in each geographic section of the city. In fact, one ghetto area showed an absolute decline in employment attributable to the entry and exit of businesses.

The industrial distribution of new businesses also suggests that they have a potentially small impact on employment problems in the ghetto. For example, over 80% of the net increase in ghetto employment, due to firms entering and leaving, occurs in either the service or wholesale and retail trade sectors; manufacturing showed an absolute decline in number of jobs. This loss of manufacturing jobs was largely attributable to one ghetto area, where it appears extremely difficult to continue a self-generating manufacturing economy.

The signs of weakness in manufacturing in the city does not apply to all types of manufacturing. Though definite conclusions on the employment situation in detailed industries cannot be based on cross-sectional data, there are indications that in food processing, electrical machinery, and fabricated and primary metal manufacturing new businesses do increase employment opportunities. There is also some evidence to suggest that manufacturing in the city shows signs of the declining importance in types of manufacturing which require production on a large scale. In the city, there appears to be a tendency towards the manufacture of specialized products which are supplied to other large-scale manufacturing industries in the metropolitan region.

The geographic distribution of total employment, that is the employment in existing firms as well as the net employment effect of entrant-exit behavior, shows that a high proportion of city-wide jobs are within the central core of the city. The net employment effect of new businesses does not change this basic finding, but it is apparent that central core employment is not likely to grow as rapidly as the employment growth in other sections of the metropolitan area.

Some policy responses to these conclusions have already been suggested. First, any assistance to new businesses should be highly selective and should link assistance directly to the employment of "disadvantaged" members of the labor force, rather than provide assistance to new entrepreneurs simply because the new business is located in the ghetto. A second series of recommendations, aimed at extending the ghetto resident's normal preference area of employment, included improvement of the public transit system within the central core. Finally, it is recommended that top priority be given to making ghetto residents more competitive in the central city labor markets. This change in the quality of labor supply may be achieved through a series of manpower training programs which are focused within the ghetto areas of the city. It is, therefore, recommended that the geographic concept used in the Concentrated Employment Program continue to be the major approach to making unemployed ghetto residents more competitive in their search for job opportunities. This is not meant to imply that this program has been successful, only that the high impact approach is the most appropriate for any labor supply policy which seeks to reduce high unemployment among ghetto residents. On the grounds of employment impact, the study provides no support for a general policy which provides aid for new businesses in the ghetto. The high priority assigned to the CEP concepts does not, of course, preclude improvements in the organization and administration of the specific programs included within specific CEP programs.

Type of Investment in Ghetto Human Resources

The nature of investment in human resources depends upon the distribution of the manpower budget among the various groups of "disadvantaged" workers. For example, should priority be given to raising the labor productivity of the unemployed before any attempt is made to increase the skills of the under-employed residents of the inner city. Experience in recruiting and training for some manpower programs has shown that the cost of retraining is higher for the long-term unemployed worker than for someone currently working either short-time or in a job which requires a lower level of skill than the worker is capable of providing (i.e., underemployed). To achieve a better benefit-cost relationship, it is recommended that more emphasis be given to retraining the underemployed than has been the usual practice in many manpower programs.

It is also necessary to set priorities among the various age groups of disadvantaged workers. The return from an investment which raises the produc-tivity of a worker is partially a function of the number of years over which the return is accrued. For this reason, long-term investment in programs designed for children and teenagers (e.g., Job Corps and some Neighborhood Youth Corps programs) produce a much larger flow of income than programs designed to retrain middle-aged unemployed workers. These examples of youth programs are cited only as illustrations. It may be that evaluation studies will show that these programs should be replaced by a more efficient type of program. The policy of concentrating on youths is the correct approach, irrespective of the some negative evaluation results. In the allocation of the manpower budget among the various programs, political and equity considerations are frequently as important as the economic costs and benefits of the programs. Therefore, the shift in priority should be achieved through additional emphasis on youth-oriented programs rather than the elimination of programs designed for middle-aged workers, provided of course that budget constraints will permit.

In recent years, several manpower programs have been concerned with increasing the labor-force participation rate of some groups of individuals. For example, the Work Incentive Program (WIN) and to some extent the administra-tion's Opportunities for Families (OFF) are designed to increase the participa-tion rate of heads of households receiving welfare assistance. Such programs are not likely to reduce the unemployment rate in ghettos but will result in some increase in the employment of ghetto residents. If the participants in these programs are successful in acquiring job opportunities, the economy in the inner city is likely to benefit. For this reason, the main purpose of both the WIN and OFF programs should be supported so long as the economic benefits exceed the costs.

There are important benefits to be gained from increasing the labor-force participation rate of women residents of the core of the city. As discussed earlier in the study, an increasingly large proportion of ghetto households are headed by women. Provided the family needs can be met at a reasonable cost without the women at home, the economic status of the family will be improved by assisting the head of the household to enter the labor force. In the case of ghetto families headed by a male, there are also obvious economic benefits to having the wife enter the labor force.

A major cost associated with raising the labor force participation is providing the day-care facilities. The cost per child varies with quality of service, the medical health of the child (costs increase substantially for handicapped children), and the size of the center. The estimated annual national cost per child for group day care ranges from $1245 to $2320 depending on quality of service.[9] If women heads of households are to be able to enter the labor force, a substantial portion of the operational cost of day care centers must be borne by the federal and/or state governments. If public funds are used for this purpose, individual benefits obviously exceed individual costs. It is not certain whether the benefits to society will exceed the costs but as far as rehabilitating the inner city, it seems clear that such programs are potentially very attractive solutions to some of the problems posed by high sectoral unemployment.

Long-Run Solutions to Unemployment in the Inner City

Many of the policies suggested as solutions to urban employment problems are not likely to have an immediate impact on the high unemployment rate in the ghetto. Urban renewal projects improve the environment in the inner city, but the cost of rehabilitation in the city is so high that only a slow, gradual change in the ghetto is possible. The expenditure of large amounts of funds will solve some urban problems, but a substantial payoff will not be achieved for many years.

One possible long-run solution is to encourage the ghetto residents to move to parts of the suburban ring where the rate of increase in job opportunities is greatest. There are several difficulties with proposals which attempt to relocate low-income residents. The economic cost of relocation is not easily borne by the long-term unemployed, and many persons living in substandard housing conditions have shown a great deal of reluctance to move to an unfamiliar area even if it has meant an improvement in living conditons. There is little evidence in the nonghetto areas of the metropolitan area, and especially in the suburban counties, that discrimination in housing is likely to diminish rapidly. Legislation to change the zoning laws in suburban areas so that it is possible to build low and middle income homes and apartments should be supported. Open housing legislation without changes in the zoning laws is not likely to be effective in moving ghetto residents to the employment growth sectors of the metropolitan area.

One of the most effective methods of giving the ghetto resident the opportunity to leave the ghetto is to raise his labor productivity. As a long-run approach, it is essential that attention be focused on future labor force participants. This requires major changes in urban educational systems. Suburban school districts frequently allocate more dollars per pupil than do city systems, despite the fact that the difficulty of educating a ghetto child frequently requires more specialized services. However, increased expenditure per pupil in urban school systems is no guarantee of improved quality of the educational product. Fundamental reforms in the structure of the system are likely to produce improvements.

Many suburban children have had preschool experience in nursery schools, and it seems that the marginal return from investing at the beginning of the educational process has a high payoff. It is therefore recommended that public education begin a year earlier than has been the traditional practice. It also seems appropriate to experiment with curriculum changes which may make it possible to reduce the number of years taken to graduate from high school. Most of these proposed changes have been suggested by educators but little has been done to implement them. Unless some fundamental change is made to increase the labor productivity of ghetto youth, relocation proposals are not likely to be successful in reducing the high unemployment in the inner city.

Solutions to the employment problems of the city are closely interrelated. Policies to reduce high unemployment in the cities must be consistent with current macroeconomic policy. For example, if the government is attempting to stimulate business activity, it may offer an investment tax credit to firms. Perhaps this tax credit could be applied to the redevelopment of urban land use for industry. It is clear, however, that unless the productivity of ghetto residents is increased, it will be extremely difficult for them to improve their economic status. An increase in productivity and skills is necessary before many ghetto residents can be employed in such a manner as to substantially raise their living standards. This vicious cycle of low productivity, high unemployment, and unstable family relationships must be broken if ghetto residents are to be helped over the long run in any significant manner.

Appendixes

Appendix A:
Data Collection and
Method of Analysis

The study involved several major problems of data collection. Some of these relate to the adaptation of employment information collected by the city of Philadelphia as a by-product of the city wage-tax system, while others are concerned with the difficulties associated with collecting original data from a sample of employees. The following discussion outlines these problems and shows how they were handled. The analytical approach used and its limitations are also discussed.

Classification of Business Enterprises

The movement of industrial activity and consequently the geographic location of labor demand are determined by decisions made by several types of enterprises. The relocation of existing establishments is only one type of movement affecting the demand for labor. To an even greater degree, geographic shifts in demand are the result of the expansion and contraction of existing operations (including the opening and closing of branch plants), the entry of new enterprises, and the death of others. In this project the various types of enterprises are categorized as follows:

Entrant. An entrant is defined as a new establishment within the city. This would include the entirely new business which emerges within the city and also establishments which have previously been in operation outside the city and have decided to move into the city. Many entrepreneurs who have incorporated or otherwise changed the legal status of their firm may regard their organization to be a new entrant. The employment impact of such a change is likely to be negligible in the short run, and consequently an attempt will be made to exclude such firms from the analysis.

Exit. An exit is a city establishment which goes out of business or which moves to a location outside the city. A firm which changes its legal status and continues in operation within the city under another name is excluded from this definition of an exit.

Relocatee. A relocatee is a firm which moves its location within the city.

Suburban entrant. A suburban entrant is a new establishment which locates in the Philadelphia SMSA other than Philadelphia county.

217

Firms not relocating. These are the firms that were located within the city before the benchmark year of the study (1967) and did not change that location during 1967.

Within each of the above firm types, the enterprise may be either a single or multiestablishment organization. In this study, the individual firms studied in depth are all single establishments.

Basic Data Sources

The mercantile license file and the wage tax records of the city of Philadelphia provided the basic data for the study. Each new establishment (for both single and multiestablishment organizations) must have a mercantile license from the city. Similarly, a change of address and exit from business must also be reported. This identified the geographic location of the firms studied. The city collects a wage tax from employers based on the wages paid to employees. The tax is paid either monthly or quarterly, depending on the amount of wages paid by the firm. In the report, the total number of employees and the amount of wages paid for the reporting period is indicated.

From the mercantile license, it was possible to collect data on each firm's address, its standard industrial classification number (SIC), and a tax account number. It was also possible to match the tax account number with the same number in the wage tax file which produced additional data on the firm's number of employees wages paid and wage tax paid. Since the study required data on segments of the population of firms (entrants, exits, and so on) the data collection procedure involved a considerable amount of manual coding as well as keypunching and machine time.

The data system which permitted matching a firm's returns for several forms of taxes through use of the master account number was a relatively recent innovation in data organization. Consequently, the study was essentially designed as a cross-sectional analysis with 1967 as the benchmark year. The selection of this year was fortuitous since it was relatively free of distortions associated with fluctuating levels of economic activity.

Separate decks of cards containing the basic data were prepared for the population of entrants, exits, and relocatees firms. The population of suburban entrants was not available from the city of Philadelphia records. A list of the 1967 entrants into two suburban counties was obtained from the Pennsylvania Bureau of Employment Security. The list also identified each firm's SIC number and estimated employment. Suburban entrants which did not have any employees (this is a fairly large number in any year) and organizations not covered by the state unemployment insurance law were excluded from the list. However, this source of data was valuable for selecting a sample of suburban entrants for detailed study.

The city records also provided a proxy for the basic data on the large group of firms which did not change their location during 1967. It was not possible, however, to secure the information for 1967. It was feasible to acquire the information on each firm's SIC number, address, employment, wages and taxes paid as of September 30, 1968 and 1969. These data on some 80,000 firms, both single and multiestablishment, provided a useful benchmark for assessing the relative importance of entrants and exits in creating job opportunities within the city.

Nature of Data and Method of Analysis

The employment implications of the behavior of firms in the central city during 1967 are based on the analysis of two major types of data. At the macro level, data were collected for the population of single-establishment firm entrants, exits, relocatees, and all existing firms. As previously discussed, these data include a limited amount of basic information on each firm's address, SIC number, employment, and wages paid. More detailed information was also collected from a sample of entrants and existing firms by conducting a mail survey and in-depth interviews with senior executives of the firms.

Mail Questionnaire

The questionnaire solicited several categories of information. Several questions focused on the personal characteristics of the entrepreneur which permitted an exploration of the entrepreneurial supply function in various industries. The questionnaire was also designed to collect data on the respondent's estimate of the advantages and disadvantages of the firm's location. Finally, the firm was asked to supply information on total employment on selected dates and details of its current occupational structure.

The mail survey sampling procedure was based on a technique which stratified the respondents by geographic area of the city and type of industry. The population of 1967 entrant firms was arrayed by geographic area and the proportion of entrants in each area. The total sample of 750 (11% sample) was distributed among the areas according to the proportion of total entrants in each area. The distribution of the sample was as follows:

Geographic Area	Proportion of Total Entrants (%)	Number of Firms in Sample	Percentage of Firms in Sample (approx.)
West Philadelphia	15	112	15
South Philadelphia	14	105	14
Center City	14	105	14

Geographic Area	Proportion of Total Entrants (%)	Number of Firms in Sample	Percentage of Firms in Sample (approx.)
Spring Garden	5	38	5
North Philadelphia	15	112	15
Northwest Philadelphia	16	120	16
Northeast Philadelphia	16	120	16
Frankford	5	38	5
Total	100	750	100

The industrial distribution was obtained by arranging the population of entrants in each area by SIC numbers. The first firm in the sample from a particular geographic area was selected at random. The second firm was selected according to an appropriate interval which would produce the necessary number of firms to be selected from the particular geographic area. This procedure was followed for each geographic area.

For comparative purposes it was also decided to survey a sample of existing firms. The sample of existing firms was chosen by a procedure similar to the one used for selecting the entrant firms. The 1967 population of firms excluding 1967 entrants was about 72,000 firms. These firms were arranged by geographic area and the sample distribution was as follows:

Geographic Area	Proportion of Total Entrants (%)	Number of Firms in Sample	Percentage of Firms in Sample (approx.)
West Philadelphia	15	144	15
South Philadelphia	11	82	11
Center City	19	142	19
Spring Garden	4	31	4
North Philadelphia	13	99	13
Northwest Philadelphia	17	122	17
Northeast Philadelphia	15	115	15
Frankford	6	44	6
Total	100	750	100

The sample within each geographic area was selected by random numbers from a list of firms arranged by SIC number.

In-Depth Interviews

The schedule for the in-depth interviews contained most of the questions posed in the mail questionnaire. This provided additional responses on a small number of employment and locational questions. In addition, the interviews produced some detailed information on the occupational structure of the firms studied and the personal characteristics (age, sex, race, residential location, and so on) of the employees. The characteristics of the entrepreneur were also probed.

The sample of firms included in the interview phase of the study is relatively small with some 200 entrants initially selected. It was therefore not possible to stratify by every major SIC or every geographic area of the city. It was decided to concentrate on the several largest SICs within each major type of industrial category. It was also decided to divide the city into "ghetto" and "nonghetto" areas and have both groups represented without being concerned about proportionate representation from each of the eight areas of the city. In addition to the sample selected from the city of Philadelphia tax records, a group of the twenty largest entrant firms listed in the Pennsylvania Bureau of Employment Security 1967 report of new businesses was also included.[a] Based on these criteria the following procedure was used in selecting the sample of entrants.

The sample was broken down into seven major groups: (1) the twenty largest BES firms; (2) large manufacturing SICs; (3) transportation; (4) finance, insurance, real estate; (5) wholesale and retail trade; (6) services; and (7) construction.

The five most important major groups were selected from the manufacturing SICs represented in the city. These groups were textile mills, apparel, printing, fabricated metal, and machinery. A total of seventy firms were chosen from these five. The seventy firms were proportionally divided among the five groups based on population.

A total of ten firms were selected from transportation. They were divided between the two largest SICs (forty-two and forty-nine). Within each SIC there was a separation into ghetto and nonghetto areas, again proportionally divided.

The next title—finance, insurance and real estate—had a total of thirty firms proportionally divided between the two largest SICs (sixty-four and sixty-five) and then subdivided into ghetto and nonghetto within each SIC.

Forty sample firms from wholesale and retail trade were selected from the four largest SICs (fifty-eight, fifty-nine, fifty-four and fifty-one). They were also distributed proportionally within each SIC into ghetto and nonghetto. Services were allocated a total of thirty firms which were proportionally divided into the two largest SICs (seventy-two and seventy-three) and then divided into ghetto and nonghetto areas. A similar procedure was used to distribute a sample of twenty-five construction firms.

Within the constraints discussed above, the cards used for the sample were selected on a random basis, by use of a random number table. Cards were

---

[a]This is an internal report of firms reporting the number of employees for purposes of Unemployment Insurance. The report was made available for research purposes by the Pennsylvania Bureau of Employment Security, Pennsylvania Department of Labor and Industry, Harrisburg, Pennsylvania.

counted out for each industrial title. Then the addressees for each card were written down from the city's master tax billing file.

Table A-1

Distribution of Sample of Entrant Firms by Industry and Geographic Area

| SIC Number | Firms | Number of Firms | | |
		Ghetto	Nonghetto	Total SIC
(1)	20 largest BES Firms[a]			20
(2)	Major manufacturing SIC			70
22	Textile		8	
23	Apparel		16	
27	Printing		17	
34	Fabricated Metal		15	
35	Machinery		14	
(3)	Transportation			10
42		1	4	5
49		3	2	5
(4)	Finance, Insurance and Real Estate			30
64		3	12	15
65		5	10	15
(5)	Wholesale and Retail			40
51		3	3	6
54		7	3	10
58		7	5	12
59		6	6	12
(6)	Services			30
72		9	7	16
73		5	9	14
(7)	Construction			25
17		12	13	25

[a]The data collected from respondent firms in this group were divided into ghetto and non-ghetto categories.

Firm Exists, Relocatees, and Suburban Entrants

Some comparative data on several categories of firms besides Philadelphia entrants and existing firms were also collected. The purpose of this was to compare the basic characteristics of the various types of firms. A sample of some fifty entrants to the suburban ring (Delaware and Montgomery counties) was selected from the records of the Pennsylvania Bureau of Employment Security list of new entrants for 1967. In-depth interviews were conducted using an interview schedule similar to the one administered to the sample of Philadelphia entrants.

Each year a large number of firms change their location within the city. Preliminary investigation showed that many firms move within the first few years after entry. It was decided to collect some basic employment and locational information from a sample of twenty relocatee firms. Similarly, a very large number of firms do not renew their mercantile license since they stop conducting business within the city. Although it is difficult to contact exiting firms, an attempt was made to collect data from twenty of these firms.

Method of Analysis

The method of analysis varies with the particular hypothesis being studied. For example, from the macro level data on the characteristics of all firms in the city, it is possible to utilize simple correlation analysis to examine the relationship between the size of firm and distance from the center of the city. On the other hand, some of the data collected at the micro level describes the characteristics of the individual firms in categorical terms, and it is necessary to rely on a standard descriptive statistical presentation of data.

The most basic feature of the analysis is the comparison of results by the firm's geographic location within the city. The geographic subdivision of the city shown in Figure 2-1 is based on the boundaries used by several federal and local agencies with programs in the city of Philadelphia. The socioeconomic characteristics of these geographic sections is discussed in Chapter 2.

Data Limitations

Some characteristics of the data pose several difficult methodological problems in addition to the usual difficulties associated with collecting data from original sources. The most important data problems associated with the survey approach are the following.

Low Response Rate and Nonrespondent Bias

The response rate to the mail questionnaire was low (about 15% responded) and the rate of useable questionnaires was somewhat lower. This low response rate was not unexpected since the population surveyed was largely composed of rather small (less than ten employees) firms who had only been in business at their current location for a short time. New entrepreneurs frequently do not have administrative assistance to handle the routine functions of payroll, tax returns, and so forth. Consequently, a questionnaire is viewed as another unnecessary administrative task which is as unpleasant to complete as business tax returns.

More important than the low response rate is the apparent bias in the industrial distribution of responses for some groups of firms. Table A-2 shows the distribution of responses for each type of firm studied. For the firms which entered Philadelphia in 1967, it is clear that although the mail and interview samples were drawn from the same population of firms, the responses by type of industry were quite different. The mail responses included a very high proportion of firms from business services and retail trade. Few manufacturing firms responded to the mail questionnaire. The interviews of entrant firms represents a wider distribution of firms by type of industry and is more representative of the population of entrant firms. The interviews also provide sufficient data in most broad industry groups to permit comparative analysis of the responses. The dearth of responses from manufacturing firms in the mail survey of entrants restricts the extent of the analysis possible.

In the interview section of city entrant firms, the system of back up samples gave a fairly good response rate with some 100 interviews successfully completed. The goal of 200 interviews was not achieved because of lack of participation and the difficulty in arranging interviews given the time schedule of the project. The higher response rate for the interviews resulted in less nonrespondent bias than was the case in the mail survey. Since there is a difference in the extent of bias in these two sets of data it was decided to present the results separately.

The mail survey of existing firms produced a somewhat higher response rate (over 20%) than was achieved in the mail survey of entrant firms. Unfortunately, there was also a lack of responses from manufacturing firms, and the underrepresentation of these firms restricts the extent to which the type of industry can be subdivided for purposes of analysis. The suburban sample contains a fairly high proportion of manufacturing firms. The proportionate distribution of industries in this sample is quite similar to the sample of entrant interviews conducted in the city. Consequently, the data from these two samples can be usefully compared.

Considerable difficulty was experienced in locating firms which had exited from the city in 1967 or firms which had changed the address of their place of business. As shown in Table A-2 the number of respondent firms is relatively small and their distribution among the twenty-two industries results in no responses from many industries. Since the number of relocatees and exits is so small in relation to the population in each category, the data collected can give no more than a superficial feel for the nature of the firms and the motivations of the entrepreneurs. In some of the substantive chapters, it was possible to merge the data from the entrant interview and entrant questionnaire. This increased the number of responses considerably and improved the reliability of the data.

Table A-3 shows the geographic location and the form of business organization of the respondent firms. For the groups of firms which were contacted personally by the interviewers, about two-thirds of the respondents are incorporated businesses. In contrast, for respondents in the mail survey, the proportion of incorporated businesses dropped to about one-third. It is expected that the sole proprietorships and partnerships are, on the average, smaller in size than corporations. Consequently, the data from existing firms and the mail entrants are probably slightly biased in that large firms are underrepresented. This is not likely to be a problem in the analysis, though small firms may have a less complex occupational structure than large firms.

Table A-3 also shows the geographic distribution of respondents from each group of firms. Both low income and high income geographic areas are well represented among all groups of city firms. There are, of course, more firms from the high income areas, but this reflects the distribution of the population of firms in the city. The specific geographic areas within both of the broad geographic classifications of low and high income areas are not equally represented, but this is not likely to affect the study's purpose of comparing firms by the socioeconomic characteristics of their geographic location. Firms located within the central business district were also included in the survey. This geographic area is a high income area, but its industrial structure and residential characteristics are quite different than the areas included in the high income category.

The problem of possible bias among nonrespondents was clearly not significant among the entrant and suburban interviews; the sampling procedure had ensured good representation by type of industry and geographic location. From what was known about the population of firms, it was evident that there was some nonrespondent bias in the mail survey. Manufacturing entrant and existing firms were somewhat underrepresented, though the extent of this bias was small, especially in the entrant category, since relatively few manufacturing firms entered business in 1967 in the city. The nonrespondent existing firms were probably slightly larger than those that responded. A small number of telephone calls were made to those who did not respond to the mail questionnaires, which confirmed the larger size characteristic among nonresponding existing firms. Most nonrespondents did not participate simply because of the trouble involved in checking records or collecting the information necessary to answer the questionnaire.

Definition of Entrant and Exit Firms

Many firms which register as new firms in a metropolitan area are not likely to affect employment since they merely represent a change in the legal form of business organization through a change in partnership, by incorporation, or by the purchase of an ongoing concern. On the other hand, new firms may either represent establishments which have been in operation outside the city or entirely new business enterprises which have emerged within the city. The

Table A-2
Distribution of Respondent Firms by Industrial Classification

SIC[a] Number		Population of Entrants in 1967 N = 2320 %	Entrants (Interviews)		Entrants (mail survey)		Existing Firms		Suburban Entrants		Exits		Relocatees	
			No	%	No	%	No	%	No	%	No	%	No	%
001-1500	Primary industries	.8	0	0	0	0	0	0	1	2.3	0	0	0	0
1501-1799	Contract construction	9.0	4	3.5	7	7.7	8	5.7	2	4.5	3	12	0	0
1800-2199	Ordinance, food & tobacco	.5	0	0	0	0	0	0	0	0	6	24	4	24
2200-2299	Textile mills	.8	6	5.3	1	1.1	1	0.7	1	2.3	6	24	4	24
2300-2399	Apparel	1.8	11	9.7	0	0	3	2.1	0	0	6	24	4	24
2400-2699	Lumber, furniture, paper	.7	3	2.7	0	0	0	0	2	4.5	6	24	4	24
2700-2799	Printing & publishing	1.7	12	10.6	3	3.3	2	1.4	5	11.4	6	24	4	24
2800-3399	Chemical, petroleum, rubber, leather, etc.	1.4	2	1.8	0	0	5	3.5	6	13.6	6	24	4	24
3400-3499	Fabricated metal	1.5	15	13.3	0	0	0	0	0	0	6	24	4	24
3500-3599	Machinery (except. elect.)	.8	8	7.1	0	0	0	0	5	11.4	6	24	4	24
3600-3999	Electrical, transportation equipment, instruments	2.4	2	1.8	3	3.3	2	1.4	4	9.1	6	24	4	24
4000-4199	Railroad & transportation services	.3	0	0	1	1.1	0	0	0	0	0	0	0	0
4200-4299	Trucking & warehousing	1.0	1	0.9	0	0	0	0	0	0	0	0	0	0
4300-4699	Water, air & pipeline transportation services	.2	0	0	0	0	1	0.7	0	0	0	0	0	0

SIC code	Industry	%	n	%	n	%	n	%	n	%	n	%	n	%
4700–4799	Transportation services	.6	1	0.9	2	2.2	1	0.7	0	0	0	0	0	0
4800–4999	Communication, pub. util.	.4	3	2.7	0	0	0	0	0	0	0	0	0	0
5000–5099	Wholesale trade	7.0	3	2.7	4	4.4	22	15.6	11	0	12	48	7	41
5100–5999	Retail trade	32.9	18	15.9	25	27.5	37	26.2	1	25.0	12	48	7	41
6000–6500	Finance, insurance	2.9	6	5.3	3	3.3	3	2.1	1	2.3	0	0	0	0
6501–7000	Real estate	3.6	4	3.5	4	4.4	5	3.5	0	0	0	0	0	0
7001–7300	Personal services	6.5	6	5.3	8	8.8	18	12.8	2	4.5	4	16	6	35
7301–9000	Business & misc. services	23.3	8	7.1	30	33.0	33	23.4	4	9.1	4	16	6	35
	Total		113	100	91	100	141	100	44	100	25	100	17	100

aThe SIC groups were merged for purposes of analysis of data.

Table A-3
Distribution of Respondent firms by Type of Organization and Geographic Location

	Entrants (mail survey)		Entrants (Interviews)		Existing Firms		Suburban Entrants		Exits		Relocatees	
	No	%	No	%	No	%	No	%	No	%	No	%
Type of Organization:												
Sole Proprietor	52	57.1	39	34.5	72	51.1	13	29.5	–	–	10	60
Partnership	15	16.5	8	7.1	18	12.8	3	6.8	–	–	1	5
Corporation	24	26.4	66	58.4	51	36.2	28	63.6	–	–	6	35
Total	91	100	113	100	141	100	44	100	25	100	17	100
Geographic Location:[a]												
Low-Income Areas												
North Philadelphia	4	4.4	21	18.6	19	13.5	–	–	6	24	1	6
Spring Garden	4	4.4	5	4.4	13	9.2	–	–	0	0	0	0
West Philadelphia	16	17.6	3	2.7	20	14.2	–	–	3	12	4	23
Subtotal	24	26.4	29	25.7	52	36.9	–	–	9	–	5	–
Central Business District:												
Center City	15	16.5	17	15.0	33	23.4	–	–	3	12	7	41
High Income Areas:												
South Philadelphia	5	5.5	17	15.0	10	7.1	–	–	2	8	1	6
Northwest Philadelphia	16	17.6	8	7.1	22	15.6	–	–	3	12	1	6
Frankfort-Richmond	4	4.4	16	14.2	10	7.1	–	–	0	0	1	6
Northeast Philadelphia	27	29.7	26	23.0	14	9.9	–	–	4	16	2	12
Suburban Areas	–		–		–		–		4	16	–	–
Subtotal	42	57.2	67	59.3	56	39.7	–	–	13	–	5	–
Total	91	100	113	100	141	100	–	–	25	100	17	100

[a]The Relocatee's location is the present location of the firm.

problem with the data derived from the mercantile license file is that no distinction is made between new "legal status change" firms and entirely new establishments. Consequently, the total employment for these firms, if derived from city records, results in a substantial overestimate of the job creation potential of new entrants.

The total employment of all firms which exit by not renewing their mercantile license is also an overestimate of the job loss created by firms going out of business. Many exit firms simply represent a change in name or ownership rather than the closing down of the establishment. It was therefore necessary to devise a method of eliminating this overcount in the employment created by entrants and exits in the city. It should be recognized that the final employment impact in geographic areas of the city has been based on estimates rather than actual employment data.

Wage Tax and Number of Employees

Employers are required to report the number of employees when they file the wage tax form. A firm may file either monthly or quarterly, depending on the amount of wage tax withheld. If the firm is liable for more than $50 tax (about four to six employees) it must be filed monthly; firms with $50 and less in wage tax file quarterly.

The different filing periods are easily handled by counting employment at the end of a quarter in the year of the study. The respondent firms are asked to report the number of employees during the reporting period. This creates a problem since they do not report the number of *jobs* but the number of employees on the payroll. Consequently, to the extent that labor turnover is substantial, the employment of both entrants and exits will be overstated. It was therefore necessary to assess the magnitude of turnover among entrant firms. This was done in the in-depth interview conducted with a sample of entrants.

Multiestablishments and the Geographic
Location of Employment

If a firm has several branches or plants within the city, it may or may not report its employment from each branch location separately. Since there is no legal requirement that firms report employment separately for each branch, there is a tendency for firms to report citywide employment from the head office. In many industries, such as in manufacturing, this does not pose a serious problem since most firms do not have a large number of plants within the city and the head offices of firms are not likely to be concentrated in any particular geographic location. However, in wholesale and retail trade many head offices are concentrated in the central business district. This means that in the section of the study which analyzes various aspects of the total employment in the city there will be some overestimate of employment in the central business district.

A similar problem exists when the head office of the multiestablishment is located outside Philadelphia. In some cases the location of the firm's city employment is not identified. When this occurred, the firm's employment was allocated according to the geographic distribution of employment in the industry. This adjustment was made for between 5-20% of employment depending on the industry. If the city employment of such firms in a particular industry is not distributed in a geographic area similar to other city firms in that industry, the results of some aggregate employment analysis will be affected.

Failure to Report Employment

The wage tax form used by the city of Philadelphia seeks information on wages paid, wage tax paid, and number of employees. Firms must report wages paid, but there is no legal requirement to report number of employees. In practice, of course, most firms (80-90%) actually report the number of employees. For the firms which did not report their employment, it was necessary to devise a method for estimating employment. This was done by comparing the relationship between wages paid and employment for all city firms within each three digit SIC which reported both their employment and wages paid. This relationship formed the basis for estimating the employment of firms which neglected to provide this information. Since all firms report the wage information this technique of estimation appeared to provide an accurate method of estimating all firms' employment.

The foregoing discussion defines the scope of the study which is primarily on the strength and nature of the labor demand created by new entrant firms in an urban area. It is designed to compare some aspects of this demand in different locations in the city and in the suburban ring. In addition, the industrial and geographic distribution of all job opportunities in the city are discussed. In this respect the study is quite unique. It is also unique in that the analysis utilizes data from a city wage tax. Since an attempt is made to generate a substantial amount of primary data from tax returns, it is inevitable that there are several limitations in the quality of the data. It was therefore necessary to develop techniques which would eliminate most of these problems. The detailed analysis of the nature of labor demand is based on interviews and a mail survey of several samples of firms in the city and the suburban ring. An attempt is made to probe each firm's occupational structure, factors affecting its choice of location, and characteristics of the entrepreneurs. Although methodological problems restrict the extent to which the results of the study can be generalized to other urban areas, it is clear that the findings will provide insights concerning labor demand in an urban area.

Appendix B:
Occupational Opportunities
in the Inner Core

This appendix contains estimates of the detailed occupational opportunities expected to be available in the inner city of Philadelphia within the near future. Since the calculations used to generate the estimates are based on a number of assumptions, the results shown in the following tables should be treated with a good deal of caution. The estimates are calculated by multiplying the 1968 employment within nineteen minutes travel time of center city by the appropriate projected ratios of occupational composition for 1975. These projected ratios were obtained from the publication, *Occupational Employment Patterns for 1960 and 1975*, Appendix C.[1]

The validity of these estimates depends on the following:

1. The accuracy of the 1968 industrial employment within the inner core of the city. In addition, even if this estimate is fairly accurate, a significant change in industrial employment in the several years after 1968 will affect the occupational estimates.
2. The extent to which the industrial structure of Philadelphia is similar to the industrial structure of the national economy. The occupational ratios are based on nationwide estimates and are not directly applicable to local areas unless the local economy is widely diversified. The highly diversified nature of the Philadelphia economy suggests that the direct application of the national occupational ratios is not likely to pose a serious problem.
3. The choice of the 1975 occupational ratios rather than 1960 assumes that the predicted 1975 ratios are valid for the period 1970-75.
4. The ratios also assume that the production function in Philadelphia industries are similar to national industrial production function. It is also assumed that over the 1970-75 period, the relationship between factor prices will not change, so that the firms' point of operation on the function will not move towards more capital-intensive or labor-intensive methods of production.

Since some of the above assumptions are fairly tenuous, it is necessary to regard the estimates of future occupational opportunities as rough guides to the potential occupational demand of new firms and perhaps general guidelines for programs designed to train ghetto residents. The estimates contained in the following tables are not intended to be precise estimates of future job opportunities.

Table B-1

Estimated Occupational Employment Pattern for Central Core: 1970-75 Estimated Number of Jobs by Major Industry

	All Industries	Contract Const.	Transportation	Wholesale and Retail Trade	Finance Insurance Real Estate	Services	Manufacturing
Clerical & Kindred	115,360	1,679	14,400	28,476	26,163	21,518	33,505
Stenos, typists, secy.	30,486	497	2,046	3,826	7,797	8,863	9,383
Office mach. oper.	5,474	22	767	1,613	2,302	441	2,165
Other clerical	79,401	1,160	11,587	23,037	16,064	12,214	21,957
Sales	46,144	103	782	37,292	11,503	911	9,966
Craftsmen, Foremen	88,755	13,585	11,200	13,639	981	7,158	53,936
Construction craftsmen	24,250	10,722	1,132	865	381	941	5,358
Metal craftsmen (excl. mech.)	9,423	405	921	67	0	118	13,769
Printing trades craftsmen	2,564	0	15	67	42	59	4,081
Transport. & public utilities	3,603	94	1,293	0	0	15	250
Mechanics & repairmen	24,804	738	4,654	8,400	321	4,336	10,021
Other craftsmen	11,224	763	1,359	2,578	149	1,264	7,634
Operatives & Kindred	115,707	3,269	28,047	20,875	220	6,790	116,588
Drivers & deliverymen	24,804	1,276	22,246	7,285	59	1,411	7,995
Transp. & public utilities	1,247	166	2,893	17	0	15	194
Semi-skilled metalworking	14,273	333	285	233	0	265	22,235
Semi-skilled textile	7,344	0	0	0	0	0	12,630
Other operatives	68,038	1,643	2,623	13,340	161	5,100	73,534
Service Workers	99,563	144	2,776	22,971	2,783	49,870	4,497
Private household	21,132	0	0	0	0	15,947	0
Protective service	9,215	25	475	166	309	750	1,305
Food service	20,647	11	285	16,450	59	4,424	278
Other service workers	48,569	108	2,016	6,354	2,409	28,734	2,915
Laborers (excl. farm & mine)	29,516	3,838	6,466	6,687	797	3,660	10,687

Table B-2

Estimated Occupational Employment Pattern for Central Core: 1970-75 (Estimated Number of Jobs in Manufacturing Industries)

	Food & Kindred Products	Tobacco Manufacture	Textile Mill Products	Apparel & Related Products	Lumber & Wood Products	Furniture and Fixtures	Paper & Allied Products	Printing, Pub. & Allied Prods.	Chemicals & Allied Products	Petroleum Refining and Related Industries
Clerical & Kindred	3,426	23	1,832	3,251	88	362	1,243	5,476	2,261	932
Stenos, typists, secy.	744	6	429	518	23	98	330	1,458	834	304
Office mach. oper.	331	2	105	213	3	18	69	219	183	83
Other clerical	2,351	15	1,298	2,516	62	246	842	3,802	1,242	545
Sales	1,482	12	285	831	24	135	322	5,585	527	156
Craftsmen, Foremen	3,985	37	2,695	2,187	238	768	2,192	7,348	2,603	1,007
Construction craftsmen	234	3	115	32	41	112	265	55	429	227
Metal craftsmen (excl. mech.)	139	5	72	48	21	31	292	109	206	94
Printing trades craftsmen	17	0	12	28	0	0	220	5,588	18	7
Transport. & public utilities	0	0	6	0	0	0	2	3	5	2
Mechanics & repairmen	1,120	12	890	401	34	82	582	313	836	252
Other craftsmen	1,228	4	605	437	79	343	170	578	199	170
Operatives & Kindred	13,335	102	13,229	31,026	626	1,870	4,994	3,805	4,822	1,146
Drivers & deliverymen	4,765	2	139	193	107	113	219	457	276	203
Transp. & public utilities	6	0	2	76	1	1	9	0	18	17
Semi-skilled metalworking	42	1	27	20	5	69	59	3	130	58
Semi-skilled textile	0	0	3,981	17,622	1	101	21	14	29	1
Other operatives	8,525	100	9,078	13,111	511	1,587	4,686	3,328	4,369	869
Service Workers	699	10	343	470	21	56	213	374	315	68
Private household	0	0	0	0	0	0	0	0	0	0
Protective service	111	1	78	68	12	22	58	32	87	23
Food service	95	1	10	20	0	0	10	9	34	9
Other service workers	493	8	254	381	8	34	146	334	193	37
Laborers (excl. farm & mine)	1,515	14	695	285	371	124	398	319	350	182

Table B2 (cont.)

	Rubber & Misc. Plastic Prods.	Leather & Leather Products	Stone, Clay and Glass Products	Primary Metal Inds.	Fabricated Metal Prods.	Machinery (Excluding Electrical)	Electrical Machinery Eqpt. & Supplies	Transp. Eqpt.	Prof. Sc. Instr. (Incl. Fire Control Eqpt.)	Misc. Mfg. Industries
Clerical & Kindred	268	243	342	401	3,458	2,037	4,883	1,600	294	1,761
Stenos, typists, secy.	67	45	81	95	1,005	637	1,955	430	92	405
Office mach. oper.	16	18	19	23	190	146	475	87	20	0
Other clerical	184	180	242	282	2,263	1,255	2,454	1,082	181	1,356
Sales	45	32	122	70	620	379	676	99	37	613
Craftsmen, Foremen	308	181	532	1,225	6,217	4,075	6,818	3,722	332	2,147
Construction craftsmen	25	5	75	156	514	159	350	927	21	173
Metal craftsmen (excl. mech.)	45	6	51	396	2,722	2,198	2,152	1,201	110	530
Printing trades craftsmen	5	1	2	7	45	18	48	10	3	91
Transport. & public utilities	0	1	1	7	3	3	257	4	0	0
Mechanics & repairmen	77	49	162	171	965	584	1,476	752	57	330
Other craftsmen	18	6	76	259	390	381	688	264	58	450
Operatives & Kindred	1,002	1,489	1,510	1,299	9,636	5,566	15,414	5,369	605	6,281
Drivers & deliverymen	7	11	333	63	324	107	173	133	8	154
Transp. & public utilities	1	1	2	16	0	3	0	10	0	3
Semi-skilled metalworking	9	1	38	332	4,001	2,775	6,919	3,033	225	1,269
Semi-skilled textile	7	272	1	0	3	2	20	33	5	267
Other operatives	978	1,205	1,135	888	5,307	2,679	8,302	2,159	367	4,639
Service Workers	35	29	52	72	382	207	595	258	23	180
Private household	0	0	0	0	0	0	0	0	0	0
Protective service	7	8	18	33	153	58	161	111	9	41
Food service	2	1	3	3	24	10	32	14	2	6
Other service workers	27	20	31	35	206	138	398	132	12	132
Laborers (excl. farm & mine)	78	57	281	388	844	292	511	396	0	269

Appendix C:
Occupational Codes

Occupations	*Dictionary of Occupational Titles:* Numbers Included
Professional	0-159, 190-199, 960-979
Management administration special	160-179
Managerial general	180-189
General Office clerical	200-209, 230-249
Account recording and business machine	210-219
Plant clerical	220-229
Sales and sales related	250-299
Retail food and drink	300-319
Personal service	320-369
Building service	370-389
Processing metal, food industry	500-599
Machinery, operation and repair	600-639, 400-499, 690-699, 950-959
Paper and printing	640-659
Machinery, wood, stone, clay, glass	660-679
Textile occupations	680-689
Bench work occupations	700-739, 790-799
Fabrications and repair of plastics, wood, sand, stone, clay, glass products	740-779
Fabrication textile	780-789
Structural work	800-839
Construction occupations	840-899
Transportation occupations	900-919
Packaging; material handling, general labor	920-949

Bibliography

Books

Banfield, Edward. *The Unheavenly City*. Boston: Little Brown & Co., 1970.

Becker, Gary S. *Economics of Discrimination*. Chicago: University of Chicago Press, 1957.

Birch, David L. *The Economic Future of City and Suburb*. The Urban Studies Series. CED Supplementary Paper, no. 30. New York: Committee for Economic Development, 1970.

Blair, John F., and Fansmith, Susan. *Model Cities Recreation and Transportation*. Philadelphia: Franklin Institute Research Laboratories, mimeo, 1971.

Chamberlain, Neil W. (ed.) *Business and the Cities: A Book of Relevant Readings*. New York: Basic Books, 1970.

Chinitz, Benjamin, (ed.) *City and Suburb*. Englewood Cliffs, N.J. Prentice-Hall, 1964.

Creamer, Daniel. *Changing Location of Manufacturing Employment, Part I: Changes by Type of Location, 1947-1961*. New York: National Industrial Conference Board, 1963.

Delaware Valley Regional Planning Commission. *1985 Regional Transportation Plan*. Plan Report no. 5, Technical Supplement. Philadelphia: Delaware Valley Regional Planning Commission, 1969.

Doeringer, Peter, and Piore, Michael. *Internal Labor Markets and Manpower Analysis*. Lexington, Mass.: D.C. Heath, 1971.

Domencich, Thomas A., and Kraft, Gerald. *Free Transit*. Lexington, Mass.: D.C. Heath, 1970.

Federal Reserve Bank of Philadelphia. *An Analysis of Shifts in Employment Among Sixteen Large Metropolitan Areas, 1959-1964*. Philadelphia: Federal Reserve Bank, 1965.

_____. *Mainsprings of Growth*: Philadelphia: Federal Reserve Bank, 1967.

Gordon, Margaret, and Thal-Jarsen, Margaret. *Employer Policies in a Changing Labor Market*. Berkeley: Institute of Industrial Relations, University of California, 1969.

Harms, Louis, and James, R. *Manpower in Pennsylvania*, vol. 2. Harrisburg: Commonwealth of Pennsylvania, Department of Community Affairs, 1967.

Harrison, Bennett. "Education and the Urban Ghetto." Philadelphia: Ph.D dissertation, 1971.

Hoover, Edgar M., and Vernon, Raymond. *Anatomy of a Metropolis*. Cambridge, Mass.: Harvard University Press, 1959.

Isard, Walter. *Methods of Regional Analysis: An Introduction to Regional Science*. Cambridge, Mass.: MIT Press, 1960.

Leibenstein, Harvey. *Economic Backwardness and Economic Growth*. New York: John Wiley & Sons, 1962.

Levitan, Sar, Mangum, Garth, and Taggart, Robert. *Economic Opportunity in the Ghetto*, Baltimore: Johns Hopkins Press, 1970.

McLennan, Barbara (ed.) *Crime in Urban Society*, New York: Dunellen Press, 1970.

Meyer, John, Kain, John F., and Wohl, Martin. *The Urban Transportation Problem*, Cambridge, Mass.: Harvard University Press, 1965.

National Advisory Commission on Civil Disorders. *Report of the National Advisory Commission on Civil Disorders*. New York: Bantam, 1968.

Netzer, Dick. *Economics and Urban Problems*. New York: Basic Books, 1970.

Ornati, Oscar. *Transportation Needs of the Poor*. New York: Praeger, 1969.

Pittsburgh Regional Planning Association. *Region in Transition*. Pittsburgh: University of Pittsburgh Press, 1963.

Rees, Albert, and Shultz, George P. *Workers and Wages in an Urban Labor Market*. Chicago: University of Chicago Press, 1970.

Regional Science Research Institute. *An Investigation of Location Factors Influencing the Economy of the Philadelphia Region*. Philadelphia: Regional Science Research Institute, 1968.

Schumpeter, J.A. *Capitalism, Socialism, and Democracy*. New York: Harper and Brothers, 1954.

Stanback, Thomas M., Jr., and Knight, Richard V. *The Metropolitan Economy*. New York: Columbia University Press, 1970.

Stefank, Norbert. *Industrial Location Within An Urban Area*. Madison, Wisconsin: Bureau of Business Research and Services, University of Wisconsin, 1962.

Sugarman, Jule M. *The Cost of Day Care*. Mimeo, 1970.

Tabb, William K. *The Political Economy of the Black Ghetto*. New York: W.W. Norton, 1970.

Vernon, Raymond. *The Changing Economic Function of the Central City*. New York: Committee for Economic Development, 1959.

_____. *Metropolis 1985*. Cambridge, Mass.: Harvard University Press, 1960.

Vickrey, William. *The Pension of the Rapid Transit Fare Structure of the City of New York*. New York: Management Survey of the City of New York, 1952.

Vietorisz, Thomas, and Harrison, Bennett. *The Economic Development of Harlem*. New York: Praeger, 1970.

Whitman, Edmund S., and Schmidt, W. James. *Plant Relocation*. New York: American Management Association, 1966.

Periodicals

Allen, Louis L. "Making Capitalism Work in the Ghettos." *Harvard Business Review* (May-June 1969), pp. 83-92.

Altshuler, Alan A. "Transit Subsidies: By Whom, For Whom?" *Journal of the American Institute of Planners* (March 1969), p. 84.

Brimmer, Andrew F. "Economists' Perception of Minority Economic Problems: A View of Emerging Literature." *Journal of Economic Literature* (September 1970), pp. 783-806.

Doeringer, Peter B. "Ghetto Labor Markets—Problems and Progress." *Program on Regional and Urban Economies*, no. 35, Cambridge, Mass.: Harvard University Press (May 1968), pp. 1-17.

Downs, Anthony. "Alternative Futures for the American Ghetto." *Daedalus* (Fall 1968), pp. 1331-1378.

Dunn, Edgar S. "A Statistical and Analytical Technique for Regional Analysis." *Papers and Proceedings* of the Regional Science Association, 6 (1960):97-112.

Foley, Eugene P. "The Negro Businessmen: In Search of a Tradition." *Daedalus* (Winter 1966), p. 107.

Gitelman, H.M. "An Investment Theory of Wages." *Industrial and Labor Relations Review* (April 1968), p. 329.

Goldner, William. "Spatial and Locational Aspects of Metropolitan Labor Markets," *The American Economic Review* 45 (March 1955): 113-129.

Graham, Robert E. Jr. "Factors Underlying Changes in Geographic Distribution of Income." *Survey of Current Business* (April 1964), pp. 15-32.

Holland, Daniel M. "An Evaluation of Tax Incentives for the On-the-Job Training of the Disadvantaged." *The Bell Journal of Economics and Management Science* (Spring 1971), pp. 293-327.

Kain, John F. "Coping with Ghetto Unemployment," *Journal of American Institute of Planners* (March 1969), pp. 80-83.

_____. "Housing, Segregation, Negro Employment and Metropolitan Decentralization," *Quarterly Journal of Economics* (May 1968), pp. 175-97.

_____. and Pershy, Joseph. "Alternatives to the Guilded Ghetto," *Public Interest* (Winter 1969), pp. 74-88.

Machlup, Fritz. "Strategies in the War on Poverty." In Margaret S. Gordon (ed.) *Poverty in America.* San Fransisco: Chandler Publishing Co., 1965, pp. 445-65.

Marshall, F. Ray and Hefner, James. "Black Employment in Atlanta." In Somers (ed.) *Industrial Relations Research Association, Proceedings*, 1970, pp. 45-54.

Mooney, Joseph D. "Housing Segregation, Negro Employment and Metropolitan Decentralization: An Alternative Prospect." *Quarterly Journal of Economics* (May 1969), pp. 299-311.

Newman, Dorothy D. "The Decentralization of Jobs." *Monthly Labor Review* (May 1967), pp. 7-13.

Noll, Roger. "Metropolitan Employment and Population Distribution and the Conditions of the Urban Poor." *Financing the Metropolis: The Urban Affairs Annual Review*, vol. 4, Sage Publications, 1970, p. 506.

Park, Se-Hard, "A Statistical Investigation of the Urban Employment Multiplier." *Mississippi Valley Journal of Business and Economics*, (Fall 1970), pp. 10-20.

Rees, Albert. "Spatial Wage Differentials in a Large City Labor Market." Industrial Relations Research Association, *Proceedings* (December 1968), pp. 237-47.

Samuels, Howard J. "Compensatory Capitalism." In Haddad, William F. and Pugh, G. Douglas (eds.), *Black Economic Development*, Englewood Cliffs, New Jersey, Prentice-Hall, 1969, pp. 60-73.

Sundquist, James L. "Jobs, Training, and Welfare for the Underclass." In Kermit Gordon (ed.), *Agenda for the Nation*, Washington: The Brookings Institution, 1968, p. 58.

Tabb, William K. "Government Incentives to Locate in Poverty Areas." *Land Economics* (November 1969), pp. 392-99.

Tulpole, A.H. "Dispersion of Industrial Employment in the General London Area." *Regional Studies* (April 1969), pp. 25-40.

Zumeta, Bertram W. "How Many Jobs Can One Job Make?" *Business Review*, Federal Reserve Bank of Philadelphia (June 1966), pp. 9-15.

Government Publications

City of Philadelphia, Planning Analysis Section. *Trends in Population, Housing and Socio-Economic Characteristics*, 1963.

U.S. Congress, House Committee on Banking and Currency. *Hearings*, October 14, 1969.

U.S. Department of Commerce, Bureau of the Census,
County Business Patterns 1959-1968
1963 Census of Business (area statistics)
1963 Census of Manufacturers (area statistics)
1960 Census of Population

U.S. Department of Labor, Bureau of Labor Statistics. *Urban Employment Survey*. BLS Report no. 376, October 1969.

_____ . Manpower Administration. *Manpower Report of the President*, various years.

_____ . *Report on Manpower Requirements, Resources, Utilization and Training*, 1967.

Notes

Chapter 1
Introduction: Urban Unemployment

1. For a similar argument see James L. Sundquist, "Jobs, Training and Welfare for the Underclass," in Kermit Gordon, ed., *Agenda for the Nation* (Washington: The Brookings Institution, 1969), p. 55.

2. Bennet Harrison, "Education, Training and the Urban Ghetto" (Philadelphia: University of Pennsylvania, under grant from the Dept. of Labor, Manpower Administration, 1971, (Ph.D. dissertation), p.103.

3. *Manpower Report of the President, 1971*, p. 93.

4. *Manpower Report of the President, 1971*, Ibid., p. 99.

5. Replaces Area Redevelopment Act of 1961 and Public Works Acceleration Act of 1962.

6. Howard J. Samuels, "Compensatory Capitalism" in William F. Haddad and G. Douglas Pugh (eds.), *Black Economic Development* (Englewood Cliffs, N.J.: Prentice-Hall, 1969) p. 62.

7. William Goldner, "Spatial and Locational Aspects of Metropolitan Labor Markets," *American Economic Review*, 45 (March 1955) : 113.

8. The penetration strategy for improving the labor force status of minority groups includes penetrating both entry-level jobs and the higher skilled jobs in the firm's occupational structure. The policy being advocated in this study refers only to the penetration of entry-level positions. The operation of the firm's internal labor market was not studied. For a discussion of the operation of penetration strategy in one metropolitan area, see F. Ray Marshall and James Hefner, "Black Employment in Atlanta" in Somers (ed.) *Industrial Relations Research Association, Proceedings*, 1970, pp. 45-54.

Chapter 2
Trends in the Urban Supply and Demand for Labor

1. Norbert Stefanik, *Industrial Location Within an Urban Area*, Madison, Wisc.: Bureau of Business Research and Services, University of Wisconsin, 1962, p. 10.

2. Dorothy K. Newman, "The Decentralization of Jobs," *Monthly Labor Review* (May 1967), pp. 7-13.

3. E.N. Dobson as cited in Peter B. Doeringer, "Ghetto Labor Markets—Problems and Programs," paper read at Conference on Transportation and Poverty, mimeo, June 7, 1968. American Academy of Arts and Sciences, Brookline, Massachusetts.

241

4. National Advisory Commission on Civil Disorders, p. 248.

5. See, for example, R. Vernon, *Metropolis 1985*, especially pp. 135-49 for the case of New York.

6. For more details of the procedure as applied to metropolitan regions compared to the national economy, see Edgar S. Dunn in *Papers and Proceedings* of the Regional Science Association, vol. 6, 1960 and Robert C. Graham, in *Survey of Current Business*, U.S. Dept. of Commerce, April 1964. For the Philadelphia area work see Federal Reserve Bank of Philadelphia, *An Analysis of Shifts in Employment among Sixteen Large Metropolitan Areas, 1959-1964*, Phila: 1965.

7. Thomas M. Stanback, Jr. and Richard V. Knight, *The Metropolitan Economy*, (New York: Columbia University Press, 1970) p. 251.

8. Ibid., p. 128.

9. Ibid., p. 152.

10. Roger Noll, "Metropolitan Employment and Population Distribution and the conditions of the Urban Poor," in *Financing the Metropolis: The Urban Affairs Annual Review*, vol. 4 (Sage Publications, 1970) p. 506.

11. John F. Kain, "Housing Segregation, Negro Employment and Metropolitan Decentralization" *Quarterly Journal of Economics*, May 1968, p. 189.

Chapter 4
Occupational Structure and Employment
Characteristics of New Businesses

1. See A. Rees, "Spatial Wage Differentials in a Large City" in Somers (ed.) Industrial Relations Research Association *Proceedings*, December 1969.

2. See Gary S. Becker, *The Economics of Discrimination*, Chicago: University of Chicago Press, 1957.

3. The phrase "gilding the ghetto" was coined by Professors Kain and Perskey, see John F. Kain and Joseph J. Perskey, "Alternatives to the Gilded Ghetto," *The Public Interest* (Winter 1969), p. 74.

Chapter 5
Decentralization of Employment within the City

1. See J.F. Kain and J.J. Persky, "Alternatives to the Gilded Ghetto," *The Public Interest* (Winter 1969), p. 74.

2. For a detailed discussion of the data source, see Delaware Regional Planning Commission, *1985 Regional Transportation Plan*, Plan Report no. 5, Technical Supplement, (Philadelphia, Pa. Delaware Regional Planning Commission 1969).

3. U.S. Department of Commerce, *County Business Patterns,* 1959 and 1968 (Washington, D.C., Government Printing Office, 1960, 1969).

4. The public transit commuting time was adopted from Delaware Valley Regional Planning Commission, *1985 Regional Transportation Plan*, Philadelphia, 1969.

Chapter 6
Employment Concentration in Sublabor Markets

1. For a detailed discussion of the advantages and disadvantages of the location quotient, see Walter Isard, *Methods of Regional Analysis: An Introduction to Regional Science* (Cambridge, Mass.: The M.I.T. Press, 1960) pp. 123-26.

2. For a discussion of the construction of the localization curve see Isard, *Regional Analysis*, pp. 255-58.

3. For an example of a statistical estimate of the urban employment multiplier in a metropolitan area see Se-Hark Park, "A Statistical Investigation of the Urban Employment Multiplier," *Mississippi Valley Journal of Business and Economics*, Fall 1970, pp. 10-20.

4. For a discussion of the job generating potential of manufacturing industries, see Bertram W. Zumeta, "How Many Jobs Can One Job Make," *Business Review*, (Federal Reserve Bank of Philadelphia, June 1966).

Chapter 7
Size of Firms and the Location of Employment Opportunities

1. For a review of the hypotheses associated with the distance of firms from the center of an urban area and the empirical difficulties in testing them, see A.H. Tulpole, "Dispersion of Industrial Employment in the Greater London Area," *Regional Studies*, April 1969, pp. 25-40.

Chapter 8
Locational Choices within the Metropolitan Area

1. Edgar M. Hoover and Raymond Vernon, *Anatomy of a Metropolis*, Cambridge, Mass.: Harvard University Press, 1959.

2. Pittsburgh Regional Planning Association, *Region in Transition*, Pittsburgh: University of Pittsburgh Press, 1963.

3. For a brief analysis, see Regional Science Research Institute, *An Investigation of Location Factors Influencing the Economy of Philadelphia Region*, 1966.

Chapter 9
Location of Business and the
Employment of Local Residents

1. William Goldner, "Spatial and Locational Aspects of Metropolitan Labor Markets," American Economic Review 45 (March 1955):113.

2. See J.R. Meyer, J.F. Kain and M. Wohl, *The Urban Transportation Problem*, (Cambridge, Mass: Harvard University Press, 1965) pp. 122-23.

3. See Meyer, Kain, and Wohl, *Urban Transportation Problem*, p. 130.

Chapter 10
The Entrepreneur and the Manager in Urban Enterprises

1. For a more detailed discussion of the entrepreneurial supply function see Harvey Leibenstein, *Economic Backwardness and Economic Growth* (New York: John Wiley & Sons, 1962) pp. 121-46.

2. J.A. Schumpeter, *Capitalism, Socialism and Democracy* (New York: Harper & Brothers, 1954) p. 132.

3. Eugene P. Foley, "The Negro Businessman: In Search of a Tradition," *Daedalus*, (Winter 1966), p. 113.

Chapter 11
Public Policy and Urban Labor Markets

1. See also William Tabb, *The Political Economy of the Black Ghetto* (New York: Norton, 1970) especially chapter 4.

2. For a detailed discussion of the case against the tax incentive for human resource development, see Daniel M. Holland, "An Evaluation of Tax Incentives for On-the-Job Training of the Disadvantaged," *The Bell Journal of Economics and Management Science* (Spring 1971), approach as a method of reducing poverty see Fritz Machlup, "Strategies in the War on Poverty," in Margaret S. Gordon (ed.), *Poverty in America*, (San Francisco, Chandler Publishing Co.) p. 455. Machlup discusses several other strategies which are equally relevant to the problem of reducing high sectoral unemployment.

4. For a discussion of possible approaches to reducing crime in urban areas, see Barbara McLennan and Kenneth McLennan, "Public Policy and the Control of Crime" in Barbara McLennan (ed), *Crime in Urban Society* (New York: The Dunellen Press 1970) pp. 125-47.

5. See Machlup, "War on Poverty," p. 456.

6. For a discussion of the difference between feasible and acceptable policy solutions see Banfield, *The Unheavenly City*, (Boston: Little Brown, 1970).

7. John F. Blair Jr. and Susan Fansmith, "Model Cities Recreation and Transportation" (Phila.: Franklin Institute Research Laboratories), mimeo, 1971.

8. The case for differential pricing schemes on subway systems is not new. An extensive proposal for differential pricing in the New York subway system is contained in William Vickrey, *The Revision of The Rapid Transit Fare Structure of the City of New York*, (management Survey of the City of New York 1952).

9. Jule M. Sugarman, *The Cost of Day Care*, mimeo, unpublished paper 1970.

Appendix B
Occupational Opportunities in the Inner Core

1. Bureau of Labor Statistics, U.S. Department of Labor, Occupational Employment Patterns for 1960 and 1975, Bulletin no. 1599 (Washington, D.C., U.S. Government Printing Office, 1968).

Index

Accessibility, importance to location, 134–143

Advertising, effective for hiring new workers, 63

Amenities, residential, important to employees, 159

Analysis, occupational, from interviews, 63

Appalachian Regional Development Act, 3

Apparel industries, declining, 6

Base industries vs. nonbase, 13

Benchwork operations in, 66

[Pennsylvania] Bureau of Employment Security (BES), 31n, 221–222

Binkley, David, xxv

Black capitalism, programs for, 103, 175

Budd Co. of Philadelphia, 33

Bureau of Employment Security (BES), xxv, 31n, 218, 221–222

Burton, Harry, xxv

Business district, central, not attractive to new businesses, 59

Businesses, new: in ghettos, ineffective, 59; in metropolitan area, 65; isolated from competition, 200; occupational and wage differentials of, 10; occupational structure of, 64–65; racial characteristics of, 74–78; structural characteristics of, 61; variations in, 172; wages and salaries in, 67

Bussey, Ellen M., xxvi

Center City, travel time to, 98–100

Central Business District (CBD), 27, 155

Changes, demographical, 37

Chi Square test, 74, 174n, 175

Cities, central, specializing in occupations, 32

Concentrated Employment Program (CEP), 11, 21, 27, 103, 211

Cities, new, special problems of, 38

Cliff, Nancy, xxv

Construction jobs, better paid in cities, 69

Core of city, occupational opportunities in, 231

Craftmen operations, 66, 69

Crime rate, high in ghettos, 39, 201

Crummett, James, xxv

Data, basic sources of, 218; limitations of, 223

Delaware Valley Regional Planning Commission, 88

Demographic change, 20

Demographic characteristics of new firms, 174

Dictionary of Occupational Titled (DOT), 64

Differentials, occupational, 66

Disadvantages of firm's location, 147–152

Disadvantages to workers in central city, 34

Dittenhafer, Brian, xxv

Diversity of firms desirable, 7

Duskin, G. L., xxvi

Education: requirements lowered, 63; role of, in entrepreneurs, 178, 185–186; urban systems in need of change, 213–214

Employment, hypotheses on, 42–43

Emergency Employment Act of 1971, 12

Employees: affected by entries and exits, 48; city workers in manufacturing, 66; disadvantages to, in certain manufacturing, 66; managerial-professional, 66; occupational structure in new businesses in metropolis, 66; racial characteristics of, 63; travel facilities to suburban firms, 169–170

Employment: distribution of, 26, 33; estimated pattern in city core, 232; generated by new businesses, 7; ghetto vs. nonghetto, 44; growth higher for city entrants, 72; increases largely in services, wholesale, and retail sectors, 48; losses in various industries, 57; net, in entrant and exiting firms, 48; nonwhite, related to segregation, 38; "potential" growth of, 35; uneven impact on city sectors, 59

Entrant firms, definition of, 225; distribution of, 222; trend to higher salaries, 69; percentage of entrant and exiting family businesses, 52

Enterprises; classification of business, 217; new, usually small-scale, 62

Entrepreneurs: black, 172–173, 192; differentials in, 175; entrant, suburban, and existing, 171; in family business, owner-operated firms, insurance, real estate, 51; in ghetto, 13, 84; personal characteristics of, 176–178, 185; racial distribution of, 184

Environment: adverse, e.g., by crime, poor housing, inadequate educational facilities, 197; importance of, to firms and

247

About the Authors

Kenneth McLennan holds a B.Sc. (Econ.) from The University of London (1957), an MBA from the University of Toronto (1961), and a Ph.D. from the University of Wisconsin (1965). He has had a wide background in research and teaching in Canada and the United States. He is the author of numerous monographs and articles in labor economics and labor relations. He has worked. as an arbitrator, mediator, and factfinder in many labor relations disputes and has been a consultant to the U. S. Department of Labor's Middle Atlantic Regional Manpower Advisory Committee since 1967.

Professor McLennan has taught at several universities in the United States including Rutgers, The State University (1964-67), The University of Wisconsin, and Temple University since 1967, where he has served as Chairman of the Department of Economics.

He is presently on leave from Temple University working for the United States Department of Labor as Deputy Assistant Secretary of Labor for Policy Development.

Paul Seidenstat is presently Associate Professor of Economics at Temple University after having taught at the University of Delaware. He received his Ph.D. in Economics from Northwestern University. Professor Seidenstat has had wide experience as a consultant for agencies of the federal and local governments. He has written several monographs and articles in the fields of urban economics, environmental economics, and water resources.